S0-BNQ-866

About the author

STEUART HENDERSON BRITT has had a distinguished career, as professor, author, editor, psychologist, lawyer, and business and marketing consultant. He also served notably in World War II, both as a civilian and as a Naval Officer. His Ph.D. is in psychology (Yale), and Dr. Britt is the author and editor of several books and dozens of articles on social psychology and on marketing.

After many years in business, he returned to teaching in 1957, as Professor of Marketing and Advertising, Northwestern University. He is also Editor of the *Journal of Marketing*, co-author of *Advertising Psychology and Research*, and Consulting Editor for the McGraw-Hill Series in Marketing and Advertising.

The Spenders

McGraw-Hill Series in Marketing and Advertising

Steuart Henderson Britt, *Consulting Editor*

Baker—Advertising Layout and Art Direction

Baker—Visual Persuasion

Barton—Advertising Agency Operations and Management

Britt—The Spenders

Crisp—Marketing Research

Crisp—Sales Planning and Control

Dunn—Advertising Copy and Communication

Haas—How to Develop Successful Salesmen

Hattwick—The New Psychology of Selling

Lapp—Successful Selling Strategies

Lazo and Corbin—Management in Marketing

Levitt—Innovation in Marketing

Lucas and Britt—Measuring Advertising Effectiveness

Martineau—Motivation in Advertising

Mauser—Modern Marketing Management

Messner—Industrial Advertising

Seehafer and Laemmar—Successful Television and Radio Advertising

Stebbins—Copy Capsules

Turner—Sales Promotion That Gets Results

Weir—On the Writing of Advertising

Weiss—Merchandising for Tomorrow

Wolff—What Makes Women Buy

Wright and Warner—Advertising

Yeck and Maguire—Planning and Creating Better Direct Mail

658.85
B77
83046

HC
110
C6
B7

The Spenders

Where and Why Your Money Goes

Steuart Henderson Britt, Ph.D.

PROFESSOR OF MARKETING AND ADVERTISING

NORTHWESTERN UNIVERSITY

WITHDRAWN

McGRAW-HILL BOOK COMPANY, INC.

New York   Toronto   London

GOSHEN COLLEGE LIBRARY.
GOSHEN, INDIANA

THE SPENDERS

Copyright © 1960 by the McGraw-Hill Book Company, Inc. Printed in the United States of America. All rights reserved. This book, or parts thereof, may not be reproduced in any form without permission of the publishers. *Library of Congress Catalog Card Number: 60-14994*

v

07930

$5.45

3-12-65

McGraw-Hill

Dedicated to the American Consumer

and P. Y. E.

What This Book Is About

The word "spender" is a naughty word for many people. It means using money, often thought of as the root of all evil. Spending is associated with words like "squander" and "extravagant" . . . and with such phrases as "shoot the works," "throw dollars away," "scatter money to the winds," "a fool and his money are soon parted."

But the father of our country said: "It is not a custom with me to keep money to look at" . . . and Abraham Lincoln mirrored the same idea: "Money is only valuable while in circulation."

W. Somerset Maugham and Carl Sandburg have had their say, too. The former: "Money is like a sixth sense without which you cannot make a complete use of the other five." The latter: "Money is like manure—good only when spread around."

This book is about the spenders—those who spread money around. The spenders are you and you and you, American consumers who have more money and time to spend for what you want than any people in all history. You can spend for essentials or nonessentials or both.

The Spenders will give you new insights into your own actions and reactions as a consumer. It tells you about the products you buy—how they are marketed and advertised for your benefit.

Business is looked on by many people as some mysterious force that may entice them to spend their money rashly or recklessly. *This book shows you why American business is not your callous master . . . but rather the servant of you, the American consumer—the spender.*

Small minds talk about people . . . average minds discuss events . . . and great minds converse about ideas. *And so this book is a conversation with you about ideas.*

The first five chapters tell you something about your motives, your "frames of reference," your wants and needs, why you as consumer are king, and why all business is your business.

The next three chapters explain your many freedoms of choice, your special opportunities to spend your money and your leisure time, and what you spend your money for.

Chapters 9 through 14 show you why you buy the products you do, what chances of success these products have, what brand images and packaging mean to you, how advertising helps you, what your stores are like psychologically, and how prices affect your buying.

The use of marketing research to learn more about your wants, and possible applications of motivation research, are the subjects of Chapters 15 and 16. Because women control so much money and influence so much spending, Chapter 17 is devoted exclusively to them. The last two chapters of the book reveal some future trends, and how these will affect you as a consumer.

Purposely *The Spenders* is not cluttered with tables and graphs . . . but it does contain what I call "living statistics," to make the book come alive.

I am a teacher of marketing; but my doctoral degree is in psychology, and my professional life (both in business and in academic work) has been primarily as a social psychologist. My background as a psychologist and marketing man has been drawn on to try to understand and to explain why so many consumers are suspicious of business, and especially of advertising, selling, and merchandising. A good part of the explanation has to do with money—with *spending*.

The original idea for *The Spenders* was inspired by conversations with A. Edward Miller, formerly assistant to the publisher of *Life* magazine, and now publisher of *McCall's*. Mr. Miller also has been kind enough to read the entire manuscript and to make some valuable suggestions concerning it.

Real inspiration and encouragement in writing the book came from Prof. Harper W. Boyd, Jr., chairman of the Department of Marketing, Northwestern University.

Several members of the business staff of *Life* magazine provided help in the development of information relating to the *Life* Study of Consumer Expenditures, especially Robert T. Elson, general manager, and Dr. Richard H. Ostheimer, director of research; and Richard Kool was helpful on design. The views of Andrew Heiskell, Chairman of the Board of Time, Inc., were also very useful.

In developing the book, a good many valuable criticisms and ideas were obtained from a group of graduate students in a marketing seminar at Northwestern University—especially from Lewis L. Dail, now with the Vendo Company; Burr Preston, now with International Business Machines; and David K. Robson, now with The Pillsbury Company.

The following people have been of great help by reading the complete manuscript and giving me the benefit of their advice, which I frequently have taken; but if you don't like certain parts of the book, don't blame them. Their names are given alphabetically: S. R. Bernstein, editorial director of *Advertising Age;* John S. Coulson, vice-president and director of research, Leo Burnett Company, Inc.; Dr. Vernon Fryburger, professor of advertising and marketing, Northwestern University; Dr. D. B. Lucas, chairman of the Department of Marketing, New York

University; Mr. Selden C. Menefee, former editor and publisher of the *San Juan Record* (Fair Oaks, California); DeWitt O'Kieffe, senior vice-president, Leo Burnett Company, Inc.; Irwin A. Shapiro, teaching assistant in marketing, Northwestern University.

The greatest thanks go to my former research assistant, Mrs. Betty Stephenson Lippincott, and to Mrs. Jean M. Sands.

S. H. B.

September 30, 1960

Contents

What This Book Is About   vii

1. **What's on the Consumer's Mind?**
   The Riddle of Motives   1

2. **Consider Your Motives**
   1. Frames of Reference   10
   2. Personalized Motives   15

3. **What Do You Want?**
   1. Needs and Wants   23
   2. Running out of Wants?   30

4. **The Consumer Is King**
   1. Speaking for the Consumer   35
   2. The Consumer's Range of Choice   38
   3. The Middle Majority   42

5. **Business Is Your Business**
   1. Our Marketing Revolution   49
   2. Dependence on You!   54

6. **Spend Your Money and Take Your Choice**
   1. Let the Seller Beware!   57
   2. Fads and Fashions   60
   3. The Consumer Be Pleased!   67

7. You Have the Money and the Time

1. Dollars and Discretion 74
2. Time on Your Hands 79

8. Who Spends for What?

1. The *Life* Study of Consumer Expenditures 86
2. Some Patterns of Spending 89
3. Diplomas and Dollars 94
4. Profile of the U.S. Consumer 97

9. Vive La Product Différence!

1. Discernible Differences 102
2. America's Silent Salesmen 107

10. Are They Tops or Flops?

1. Products and People 116
2. Failures and Successes 120
3. Counsel from Consumers 126

11. What Do You Imagine?

1. The Priceless Ingredient 130
2. Pictures in Our Heads 137

12. You Learn through Advertising

1. Advertising: Servant or Sinner? 147
2. Education through Advertising 159

13. Your Stores Have Personalities

1. Friend or Foe? 168
2. You and Your Shopping 175

14. How about Price?

1. Prices on Trial 179
2. Getting Your Money's Worth 186

15. Marketing Research Can Help

1. Under the Marketing Microscope 193
2. Samples and Surveys 198
3. Pass Key to Better Products and Easier Shopping 204

16. Is Motivation Research the Answer?

    1. The Meaning of M.R.   211
    2. Projective Techniques   214
    3. Motivation Research in Use   222

17. Women Are Here to Stay

    1. Woman's Changing World   230
    2. Woman's Changing Role   235

18. There'll Be Some Changes Made

    1. Patterns of Today   244
    2. Patterns of Tomorrow   250

19. Your Future Is Here

    1. The Soaring Sixties   256
    2. Blueprint for Tomorrow   261

Some Suggested Readings   267
Acknowledgments   273
Index   283

1

What's on the Consumer's Mind?

The Riddle of Motives

Why do you use Ethyl gasoline in your car? Why did you buy the suit (or dress) you are now wearing? And why did that friend of yours, who is very much like you in so many ways, astonish you by buying that hat which seems to you so ridiculous? Why did that other friend pay $30 for a pair of shoes instead of $15?

A lady I know told me she had bought some towels—some gray-green ones, even though they were the same brand and more expensive than the other towels on display. She liked and wanted that particular green, and was willing to pay a bit more to get it.

Why have these people bought what they have . . . and why do you buy what you do? The answer is that *all selling takes place in the mind of the consumer*. This is where the sale is actually carried out—in your mind and in mine.

Every manufacturer has to speculate on what the psychological factors are that cause us to spend our money the way we do. He probably wishes he could get inside his customer's brain to find out what really makes him buy. Or is it just the customer's brain? This would neglect the autonomic nervous system and the glandular system, important factors in our thinking behavior.

Anyhow, businessmen didn't have to know so much about the consumer fifty years ago. The problem then was more one of *how to produce* than of *how to sell*. Today the problem is— *what's on the consumer's mind?* A company must learn everything possible as to what new products are likely to be accepted ... and for products already on the market, how they can be sold most acceptably. This is because of constantly increasing competition in the market place.

The Dayco Corporation (formerly called the Dayton Rubber Company) developed a new type of foam rubber, with many usage possibilities. The question was—what should be done with it? After psychological studies by the Institute for Research in Mass Motivation of various kinds, it was decided that this new product would be called "Koolfoam," to stress comfort and to avoid the notion that rubber is hot. The slogan used was, "Gives you the rest of your lifetime"; and Dayton became a leader in its field with this product. The company found what consumers wanted, and matched this desire with a right product and appropriate advertising.

Consumer desires also guided the Sheaffer Pen Company in its development of the snorkel pen. Through similar psychological research, it was learned that a prime objection to fountain pens was the uncomfortable business of dunking and wiping after refilling. In large part this led to the development of the snorkel.

The Florsheim Shoe Company found through psychological studies that more men were wearing "loafers" at home, but wanted shoes with the same comfort and yet dressy enough for regular wear. So a new, lighter, slip-on shoe was developed, both comfortable and good looking.

Yet businesses do not always have to carry on psychological research in order to hit on useful marketing ideas. There are still such things as creativity and the old-fashioned quality of just being bright. For example, adman David Ogilvy has pro-

duced famous advertisements for Schweppes Tonic, showing
Commander Edward Whitehead, red beard and all ... and a
product formerly almost unknown among Americans—gin and
tonic—has become an important drink.

As to drinking patterns, what about the sales success in recent years of an alcoholic product which you can't even taste
or smell? I am referring to a product called vodka, and the important brand name is Smirnoff. Americans buy Smirnoff in
spite of anti-Russian sentiment, and have learned that it im-
proves their social status to know that a "screw driver" is not
just a tool found in the tool kit.

But the fact remains that there simply is not enough information about the *why and wherefore of consumer behavior.*
Business has access to all kinds of marketing data and to
tremendous handbooks of facts and figures. After proper probing in libraries and files, all kinds of authoritative and complete indexes can be found of buying power for all consumer
markets—the national market, the farm market, the state
market, the city market, and so on. Excellent estimates can be
obtained of present market sizes, but without learning very
much about *people.*

Dozens of studies have been made of automobiles, asparagus,
atomizers, appetizers, or what not, that have never come to
grips with the fundamental problem of *why* people buy. For
example, there are detailed reports on the soft-drink market,
which tell the seasonal fluctuations in the consumption of soft
drinks, types of beverages purchased, percentage of families purchasing, and similar information. But still not very much is
known about the very complicated motives that result in the
sipping, swallowing, and guzzling by Americans of almost 1.5
billion cases of carbonated beverages annually. What causes
millions of us—men, women, and children—to take into our
intestinal tracts various kinds of sweetened or bubbling liquids
in a variety of different colors and flavors is not easy to explain.

The point is that the soft-drink industry has not learned as
much about human motivation as you might expect. The same

goes for other major industries, whether automobiles, refrigerators, canned goods, or household furnishings. Millions of dollars have been poured into product research, but relatively little in trying to discover the fundamental motives of consumers. Only "peanuts" are invested in research on human behavior.

You might expect psychologists to have a lot of the answers about motivation. After all, buying is an important form of human behavior, and the field of psychology is usually described as dealing with the prediction and control of behavior. So... why shouldn't we turn to psychologists to get their answers about buying motives? There are several reasons.

First of all, the subject of psychology covers a broad area and includes such diverse fields of specialization as child psychology, abnormal psychology, social psychology, industrial psychology, personnel psychology, clinical psychology, experimental psychology, and so on. Every psychologist of any repute tries to keep up in his own field of specialization and rarely knows much about the other areas of specialization.

As an analogy, you wouldn't go to a corporation lawyer and expect him to give you the best advice on a problem of domestic relations, nor to a criminal lawyer in order to get tax advice. You wouldn't go to a cardiologist to have your feet treated, or to a chiropodist for a cardiograph.

And you shouldn't expect most psychologists to be experts on the psychology of business or buying behavior. Only in recent years have a relatively small number of psychologists been studying human behavior in the market place. Of the 18,000 members of the American Psychological Association, less than 800 are industrial psychologists.

A second consideration is that such terms as *psychology, psychiatry,* and *psychoanalysis* produce unfortunate images in the minds of most people. The businessman has heard plenty of anecdotes about the "head shrinkers." It is only natural that he has developed some hostility and even aggression toward this strange brand of individual called a psychologist.

Perhaps there is the fear, almost unconscious for many, that, if I deal too closely with psychologists, "they might find out something bad about me." One popular definition of a psychologist is that he is an individual who when a good-looking girl enters the room, watches everybody else! There is also the story of the secretary who refused to take a job working for a psychologist because she felt that if she arrived at work early, he would think she was anxious . . . if she came on time, he might suspect she was compulsive . . . and if she reported late, he might judge her to be hostile!

The attitudes of business executives toward psychologists are probably affected also by their own earlier contacts in college with the subject of psychology. A great many men recall that their own course in psychology seemed to them to deal just with graphs of learning, and that there was lots of discussion of the physiology of the eye and the ear. So, in their business life, they feel that their own opinions of human behavior are just as good as those of the psychologists . . . even better! They have also discovered to their dismay that different psychologists come up with different answers. It may be necessary for there to be differing opinions among businessmen, but in turning to psychologists for counsel most businessmen hope for certainty.

Most basic of all in the resistance to psychological findings is suspicion of the new and unknown. Nothing is so unpopular as a really new idea that other people do not fully comprehend. As Prof. Joseph W. Newman of Stanford University says, "Opposition is likely to be vigorous when the new idea relates to the nature of man and his behavior—a subject on which most people fancy themselves more or less expert."

Yet how can we ignore the *why* of buying behavior? How can we understand more and more about the consumer . . . the kind of person who buys "The Chipmunk Song" or Beethoven's "Fifth" . . . who idolizes a middle-aged gentleman with a toupee named Bing Crosby or a young crooner named Fabian?

A classification of motives that has interested me is the one by the late W. I. Thomas of the University of Chicago. He recognized that his classification was not a complete explanation of motivation—no classification is—but it may be useful in gaining insights into consumer behavior.

According to Dr. Thomas, there are four wishes or desires which are so fundamental that they probably include all the others—the desires for (1) new experience, (2) security, (3) response, and (4) recognition.

1. The desire for *new experience* expresses itself in courage, advance, attack, and pursuit. It implies, therefore, motion, change, danger, or instability. It satisfies the love of adventure, which is present in such activities as gambling. It also satisfies such curiosity as occurs when we are creating or building something or solving a problem.

2. The desire for *security* is opposed to the desire for new experience. It expresses itself in timidity, avoidance, and flight. The desire for security makes a person cautious, conservative, and apprehensive, tending to regular habits, systematic work, and the accumulation of property.

3. The desire for *response* causes people to seek intimate contacts with other people. It is the most social of the four wishes, and contains both a sexual and a gregarious (crowd) element.

4. The desire for *recognition* is expressed in the general struggle of men for position in their social group. It makes people desire a recognized and advantageous social status. The desire for recognition includes such feelings as vanity and ambition.

It is reasonably easy to make an analysis of any bit of behavior in terms of these four wishes. Take such a simple act as putting into one's mouth the tip of a rolled piece of white paper containing some brown shreds, and then removing the tip and blowing out smoke. Why do people engage in this unique pastime? Certainly many a person achieves *new experience*. He does this, however, with a modicum of *security*. He achieves a certain amount of *response;* and he certainly can achieve some *recognition* as being "in the know" and not an outsider—no longer does he wonder what to do with his hands!

Such analyses, however, are merely classifications of motivated behavior. They certainly are *not* explanations or answers to all problems of motivation. No single set of wishes can account for the countless ways of behavior of countless people in all sorts of situations. Also there is no universally accepted list of motives. Moreover, none of the various lists of motives is either universally or specifically applicable to the *why* of buying goods and services.

Thorstein Veblen, of *The Theory of the Leisure Class* fame, did not need to have a list of motives before him when he made the sage observation that a "fancy bonnet of this year's model appeals to our sensibilities today much more forcibly than an equally fancy bonnet of the model of last year; although ... it would be a matter of the utmost difficulty to award the palm of intrinsic beauty to the one rather than to the other of these structures." Nor did Veblen have a list of motives in mind when he remarked that "the high gloss of a gentleman's hat or a patent-leather shoe has no more of intrinsic beauty than a similarly high gloss on a thread-bare sleeve." He gave numerous examples of how a thing which is basically beautiful, but which is not expensive, is not thought of as beautiful by most consumers. Some intrinsically beautiful flowers—for instance, dandelions—pass for nothing more than offensive weeds, whereas in the florist shop those flowers which are the most expensive are usually considered most beautiful.

After all, man is a complicated animal. Because of his superior intelligence and highly developed desires, however, he succeeds in making life even more complicated for himself than it already is. But man is more than an animal or a physiological being. In addition to his basic drives, he is also a social being.

Man the Consumer belongs to a particular nationality group —he is a member of a certain community—more often than not, he is affiliated with a church—he shows allegiance to a

political party—he pays dues and maintains a membership in
his labor union or professional organization—he pays additional dues to belong to a lodge or fraternal order—and he may
belong to a club of some kind. Each and every one of these and
other social institutions has an "emotional pull" for him. Here
is where we find out about his basic loyalties, beliefs, and
prejudices. Consider his nationality, his labor union, his club
—it is areas like these that need investigation in order to obtain an adequate picture of Man the Consumer.

We also need to find out about his special likes and dislikes,
and how he got them. It is not enough to know that a green
package is more effective than a red package (or vice versa) in
getting attention for a certain product. It is not enough to know
that most men prefer cigarettes to other forms of smoking. It
is not enough to know that young women use more hand lotions
than older women. The purpose is to find out *why* people have
these preferences.

As psychologist Arthur W. Kornhauser has asked: "Why does
a man purchase the clothes he does? Is it enough to learn that
he looks for a suit that fits well or that has style and quality? Certainly these attitudes tell something beyond explanations per-
taining to store location, brand name, window display, etc., although these, too, are significant. But 'fit' may, in terms of more
general desires, mean primarily bodily comfort to one man, social distinction to another, security from disapprobation to a
third, or the increased affection of his lady-love, or a feeling of
effectiveness and proper workmanship."

No list or classification of motives—including the one given
earlier—*is sufficient to answer all questions about consumer
behavior.* Such a list, however, can provide us with a suitable
check list, and we can then use the list as a guide in attempting
to understand our actions better.

Actually every social situation is different from every other
and requires a separate analysis. This means that *there is no
such thing as a universal set of explanatory motives.* Any list
of motives can be classified under a number of different head-

ings; and then someone else can rearrange that same list and assign them to different headings.

Also, the consumer often is a very unpredictable fellow, impossible to satisfy continuously and sometimes as changeable as tomorrow's weather. As Dr. Ruth P. Mack of the National Bureau of Economic Research has so well said, "An individual's buying is a function of what he is, what he has, the recent history of his purchases, what others have or buy, what he expects, what he hopes, the habits that he has established, and nearly everything else." *That is why the riddle of human motivation is so tough.*

Although many people have developed a rather formidable psychological jargon—including such terms as "motivation," "ego involvement," "superego," "id," and "emotional impact" —a great deal remains to be learned about such concepts. We don't have to interpret *every* act of spending behavior as having deep psychological significance, but we should try to solve the "riddle of motives" which involves every one of us as consumers.

2

Consider Your Motives

1. Frames of Reference

One of the keys to unlocking the riddle of motivation is what social scientists call the "frame of reference."

Here is a simple example of a frame of reference. Think of two men, Charlie and Henry, standing before three buckets of water. These buckets contain water at three different temperatures—hot, room temperature, and cold. Charlie puts his hand in the ice-cold water, and Henry puts his hand in the hot water. Then both take their hands out of the water and put them in the room-temperature water. When asked, Charlie will say that the room-temperature water is hot, and Henry will say that the water is cold. The frames of reference for Charlie and Henry are different.

British psychologist Dr. J. A. C. Brown describes a London slaughterhouse where six girls worked in a small, cold basement room. Their job was to sort out and wash the glands, intestines, and other internal organs of slaughtered pigs. The dimly lit basement room was damp from the water and blood which covered the floor, and the odor from the contents of the intestines added nothing pleasant to the total picture.

The industrial physician was appalled; and since no immediate change could be made in working conditions, he recommended that the girls be transferred to other parts of the plant and that men take over their jobs. But the six girls raised such a storm of protests that the order was immediately withdrawn. Why, asked the girls, were they being "picked on"? If they were not doing their job well, why didn't management come out and say so in order that they would have an opportunity to do something about it? Here was an example of working conditions at their worst, and yet the girls refused to get out of the "hole" in the slaughterhouse.

The doctor had in his own mind a set of standards (a frame of reference) which undoubtedly was higher than that established by the girls. His frame of reference was such that he viewed these working conditions as bad. In addition, according to his frame of reference, if bad working conditions cannot be changed, then men, not women, should do the job.

But the doctor was looking only at the physical working conditions and not the "mental" conditions. The six girls were a very close working unit separated from the rest of the plant. They saw their job as requiring skill; their supervisor did not control them closely; they were on friendly terms with one another and laughed and sang all day long. They viewed this job as being a "good" job and resisted giving it up.

Another example: A psychologist gave a group of rich children and a group of poor children a number of disks and coins of exactly the same size. For all of the children, the coins *seemed* larger than the disks ... and the poor children "saw" the coins as even bigger than the rich children! Their frames of reference were different.

Of course, frames of reference are not limited to girls in a London slaughterhouse or to rich and poor children. They affect people like you and me as well. An illustration of how a frame of reference may affect attitudes can be illustrated by an office situation. The boss calls into his office one of two assistants and closes the door. Immediately through the mind of the other assistant race a dozen different questions: Is the other man being granted a special favor? Is he going to be given additional responsibility? Or is the other man being reprimanded? Is he being "told off"? A lot will depend on the "frame of reference" for the relations among the three men.

As psychologist Hadley Cantril says, "We are constantly seeing things not as they are but as we are.... Man sees what he wants or expects to see in people as well as things."

Dr. Mason Haire, professor of psychology at the University of California, conducted the following experiment. He showed pictures to different groups of executives. The pictures were of two men of normal appearance and with little expression. All that the viewers were told was that both men were forty-six, married, healthy, and successful in their work.

The two sets of pictures were *identical,* but what the two groups *perceived* were quite different characteristics. When members of one management group were told that one of the men in the picture was a *union official,* 58 per cent found him "aggressive," 60 per cent "argumentative," 58 per cent "opinionated," and 58 per cent "outspoken."

But when the other group was shown *the same picture* and was told that the man's job was *plant manager,* only 18 per cent found him "aggressive," only 8 per cent "argumentative," only 10 per cent "opinionated," and only 5 per cent "outspoken."

At this point you will no doubt say, "But what on earth do all these examples have to do with buying and spending?" The only reason these instances have been given is so that the concept of frame of reference will be clear.

Frames of reference can and do affect your attitudes toward various products and influence which ones you buy. For example, some work for a pharmaceutical firm showed that medicines which had been sweetened and "tasted good" were not selling as well as medicines which "tasted bad." Psychologically the frame of reference for most people is that certain medicines are not very effective if they taste good.

In some work I carried out with some housewives concerning maple syrups, I found that the color of the syrup influenced their judgments whether the syrup was thick or thin. The darker the color of the syrup, the thicker these women thought the syrup was. Almost unconsciously this affected their decisions as to which kinds of syrups they bought.

Another instance is that of a company manufacturing electric mixers for use in the kitchen. The manufacturer brought out a new model which was practically noiseless, believing that this was what consumers would want. To his amazement, the new model just did not sell. The frame of reference of the consumer was well described by one woman who said that the mixer didn't seem to have any power—it didn't make enough noise!

One study carried out by two social scientists showed the effect of wrapper design on soap sales in a grocery store. When the same bar of soap was placed on the store shelves in two different types of wrappers, the soap in one wrapper outsold the other wrapper nearly two to one! It would, of course, be absurd to contend that housewives actually consider wrapper designs or containers in most instances consciously and logically. The point is that frames of reference influenced the purchasers of the soap bars, just as they always influence our buying behavior.

In 1958, Lever Brothers brought out Lux soap in wrappers of five different colors . . . and the soap also was in five different colors. Even though the soap lather always ends up white, this was a different way of getting the shopper's attention—by giving her a choice of colors. So to meet the competition, Procter & Gamble's pink Camay began to be packaged and offered also in a variety of colors. And even a meat packer's soap, Dial, joined the color parade with more than one color for Dial soap.

You and I form thousands of different attitudes, and many of these are fairly enduring. To quote psychologists Muzafer Sherif and Hadley Cantril: ". . . Attitudes are formed in relation to objects, persons, and values which may or may not have motivational appeal at first. Almost any food may satisfy hunger, but we may develop a special liking for a special food,

even for a special restaurant, and even a special table in that
restaurant. When these particular likes or dislikes are more or
less fixated, we have formed attitudes in relation to these particular objects."

The way we react to any buying situation depends not simply
upon the character of the thousands of stimuli which are
bombarding us, but also upon the character of our own attitudes at that particular time and place.

Most of us have built up over our lifetimes what we think
is an adequate picture of the world around us. It is adequate
in that it is true for us. We have adapted ourselves to our
environment in terms of what we believe to be true. We know
what to expect of certain people and certain places. Our mental
pictures may not always correspond with reality, but at least
they enable us to feel at ease.

As consumers, we do not want interference with our interpretations . . . our frames of reference. We hear and see largely
what we want to hear and see, and as we grow older we associate for the most part with people who perceive things as
we perceive them and not with those "awful" people who see
things differently. We often select those newspapers and magazines which reinforce our own attitudes; and we buy those
products which help to support the images we have of ourselves.

Drs. Eugene L. Hartley and Ruth E. Hartley, experts in the
field of social psychology, have discussed how each of us looks
at things differently. "Objects and events take on perceptual
organization and perceptual importance as a result of several
factors: their connection with the satisfaction of body needs,
their repeated occurrence as total patterns of the environment,
the stimulation they offer the organism, and the emphasis given
to them by interpersonal communication."

This is why the symbolic function of language is very real.
Every one of us is influenced by concepts and abstractions.
Take such words as "sacrifice," "mystery," and "honor," which
are difficult to reduce to precise meanings, and yet each of us
has his own ideas of what they mean and how they affect his

life. Yet words that cannot be precisely defined have tremendous social force.

In your purchasing behavior, how meaningful are such words as "small" or "super"? Actually if you try any more to find something in the drug store or five-and-ten labeled "small," you may have to look for a long time. The small package today is labeled "regular" or even "personal." What used to be the medium-size package of toothpaste is now "family" or "economy" size, or even marked "large." And what was formely the large package is "giant" or "super" today.

In 1959 the *Deluxe* model of the Rambler car was the *bottom* of the Rambler line . . . and the *Super* was a step above the *Deluxe!* Our frames of reference are changing. As consumers, we continually make use of signs and symbols. These are powerful in influencing us to buy or not to buy. But if the communication between seller and potential buyer does not adequately convey the image of the product, its effectiveness is lost. And this may be due to our *frames of reference.*

2. Personalized Motives

No wonder we have such a difficult time understanding our own motives. Most of us kid ourselves into believing that we are logical, rational human beings, and neglect the fact that most of our thinking is not based on reason.

We like to think of ourselves as logical people who are information seeking; but unless our information is dressed up with a good deal of entertainment we may not want it.

Too many observers of human behavior have stressed man's rational character and objective thought processes, and have overlooked the tremendous importance of unconscious factors and of free association of ideas. Although man is called *Homo sapiens,* probably very little logical reasoning goes on with the great majority of people if they can possibly avoid it. We do not always think things through in logical steps.

How many of your decisions today were based just on simple habit? In deciding what to eat at lunch . . . which newspaper or magazine to buy . . . which brand of cigarettes to spend your money for—to what extent were these decisions made on a logical basis?

Use yourself as a guinea pig and actually check up on the number of instances where you have reasoned things out objectively. Examine every detail of your behavior during a single day and see what a large percentage of your activities is carried on primarily on the basis of the autonomic nervous system or through sheer habit, and how few of your decisions are actually determined by reasoning and sound logic.

Consider, for example, the tremendous number of things you do just through habit. This morning you put on your right shoe before your left, or else your left shoe before your right. But, whichever way you did it, probably you will do it the same way tomorrow morning and the next morning, and every morning thereafter. At least I hope this is true, because if you have problems making a decision of this sort, then you are in need of professional counseling.

Perhaps one of the best ways for you to demonstrate how habitual many of your acts are is to clasp your hands together. Be sure your fingers are interlocked and that one thumb is on top of the other. Note which thumb it is—left or right. Now, unclasp your hands and clasp them again, but this time with the other fingers and thumb on top. Feels strange, doesn't it? But if you don't think about it and just try clasping your hands, you'll find after thousands and thousands of repetitions that the same set of fingers and thumb is always on top!

It's a good thing. After all, wouldn't it be ghastly if you had to stop each time and make a conscious decision about something like this?

Stop and think also about how different your motives and actions may be from those of other people. As researcher Pierre Martineau has said in the *Harvard Business Review:* "The difference between the man who buys a heliotrope shirt and the man who doesn't, between the man who smokes a pipe and the man who doesn't, between the woman who loves to cook and the woman who dislikes all housework, between the woman with high-brand loyalties and the woman with almost none—all these are apparently personality differences."

This suggests the need for more psychological studies of people, to see what are the personality characteristics that cause men to buy, let's say heliotrope shirts. From theoretical work by Dr. Cyril Herrmann of Arthur D. Little, Inc., and Dr. John B. Stewart of the Harvard Graduate School of Business have come some interesting suggestions about why people buy; one of the basic ideas is that *a sale depends on whether the potential customer believes that the purchase of the product will raise his own evaluation of himself.*

If you can buy a product which will increase your own ego, that's pretty important. But as to what you buy and how you behave will depend upon your social status and your personality characteristics and a host of other things. Just look around your own neighborhood. To quote Pierre Martineau again: "One of your neighbors is a very stodgy conservative who prefers brown suits and cars that last eight years. He never tries anything new, is very meticulous and fussy, and almost miserly in the way he bargains and schemes to save a few pennies.

"Next door is the exhibitionist, who makes a virtue of being different to attract attention. The test for most of his actions, for almost everything he buys, is whether or not it will create comment.

"And right across the street from you are the striver and his wife who are inordinately ambitious to move upward in the social scale. Each step they take is just as calculated as a move in a chess game. They pick their friends just as coldly as they choose their furniture, their vacation spots, their brands of liquor, and their children's schools. Everything must fit into a grand design to facilitate their upward movement."

Human nature varies tremendously from one person to another and from one group to another. We are even influenced by the region in which we grow up and where we now live. As sociologist Joyce O. Hertzler pointed out in discussing regionalism, "The culture of a region is compounded out of a complex of such factors as topography, climate, and natural resources"; and these affect our basic attitudes. In spite of many uniformities of behavior, there are distinctive social patterns of the South, New England, the Middle West, and other regions. Each region gives rise to special sentiments, wishes, interests, loyalties, attitudes, thought patterns, habit systems, and forms of public opinion.

Have you ever moved from one region of the United States to another? If so, you probably found some of your interests, attitudes, habits, and opinions at variance with those of the people who have lived in the other region for some time. For a while you were an "outlander"—not quite in step with the others.

Psychologist A. H. Maslow says that "we must treat the individual first as a member of a particular cultural group, and only after this can we attempt to treat him as a member of the general human species."

When you make up your mind to follow a certain course, this action may be based only partially upon your thinking just prior to the action. The actual roots of your behavior may lie in activities engaged in a long time before. You and I are even influenced by what countless millions of other humans prior to us have thought and done, and by what countless millions of others (not personally known to us) are now thinking and doing.

Conformity to the standards of the group is important. Every group has its own norms of behavior which affect the behavior and personalities of those who come in contact with them.

These are important factors to remember when analyzing how we consumers spend our money. *All consumers are not the same,* and what proves to be an effective sales appeal to one of us may be taboo for someone else. Cigarette smoking or beer drinking might be examples.

Child psychologists and pediatricians agree that many of our principal characteristics are acquired before we are five years old. By that time we have become creatures of habits, conventions, and attitudes from which we never completely escape. Some would even put the age earlier and say that by age three our personalities are fairly well developed.

There are many instances, for example, of children only two or three years old who have developed well-marked food preferences and food avoidances. Yet most of these early attitudes about foods are not traced to the gustatory aspects of the particular food, but rather to the environmental factors which accompany early childhood feeding habits.

In fact, early childhood conditioning helps to explain many of our adult attitudes about spending. At a later time, of course, environmental factors may change our personalities; but generally the type of treatment which we received in our early years affects our later attitudes and behavior.

Most of our traits do not change much in adult life. As behaviorist John B. Watson said: "After thirty, personality changes very slowly owing to the fact . . . that by that time most individuals, unless constantly stimulated by new environment, are pretty well settled in a humdrum way of living. Habit patterns become set. If you have an adequate picture of the average individual at thirty, you will have it with few changes for the rest of the individual's life—as most lives are lived."

Our social class certainly affects our buying patterns. Most boys and girls grow up believing that the people on the "other side of the tracks"—no matter which side—are not only different but inferior. There are very few, if any, "natural" prejudices. Even though you have had certain beliefs as long as you can remember, you were not born with them. After all, how much of your life can you remember before age five? Your biases exist because of your own conditioning, which is largely due to the beliefs and customs of the social class in which you live.

All of us fall into patterns of behavior which, once established, are very hard to change. It is usually difficult to stop doing something that you have started doing, as the great psychologist E. L. Thorndike used to point out. Whether it is playing a game or working, once started on a pattern of behavior, it is sometimes hard to stop.

After you have once established certain habits, why should you have to stop and rethink your behavior? This would certainly be a waste of time. As to your buying habits, once you have found a brand of something that pleases you, why should you spend lots of time thinking about what brand you should buy next time? If you like a brand, why worry about whether this is really the correct brand for you?

However, because many of us are restless people with an "itch" to try out new things, we are willing to experiment and try something new.

Yet in broad, general terms . . . what motives underlie consumer purchasing behavior? What actually determines buying decisions? It may not be possible to obtain answers to such broad questions. The task is enormous. The answers are complex. Each of us has almost infinite likes and dislikes, and there are more likes and dislikes and shades of likes and dislikes than there are people. And each individual's likes and motives are subject to change with different circumstances.

What fits one buying situation may have little or no relationship to another. Things that may be learned about one buyer situation in one locality with respect to one kind of product may have little or no applicability to another buyer situation in another locality with respect to another kind of product. The question of *"What's on the consumer's mind?"* must be answered not in generalities but according to specific and personal circumstances.

To discuss this problem in down-to-earth terms, think of a young married couple making a very unexotic purchase—orange juice. Why do they buy what they do? At least three factors are involved: they buy what they *like* . . . they buy what they *need* . . . and they buy what they can *afford*.

What do they *like?* They probably wonder themselves at times. Both like orange juice very much. But they like frozen orange juice better than canned, Snowcrop better than the A&P brand, and fresh orange juice better than any preserved kind. The husband likes California oranges best, but the wife prefers Florida oranges. What can they *afford* on their limited budget? After all, he makes only $325 a month, and they have other living expenses. Canned orange juice is cheapest, but neither one *likes* it! Good oranges are more expensive than frozen orange juice, and Snowcrop is more expensive than A&P. Do they really *need* orange juice or would they settle for grape juice or prune juice ... and what brand and at what price?

This example is fairly simple, but every purchase involves an unconsciously intricate balancing of decisions on these subjects. And there are an infinite number of combinations of *liking, needing,* and *affording*—it all depends on the time, circumstances, and article to be purchased.

On some occasion you may buy something on impulse. You may have walked by a given product a hundred times and on the one hundred and first time will buy it! On another occasion you may be shopping for some fairly expensive item—furniture, appliances, or even a car. Now, liking, needing, and affording will really play a big part—all the factors will have to be weighed carefully, though the final decision may not be completely rational.

More specifically, what do the terms *liking* and *needing* mean? When you say that you like something, you mean that it appeals to you, but you may not be able to explain why—and the same item may be displeasing to me or someone else.

Psychologists have attempted to break *like* and *need* into their many facets. Each particular aspect is part of a chain reaction that takes place in our minds. The first step is a *sensation*—the thing that "triggers" our minds through some stimulation (touch, taste, sight, etc.). This creates a mental *image* that is colored by all our past experience—our parents' influence on us, our environment, our family, and so on. Next we mentally *judge* the image. Will buying the particular product raise our status in the eyes of others; or help us to protect our loved ones; or nourish our bodies and fill our stomachs? The split-second and intricately balanced chain reaction ends with the development of attitudes toward the product—the extent to which we *like* and *need* the product—and once these attitudes are developed we can make any rationalization we want.

As for being able to *afford* something, this depends on how much we like and need it—our attitudes. Whether or not we have the cash at hand may make little difference—we can charge it or pay for it in installments. Lots of times it is not a question of whether we can afford it—it is a question of whether we can afford to be without it!

Eventually the question of consumer motivation will be explained on a more scientific basis. It is no answer to say that human behavior is too complex to classify and understand. That same sort of statement used to be made about the stars and planets . . . that they were too complicated to be understood . . . but men like Copernicus and Galileo demonstrated otherwise, and so have today's atomic scientists and astronomers. The Copernicus or Galileo of human motivation will also be found.

3

What Do You Want?

1. Needs and Wants

There is a school of thought popular among certain intellectuals that goes like this: advertising and selling are pretty nasty because they force people to buy things that they do not *need*. This is double nonsense.

It is double nonsense because, in the first place, no advertising or selling of any kind has ever *forced* you or any other consumer to do anything you didn't want to do. You have freedom of choice. True, advertising and selling encourage you to buy various products. And if you and I and a lot of other people quit buying, our economy will suffer. *But you are not forced to buy*—at least not by the influence of advertising and selling.

In the second place, to say that you buy things which you do not need is also nonsense, because the people who say this usually are confusing needs and wants. You and I buy things all the time—everybody you know does—which we do not *need*. What we are doing is buying things which we *want*.

If you are male, you do not need a necktie; and if you are female, you do not need jewelry. If you feel you must have a

23

necktie, or a piece of jewelry, one will do and will last you for many a moon. But actually you possess quite a number of neckties or pieces of jewelry.

I could get along with only one suit of clothes. When I was in college, I had a professor who wore the same suit all year. We had a pool on this; we chose dates when he would change the suit, and whoever chose that date was to win. But nobody won because he always wore the same suit. This man didn't need more than one suit, and he didn't *want* more than one suit.

Consider some of the things you purchase—you certainly do not need dozens of phonograph records, but you may have acquired them . . . and if you sat down and tried to play continuously all of the records which you have acquired you'd be awfully busy for several days. But you have learned to want lots and lots of things like this.

The result is that new products which have come on the market only in recent years are sold on a tremendous scale. We might not have been able to predict this a few years ago. I am quite sure that in the 1930s or early 1940s, no *man* (and I underscore the word *man*) would have dared to be seen in a pink shirt . . . but in more recent years it became all right for men to wear pink shirts, and they didn't even get whistled at. And no self-respecting adult male would have been seen working in his garden or cutting his lawn in mauve-colored pantaloons or a chartreuse whatnot . . . and not many men in the suburbs would have been proud to have been seen cooking outdoors, wearing an enormous chef's hat and a fancy apron. These are things which no one needed but which apparently people wanted.

A Vermont friend has pointed out that in the state of Vermont the habits used to be for people to eat indoors and to "go to the bathroom" outdoors. But in modern living these two important activities have been reversed! It has become somewhat stylish—especially for the "summer folk"—to eat out of doors and to have lots of modern plumbing inside the house. We *are* an unpredictable lot!

Alfred Marshall observed half a century ago that, as the economy expands and man progresses, "his wants become rapidly more subtle and more varied; and in the minor details of life he begins to desire change for the sake of change."

Let us consider two different aspects of spending behavior:

1. Long-term trends in purchasing power of consumers
2. Changes in buying habits due to changes in income

As to *long-term trends in purchasing power*, every indication is that the "leveling process" of having a huge middle majority is not just a matter of income. It is also that people are becoming more and more uniform in their patterns of living. Strangely enough, in an economy where there is the greatest freedom of choice in the world, we have tended as consumers to become more and more alike in what we do and how we spend our money!

Our psychological feelings of insecurity have not always led us to try to keep up with the Joneses just to prove that we are somebody, because it's no longer necessary to keep up with the Joneses—we are the Joneses! Instead, we have tended again and again to buy the same kinds of products which everybody else has, and not to deviate from this very much, because we do not want to appear too different from our neighbors.

Drive through certain suburbs of any city and see the new homes—small, "ranch-type" homes (ranch-type really means one-floor homes) with huge picture windows. Originally a picture window was designed so that you could look out on something beautiful. But now you look out through your picture window and there's traffic, only a few feet away. And then you have a little table in the center of your picture window, and on this you have a lamp, don't you?

Just look about you for the many other examples of uniformity. How about the automobile designs of recent years? And they are not the result of an automobile manufacturer dreaming up something just for the fun of dreaming it up. The manufacturer dreams up something because he believes it will sell. He believes that people will spend their money for what they want.

In the late 1950s our automobiles developed such a look-alikeness that the Fleetwood Cadillac didn't look too different from the Fairlane Ford. Practically all cars had bigger and better tail fins . . . and tail lights became so inflamed that driving behind another car at night, you could be almost blinded by a red-eyed monster. Uniformity in automobiles became so great that almost all of them looked like small-sized ferry boats, coming at you gnashing their teeth.

Along with the greater and greater uniformity in many products we buy, our spending power is also becoming greater and greater. The possibilities of buying more and more appliances and more and more luxury items seem unending. And how about the so-called gourmet-type foods—have you had your snails lately? Almost any of us today can improve our standard of living—and what our neighbors think of us—through our choice of how we spend our money.

How do spending habits change with changes in income? The trends will continue of our becoming more and more a middle-class market. But this huge middle-class market may not always be content with tendencies to uniformity. Perhaps people will want to "upgrade" their living more, and will no longer be satisfied with 6 neckties but may want 20, and not 6 pieces of jewelry, but 20. The spenders have the power to do what they want to do.

This includes the development of more leisure time and decisions as to how this leisure time is used. As a young man in the 1920s, I took it for granted I would work for the law firm that employed me six days a week, all day, from 8:30 A.M. until 5:00 or 5:30 Monday through Saturday. I don't need to tell you that times have changed. The pattern now is 9:00 to 5:00 in most offices, five days a week—and this 9:00 to 5:00 even includes the 1-hour lunch plus 15-minute coffee breaks morning and afternoon, so the actual number of working hours may be even less than 35. But people still like to come home from work and feel important by telling others how tired they are.

Today most of us have an enormous amount of free time, to do with what we wish. For most people, there is more and more leisure time, and the question is—what are people going to do with it? For producers, the opportunities to manufacture all kinds of leisure-time materials are excellent—television sets, radio sets, bowling balls, golf sticks, automobiles, garden equipment, and household gadgets of every kind. In recent years people have been buying hi-fi equipment and stereo hi-fi on a fantastic scale, not because people's ears have improved so that they know the technical differences between hi-fi and low-fi, but because they have learned to *want* hi-fi, and this is *the* thing to do. So now lots of people seem to be able to "blast" their friends and neighbors out of the room with loud hi-fi.

The same kind of phrenetic activity goes on in our picture taking and slide making and movie making. Despite "like-sleeping-on-a-cloud" mattresses, insulated homes, mosquito-proof screens, and refrigerators, people are accumulating gypsy equipment. (There's just nothing like getting your face rained on while sleeping under the stars.) And after they've stored the tents, people slide out the skis and start waxing for the winter trek to the mountains—lots of money for equipment, travel, lodging, and orthopedic surgeons! And all this spending is fine for the economy.

A sociological question is this: How soon will people who have long week ends and lots of leisure time become completely satiated with themselves and with spending a good part of the week end reading magazines and newspapers, looking at television, and smoking cigarettes? Many are already wondering what to do with all the leisure time they have on their hands.

A gnawing complaint of many housewives is that they don't know how to spend their spare time effectively. A housewife raising small children works extremely hard, probably much harder than most men at their jobs, but in the life cycle of a woman a point is reached where there are just lots of hours and not much to do with them. In spite of the lethargic way some of us spend our leisure time, there are many opportunities for the American people to spend their time creatively and rewardingly. There may be a developing market for books, handicraft, weaving, all sorts of do-it-yourself projects which have begun in the last few years and which might be extended greatly.

Actually there is considerable uniformity as to the percentage of the dollar income which goes into recreational activities, regardless of the amount of family income. The *Life* Study of Consumer Expenditures (see Chapter 8) shows that out of every dollar spent by the consumer, 5 cents goes for recreation and recreation equipment, such as games, toys, pet foods, photographic equipment, radio sets, TV sets, phonographs, spectator admission fees, sporting goods, and items of that sort. The really startling thing is the *consistency* among various households in the percentage of total expenditures allotted for recreation—about 5 to 6 per cent, regardless of income.

Consider also the technological changes which we have had and will continue to have in the United States.

In the first place, think of the things which have grown up in your lifetime, which you take for granted. Rayon and nylon clothing—all sorts of things you can wash and wear again tomorrow . . . mechanical refrigeration . . . the deep freeze . . . kissproof lipstick . . . television sets . . . power steering . . . power brakes. Deodorants exist on such a tremendous scale that someone has wisecracked that deodorants represent the American way of life. Little wonder, when you think of all the different kinds you can spend your money for—apply your deodorant with your fingers, with a spray, with a rub-on, or with a little revolving ball. Your wants can be satisfied in so many different ways.

Next, look ahead to the sorts of things that are going to be developed in the future. I cannot begin to describe them. They fall into two categories—first, those things which people have thought about and dreamed about a little bit, but which have not quite been perfected; and, second, the number of things which almost nobody has really thought about sufficiently, but which I am sure are going to be invented.

In the first category are such things as a golf ball that will have some sort of transmitter equipment on it so that you can locate the ball when it is lost in the rough. Television sets so that the picture will be projected on a wall or movie-type screen. Highways that will be equipped so that driver and passenger can play cards while the car goes down the highway. Homes heated by stored sunlight.

But in the second category, it is difficult to know what to list. I know of no one bright enough to tell you what these things are. But we can be sure that within the present century we are going to be spending our money for plenty of products which do not now exist because they have not been thought of as yet.

Is there anything new to be developed? Well, the combinations of new things are tremendous—new ways even of putting something together, new ways of packaging. Consider such a simple example as the little plastic bandages that go on your skin when you have a cut or wound of some kind. Until a few years ago these were absolutely white—suggesting purity. Then what happened? What was the next change? Putting little battle stars and designs on them, so that when a child puts on a Curad he can really be proud of it and show it to people. He can subtly call attention to himself, and have people say, "Oh, you poor thing." The product is the same, but it is put out in a different form.

As consumers, we want all sorts of things, and because we have learned to want all sorts of things, and because we like to have all sorts of things, a lot of products have become more and more expensive. There is more to it than that, of course—but to some extent variety is the spice of price. Take men's shirts, for instance. According to Prof. William J. Regan of San Francisco State College, in a recent year one manufacturer of men's shirts made 42 different collar and cuff styles in the *white* shirt alone. The company made 51 different collar styles and sleeve-length combinations. This combination of collar styles and sizes alone made a total of more than 2,000 different specifications for the white shirts.

Whether you are a man or a woman, you take it for granted that when you go into a store to buy a shirt, you can find it in I don't know how many different colors and patterns ... and you also expect to be able to get it in a number of variations of sleeve length and collar size ... and then there will be all sorts of variations in the shirt itself, such as whether it will be a cuff-link shirt or one with buttons on the sleeves, or whether the collar is a tab, button-down, or spread collar (and for some people the collar must have a little button right in the back) ... and then there are the variations in the material itself, from the very lightest weight to the heaviest weight ... and it can be any of all sorts of different grades of cotton, of which there are many, or wool, or mixtures, or even rayon, nylon, and so on and so on.

And what happens? The requests are so varied, because of what we want, that not only is the manufacturing problem an expensive one, but the warehousing and transportation problems are considerable. For the retailer, the problem of making enough room on the store shelves is a very tough one.

Yes, we do have many and varied wants for which we are willing to spend our money. And how different many or most of these are from our needs—those items which we must have to continue living. A tremendous amount of our spending is for these psychological *un*necessities. We want lots of variety, and we are willing to spend our money to have it.

2. Running Out of Wants?

In 1958 I attended a week-end conference at Arden House in Harriman, N.Y., attended by 35 of the nation's leading economists and experts on marketing. It was the almost unanimous feeling of this thoughtful group that there should be no attempt to try to "tone down" the number of consumer wants.

There is no final saturation point to the number of wants that may be created, because of the enormous complexities of personality of millions of different kinds of people. Each consumer will himself become satiated or saturated as to some kinds of wants, but in other areas this same consumer may find that new wants, or needs, arise as he moves along in his own life cycle.

In summarizing the conference, Dr. Henry C. Wallich, professor of economics at Yale University, wrote: "We are far from running out of consumer wants, contrary to what some social critics have been arguing. Research will provide new goods, and advertising will make them known. To argue that wants created by advertising are synthetic, are not genuine consumer wants, is beside the point—it could be argued of all aspects of civilized existence."

True, we have thousands of different gadgets. But we are not surfeited with them. At least the great middle majority of our population are not . . . and our lower-income groups can only dream about ever having a lot of the comforts that some of us seem to take for granted.

No, we are not running out of wants. There is still room for useful improvements in the mechanics of our existence.

This issue of whether we might be running out of wants so stirred the Arden House conference that the group actually took a vote on it; and an overwhelming majority of these experts believed in the limitlessness of human wants. Here is what two of them said:

Alfred Politz, president of Alfred Politz Research, Inc.: "Some people say that high saving is evidence of shrinking wants. But for most people, savings are simply delayed expenditures. It does not have anything to do with having or not having wants."

Dr. Ruth P. Mack, economist of the National Bureau of Economic Research, Inc.: "One of the main characteristics of this country is that people want things so badly that they will work a lot harder than they will in other countries. People will take double jobs; wives with families will work."

You will find that a considerable number of "moon-lighters" work at two jobs, to make ends meet and to satisfy their wants. About 1 out of every 20 workers holds more than one job. Remember, too, that our high American standard of living is sustained only with great difficulty by those in lower-income groups, and almost not at all by the lowest-income people with annual income per household of less than $1,000 a year.

You might well ask: "Is there a danger that meaningless wants may be stimulated, just to keep people employed?" Hardly. In the long run, research and human nature will probably keep wants ahead of our ability to meet them. Most consumers continue to "go out" for all they can get; and if their wants were ever to become generally satiated, we probably would be headed for a first-class recession.

There are, of course, a number of problems that the consumer faces and must continue to face. Three of these were discussed in some detail at the Arden House conference.

One of them is *inflation*. This is a serious, long-run threat. And inflation should not be accepted as inevitable.

Another problem for the consumer is the threat of a *possible recession*, or of recurring recessions. Here most consumers remain almost complacent, with great faith in their government. Most believe that somehow a depression such as that of the thirties just can't happen again. If the answers were only this simple!

A third problem for the consumer is that of *service*—that is, service for the elaborate gadgets and other machinery that he buys. The furnace, the hot-water heater, the refrigerator, the washer, the dryer, the TV set, the radio, the automobile, the power lawn mower, and so on and so on must be kept in order and kept repaired. The need for better and less expensive servicing of these machines, which are almost our "masters," is paramount.

But aside from such problems as these, which we'll have

with us for a long time, what about the consumer himself? My answer is that, as of the 1960s, the consumer is in fairly good shape ... and there is more right than wrong with him or her.

Not so, says August Heckscher, director of the Twentieth Century Fund: "While the more glittering kinds of consumer goods have been pouring off the production lines, the country has remained notably deficient in key areas of the intellectual and creative life. Our automobiles are better than our education, our kitchen gadgetry more central to our preoccupations than the form and livability of our cities."

It is true that education is not adequately financed, and that we still have slums in cities. It is also true that there are still several million U.S. citizens who continue to be faced with the question, not how to dispose of their surplus (of which they have none), but just how to meet their elementary needs. Some 5 per cent of our families have an income from all sources of under $1,000, and over 10 per cent have cash income below that level. We have no reason, therefore, to be complacent or to slacken in our efforts to make our living standards grow.

However, in recent years consumers have stepped up their expenditures sharply for education, health, and religious activities. Year after year, we press forward in our attack on poverty, disease, and other causes of human misery. Year after year, more and more Americans lead more comfortable lives.

Our American standard of living not only is high but has a good solid foundation. Irritation with and criticism of frills and trivia overshoot the mark. We may be overly gadget conscious, but the sale of gadgets spurs our economy. Certainly, some of our habits of consumption may be of a trivial kind. But why not? All of us know that women's hosiery made thicker would wear longer, but women still like to wear sheer hose ... and men like to see them this way, too! If it makes some of us feel better to have lots of chrome on our automobiles, aren't we just being human?

The sentiment was well expressed by an Iowa farmer: "We

could go without lots of things, but I think we ought to have things decent. You're only alive once. You might as well be all alive instead of just half alive."

Many consumers use their power to choose freely by making choices that—from someone else's standpoint—seem unwise or wasteful. But I still say, "Thank heaven, it's a free country; and God bless the man or woman who wants to spend money on something that seems frivolous to me." And I add, "May I please continue to have the freedom to do the same, if I wish!"

My view has been well put by Dr. Richard G. Gettell, formerly economist for *Fortune* magazine and now president of Mount Holyoke College: "In this less than ideal world, the exercise of consumer choice sometimes leads to trivia and waste. But as soon as we contemplate alternatives involving more government regulation, or restriction of advertising, it is felt that, first, we can afford the waste, and, second, that the sacrifice of inhibiting that sort of thing should be greater than the alternative of accepting the waste."

I am convinced that greater governmental regulation of production or of advertising would involve heavier sacrifices than any stemming from free consumer choice.

4

The Consumer Is King

1. Speaking for the Consumer

What kind of men founded America? What kind of men journeyed 3,000 miles into the unknown?

This country was settled first by adventurers. There were enough of them to reach our shores and then to push inland and gain a foothold.

Then, to push across the country and to *hold* it, other men were needed. Call them adventurer brigands, if you will. They had vision, but more than that, ruthless courage. And eventually we had land—3,000 miles of land in one direction.

But the bowels of the earth didn't just open up and spew forth the incredible natural resources of the land. No, a new type of American came into being: *the entrepreneur.* He gouged the hills for metals and minerals, cut down forests, ribboned the land with rails, changed a lot of landscape into cities, and built big industrial plants. He and his cohorts dreamed big dreams and did big things.

The entrepreneur was "king." The entrepreneurs were the magicians of ideas who worked their wonders with the wonders of the land . . . and our relatively young nation grew into a

35

young giant, flexing its muscles and bragging about how much could be produced. And produce we did. We developed a giant, sprawling complex of factories and plants.

Within 150 years we were the greatest nation the world had ever known. And the entrepreneur is still powerful, and will continue to be. But something happened in the twentieth century that never would have been dreamed of by the "robber barons" of the nineteenth century. The modern Goliaths of industry are being challenged by millions of twentieth-century Davids: over 180 million American consumers.

Not the adventurer . . . not the exploiter . . . not the "robber baron"—but *the consumer is king today*. Our nation has moved from an era of scarcity to an era of plenty, and this makes the role of the consumer more important than ever.

The U.S. consumer—beset by high prices and more-than-creeping inflation—and even accused by some of bringing on the recessions of the 1950s—is still the boss. No one has yet come forward with an adequate substitute for his sovereignty in the market place.

Because of his "dollar ballots" the consumer will continue to be king. Every day he casts these ballots at the cash registers. Yet he scarcely realizes that his decisions determine to a large extent what is to be produced. Business has no choice but to discover what he wants and to serve his wishes, even his whims. And this does not imply that he is a poor manipulated thing whose supposed wants are synthesized by the admen of New York's Madison Avenue or Chicago's Michigan Avenue.

The consumer's range of choice is still widening. This is because of a growing number of products. It is also because of a rising discretionary income; in fact, discretionary income is going up even faster than total income. (Discretionary income is what is left after taking care of essential expenses.)

It is the consumer whose wants, needs, wishes, desires, and aspirations must be fulfilled. If they are not filled by one manufacturer or retailer, some other manufacturer or retailer can see to it that they are. If consumers buy from one manufacturer or retailer, that business firm is successful. If they don't buy, it is not successful. It's that simple.

There must be excellent products and significant sales appeals in order to satisfy these consumers. The real job of a business firm is to provide the products most suitable for their consumers. And the job of the consumers is to make their wants known. This means that consumers have a greater voice in forming opinion than ever before. But they don't seem to realize it.

Many an American is both consumer and producer. Quite a few million of us "wear two hats"—some of us as people engaged in business, but all of us certainly as consumers. In our producer role, we are influential. Producer groups are vocal and powerful. But who speaks up for the American consumer? No one, really. There is no Department of Consumers in the executive branch of the Federal government. There is no formal, nationwide organization of consumers as such. There is no strong lobby in Washington to push the interests of consumers.

In fact, it is somewhat doubtful that consumers can be organized effectively *as consumers*. There are just too many kinds of people for any one person or group to say that he or it is representative.

Even without formal organization, though, most consumers do not speak up as individuals and say what they think. More and more we have tended to become a nation of conformists. The man or woman who "speaks up" doesn't make himself popular, and strangely enough, is looked on askance by most other consumers.

Are we becoming a society of bland individuals? In fact, I sometimes wonder if our problem isn't that of the bland leading the bland.

Although every consumer has the right to be vocal when he doesn't like a product, too many of us remain mute and silent.

Apparently in our rich milk-and-honey prosperity, it just isn't important enough to most of us to make much difference. We are too much involved in too many other activities.

And yet all the opportunities exist for the consumer to speak his piece. We are living in the greatest democracy ever. Ours is a land of freedom of speech and freedom of action. And the consumer is still King.

2. The Consumer's Range of Choice

Every consumer, within the limits of his income, has an infinite number of products and services to choose from. And every businessman knows that he competes with every product that makes a bid for the consumer's dollar.

But he also knows—both as a businessman and as a consumer—that you and I as consumers are free to buy or not buy, according to what we decide to do, and not according to what business tells us we have to do! There is no law that says that the consumer has to pick power steering over "heat-and-serve" dinners.

"The sales volume of individual products is being increasingly influenced by competitive pressures, rather than by the consumer's own requirements for survival," according to Fred J. Borch, General Electric vice-president and group executive, Consumer Products Group. "In 1800, 75 per cent of a working man's expenditures went for food alone, and only 8 per cent for products other than housing, fuel, clothing, and food. Today, that 8 per cent has grown to 48 per cent ... —which makes modern advertising so necessary, and causes mink coats to compete with cars, vacations with appliances. . . ."

As Beardsley Ruml so sagaciously observed, "The consumer is free today as never before—free to postpone, free to reduce, free to anticipate, free to switch from one unnecessity to another."

And what are these unnecessities? Everything except basic food, clothing, and shelter ... and, for most of us, an automobile. Today most of the things we buy represent the satisfaction of our *wants*, not just of our *needs*.

The *Life* Study of Consumer Expenditures (to be discussed in a later chapter) reveals that for the great middle-income group of households ($3,000 to $7,000 annual income), about 75 per cent goes for food, clothing, housing, and automotive. This leaves approximately 25 per cent of every dollar for other spending, or saving; and actually we have no way of knowing how many dollars really had to be spent for the essential, because after all there is a wide range of choice as to how much to spend for food, clothing, housing, and automotive.

All this adds up to the fact that the consumer's range of choice is pretty broad. You and I can spend "high, wide, and handsome," or we can pinch our pennies.

As consumers, we are free to postpone indefinitely the painting of our own houses until finally we have created our own personalized little slum. We are free to reduce our spending to keep up the interior of our homes until our teen-age kids are ashamed to bring their friends home. We are free to buy a new car while the cracks in the plaster multiply.

Or we can spend our money for whatever our fancy suggests. In the 1920s and 1930s Henry Ford sang a siren song and lured us out of our houses and put us on wheels. In the later 1940s, Dr. Du Mont was peddling his living-room vaudeville on the flickering TV tube, and overnight some of us were back in our houses; and for a while our houses were crowded with envious neighbors, so that we had a hard time nudging them aside to get a look at our own TV sets. But then the neighbors also began to exercise their freedom of choice by buying these same "unnecessities," so that we could choose our own TV programs once more.

By the late 1950s, with many of us already in almost a schizoid conflict as to which of our myriad recreations to enjoy, hundreds of thousands of us bought or were buying boats of all sizes and shapes . . . and we were having fun talking a new language about port and starboard, fore and aft, and going top-side.

The consumer's range of choice is greater today than ever before, and incomparably and immeasurably greater than in any other country of the world. Not only do we have more items on which we can spend money, but over the years we have learned how to spend our money pretty efficiently.

Our range of choice is so great today that, as an example, we can choose in the modern supermarket from as many as 7,000 or 8,000 different products, as compared with only 2,000 a few years ago. And the number of items and products—and, therefore, our choices—are becoming greater and more complex.

But we have become experienced shoppers and have learned to differentiate among products and especially among *brands*. After all, we have been living in a fast-changing business environment where many changes have taken place within a relatively few years, among them: automatic vending machines; chain stores; credit buying; discount houses; diversification of products; do-it-yourself; prepacked foods; self-service; huge shopping centers; trading stamps.

The mass of consumer goods is manufactured for the masses of people, that is, for the majority of those who want these products. Only unusual wants are difficult to satisfy. It is hard to find a place to buy salt-rising bread, or a nonautomatic pen. And throughout most of the 1950s, choice of an automobile had to be made among those over 17 feet long.

But the "off-beat" products *can* be found. The ingenious consumer can find the "semi-unique" product if he is willing to take the trouble—and actually the search is often fun.

Paradoxically, the great difficulty about consumer choices is that we have so many choices! Have you ever gone into a restaurant for lunch with the thought of something simple like a cup of soup and a sandwich, or a hamburger and a cup of coffee . . . and then been thrown into a state of indecision and frustration because of the wide range of choices on the two-page menu? Well, multiply this situation several thousandfold, and you have something comparable to the problem of choice facing you, the consumer, today.

You and I have a greater opportunity than at any time in history to know a great deal about the products we can buy. But we are "bombarded" by so many possible choices, all at the same time, that many times we have real difficulty in making rational choices. There are so many products available that often we find it hard to make up our minds, and then there is so much information about all these products that most of us cannot possibly absorb it all.

And thus the consumer may become frustrated, and even unhappy because he can't make up his mind. Some work in experimental psychology, notably by psychologist Norman R. F. Maier of the University of Michigan, has demonstrated the tendency of laboratory white rats to "break down" and develop neuroses when confronted with choice situations in which no adequate choice can be made. It is possible for the modern American to be faced with so many choices day after day throughout the year, that, although he in no sense "breaks down," at least he feels the stresses and strains of all these choice situations.

How can people understand the *differences in quality* of products? One way, of course, is based on price. Many people feel that a higher-priced item is more valuable than one that sells for less money. And decisions based on price may give some consumers considerable psychological satisfaction.

But one of the greatest needs of the consumer is for a *discernible difference* among competing products. For a great many consumer products, it is difficult, if not impossible, for us to make judgments on a completely logical, rational basis.

In general, though, consumers do an excellent job of choosing among packaged brand-name products, because we have learned over the years how to shop efficiently. A good deal of this is because of the effectiveness of advertising, which has given us a certain amount of information even *before* we shop or see the product. Advertising is one of the most powerful forces in our economy to bring to our attention the thousands of new products being developed every year. Advertising also informs us of the basic qualities of products and their variety of uses.

Regardless of whether or not these new products are developed through the guidance of marketing-research studies, they necessarily mean a "stepping up" of consumer wants. We have opportunities to satisfy wants far beyond the expectations of even a decade ago. This is a result of having moved away from an economy of scarcity to one of relative abundance.

We have learned to express our egos in new ways. And increasingly we have departed from puritanical traditions where it was felt that too much spending was a dangerous thing; and we have gotten rid of a lot of our traditional guilt feelings about having a good time.

3. The Middle Majority

What are some of the trends which must be watched by businessmen, in order to know what we'll spend our money for?

Number one—the tremendous population changes which are going on in our country. We are getting born in greater numbers than ever before, and some of us seem to live almost forever! We are "busting out" all over: we are now a population of 180 million, and it will be only a few years until we are a nation of 210 million. To put this dramatically, in the United States today within a 24-hour period about 4,200 people died . . . but there are also over 11,000 women who during the same 24-hour period gave birth to babies. With this many more births than deaths you have every indication that our economy is an expanding one.

Interestingly enough, our high fertility rate is not directly related to income status, although it is associated with our general prosperity. Although lower- and middle-income families account for the bulk of new births, babies have become fairly stylish among prosperous families as well.

But the so-called lower incomes are no longer very "low." From the standpoint of money, everybody is tending to become middle-class. The former rich are getting poorer, and the former poor are getting considerably richer.

And we are getting to be an older and older population! By 1965, we shall have 2 million more people who are sixty-five years and older, resulting in a population of something like 18 million people sixty-five years of age and older. The journey from womb to tomb is getting longer.

Along with the population changes, consider also certain geographical factors. Horace Greeley said, "Go west, young man"; and perhaps this can still be said, because the great population movement today is to the West and the Middle West. Every statistical survey indicates that a great deal of our future growth lies in these regions. The Middle West has always been (to use a mixed metaphor) both our bread basket and the backbone of our economy.

Significant employment changes are also going on. Our total population is expected to increase about 25 per cent in the next fifteen years, but the size of our labor force is not expected to gain quite so rapidly.

Another trend will be that more young people will stay in school longer than ever before. This will mean the most-educated population ever, and, thus, accompanying changes in spending habits.

Another trend is toward increasing employment of women. Back in the 1920s, it was generally questioned whether or not women should work for what was called "pin money." There seemed to be a theory that a woman who worked was taking a man's job away from him and that no woman had to work. But today, aside from young women who teach kindergarten or punch a typewriter for a year or two waiting for some unwary male to come along, the majority of women who work are doing so because they *have to*. This does not mean just to satisfy fundamental needs, although this is part of it, but because in our modern society the *wants* of an individual and a family are so great. About a third of our labor force today is made up of women, and this is by no means limited to single women. It is also made up of mothers and wives.

Consider next the changes in distribution of our income. As I have said, the rich are becoming poorer, and the poor are getting richer. There is more and more an equalization of income. It can't be said so much any more that all men are created equal, but rather that some men are more equal than others!

The result is a newly rich middle class which has evolved, particularly since World War II. The number of consumer units with incomes of $4,000 or more (this is after taxes in 1955 dollars) increased by 85 per cent from 1941 to 1955. And the number of consumer units with incomes of $4,000 or more is still on the increase.

During the first five years of the 1950s the number of consumer units increased 6 per cent. But the number with incomes between $4,000 and $7,000 increased more than 20 per cent, and those with incomes from $7,000 to $10,000 more than 40 per cent!

Back in 1929 the average family in the United States had an annual income of $2,320. By 1957 the average family income had risen to $6,130. Of course, the purchasing power of the dollar had declined over the years, and income taxes had risen. Yet if we compare income after taxes and also adjust the 1929 dollars into 1957 dollars, we find that real purchasing power for the average family had increased 40 per cent!

Today we are developing a great middle-income society. This is what Dr. Burleigh Gardner, president of Social Research, Inc., so aptly terms the vast "middle majority." Our concern about spending is not with that small percentage of people who are really rich, nor certainly with those who are very poor.

Most spending is done by the huge middle majority ... and this is *most* people.

Historically, distinctions about people's spending have been in terms of how much money they had or made. How much does a person earn? How much does a family have? And American business sold accordingly—selecting markets in terms of power to buy.

Today this is no longer true. The question is no longer one of whether or not people have money, because almost everybody has enough money to buy many of the mass-produced products. The question is, of all the products available, *which ones* will people buy?

The problem is a psychological one. What are the tastes and preferences of individuals, depending on their background and experience? I know a truck driver whose salary is more than mine as a professor. But our *wants* tend to be very different. Both of us like to have meat and potatoes regularly. But beyond our expenditures for food, clothing, shelter, and an automobile, we have a vast amount of discretion as to what we spend the rest of our money for. I like books more than beer—the opposite for him.

In our very new United States (and it is awfully new as compared with some other countries), we have tended to equate success with lots of money. It is even assumed at times that the person with money is also quite expert on all sorts of diversified subjects.

But the trends are changing. Increasingly we think of people, not just in terms of how much money they have, but more in terms of *where* they live and *what* they do.

The most important things about YOU as a spender are twofold: (1) Where do you live? (2) How do you earn a living?

1. *Where do you live?* This doesn't refer just to regional differences ... or whether you live in a big city like New York or Chicago, as contrasted with Omaha or Denver or Peoria. It refers more to *what part of your community* you live in.

GOSHEN COLLEGE LIBRARY
GOSHEN, INDIANA

This goes beyond "which side of the tracks." No matter where you live, you know that there are psychological boundaries to communities which do not appear on any maps. And to live on this or that street, as compared with a block over, may make a great deal of difference in how people are regarded, and how they spend their money. Sometimes the difference depends on whether you live on one side of the street as contrasted with another . . . or up the street or down the street. New York City's Park Avenue is ritzy, provided you are not too far uptown in the tenements.

Think about your own community . . . and you realize that there are certain sections that are fashionable and others that are not. The prestigeful and less prestigeful areas may even be next to each other . . . with only an "invisible" boundary, which is meaningful to you and others in the general community, but not always to strangers. It makes a difference whether you live in Yonkers or Scarsdale—adjoining each other in Westchester County. There are subtle differences between saying that you live in Northbrook, Illinois, or nearby in Winnetka . . . or in Prairie Village or in adjoining Mission Hills of Kansas City . . . or in San Mateo or Burlingame on the San Francisco Bay peninsula.

2. *How do you (or the head of your household) earn a living?* It makes considerable difference in how you spend your money as to whether you earn your living with your *hands* (as in factory work) or with your *mind* (as in one of the professions). Lawyering, doctoring, perhaps dentistrying are considered desirable, and along with these go lots of management jobs and banking and manufacturing. Contrast the buying habits of families headed by professional men with the types of buying of plant foremen and other well-paid workers.

This is not just a difference in amount of income. Your occupation (or that of the head of your household) is a powerful influence on what kinds of things you spend your money for. This even includes your place of residence, the kind of house or apartment you live in, how it is furnished, what car you drive, how you dress, what your hobbies are, how you use your leisure time . . . even whom you marry.

Look around you—at where you live and where other people in your community live—and note the differences in neighborhood, the size and condition of the homes and apartments, the occupation of the heads of the households, and the other sources of income . . . and you will readily see the differences in motives and ways of living and spending money.

Unfortunately, some of the top men in business have not had sufficient contact with the vast middle majority of people, and with the "lower-status" people who have such great buying power. Or if a successful businessman in his younger days ever was a member of such a group, he has "elevated" himself out of this group and no longer has any real contact with such people except to say to the man at the gasoline pump or to the elevator operator, "Good morning, Joe," or "Hello, Bill," and have the man reply, "Good morning, sir—nice day."

According to an analysis by Dr. Lee Rainwater and other social scientists of Social Research, Inc.: "The working class is the largest social class in our society, yet it is the one which most businessmen, professionals, and even social scientists know least about. This is not surprising since most of them grew up in families which had some pride in not being of that group, families which bent their efforts to being and staying part of the middle class of white collar workers, businessmen and professionals. The chances are that even those . . . who grew up in a working class family but who have moved on in adult life, no longer have a clear understanding of what a working class life is like. Such a person must 'unlearn' much of what his background has taught him if he is to be successful in his ambition to get ahead in the world."

Consideration of how a person earns his living is influenced by something that has happened to our society as we have moved from an almost completely agricultural nation and one of real craftsmanship to one where almost everything is made in the factory. Psychologically a tendency has grown up to look

"down the nose" on the individual who works with his hands.
Yet craftsmanship is one of the things that has made America
strong. The social distinction that has come about is that there
are two kinds of people—those who earn their living with their
hands, and those who earn their living with their *minds.* And
it has become more socially desirable to earn your living with
your mind than with your hands.

You may well ask, "What has all this got to do with spending behavior?" The answer is simply that these are the kinds
of things which influence what people spend their money for.

Money is no longer the complete key to our buying behavior. The wherewithal for such articles as Cadillacs, Ivy
League suits, and vichyssoise is no longer confined to the
known "aristocracy."

The fact that the United States is developing a vast middle
majority does not mean that we now have a completely classless
society. As a matter of fact, distinctions are beginning to be
made about people, not just along income lines, but along the
lines of our likes and dislikes. There are those who prefer conservative clothes and accessories, and at the opposite pole are
those who like bright colors and extreme styles. While this
situation always has existed to some extent, it now exists, not
so much because a person can afford one style of living or the
other . . . because he probably can afford either . . . but because
he himself and his associates are developing these tastes.

People can now eat "more fancy" than ever. Housewives buy
some foods because they look "so pretty," and the sale of
gourmet-type foods doubled in the last four years of the 1950s.
Caviar can now be bought in the supermarket . . . and even the
mail-order houses are selling "French snails—escargots!" along
with gingham dresses and electric irons.

5

Business Is Your Business

1. Our Marketing Revolution

If you travel in other countries and then come back to the United States, you are impressed by the fact that we have an economy which is the likes of nothing ever seen by any nation in any period of history! By the 1950s we had developed an economy that could produce faster, better, and cheaper than had ever been done before.

And the average person in the United States today has an income about ten times that of the average person in the rest of the world. *No matter how little money you may have, you are a "millionaire" compared with most people in the world.* There are fifteen to sixteen times as many people living in other parts of the world as in the United States. But we in the United States have fifteen times as many possessions as all the rest of the people in the world.

In so many countries, the great majority of the people are just hoping for enough to eat and to enable them to survive and get through the day. They start work as children, are almost always hungry, never acquire much more than the clothes on their backs, and will never know the meaning of the word "vacation."

Life in the U.S.A. is so very different. We are so prosperous that what happens to almost any part of American business affects all of us in the United States.

America's business is everybody's business. Harsh experience has taught us that a factory layoff in Detroit means tightening of belts in Pittsburgh, late mortgage payments in Wichita, smaller tips for the waitresses in San Diego.

We know this—whether we are stockholders who risk our savings in the ownership of American business . . . managers who strive to keep a company productive and profitable . . . or workers who both make and buy the wonderful myriad of goods that has made our standard of living the envy of the world. Whatever our role, each of us—and our families—has an increasingly communal stake in the future of the economy of the United States.

In 1957–1958, we had a wonderful example of this. When I say "wonderful example," I use the words in the same sense that a bone surgeon might say, "I just saw a beautiful example of a broken arm." In other words, it was interesting (but not exactly fun) for us in the United States to go through a mild depression . . . the polite name for which has now become "recession." Goods piled up on the shelves of the retailers and in the warehouses, because people were not buying enough. It didn't take very much of this stockpiling to cause production to be cut back . . . and when you cut back production, you "lay off" people, particularly in the motor capital of Western civilization, Detroit . . . and the steel capital, Pittsburgh. Then, in turn, because there are hundreds of other industries dependent on Detroit and Pittsburgh, lots and lots of people are laid off, and it isn't long before those people who have not been laid off begin to ask themselves, "Should I buy now, or should I postpone my purchases?"

Industry's genius for discovering new ways to make old products better and new ways to make new products possible will in the next decade provide us with a continuing abundance of goods. But industry, though bustling and prosperous today, is also vulnerable. The continued success of its mass-production methods rests on one vital theorem: *the more we produce, the more we must consume.*

If industry fails to sell its products, inventories pile up, factories slow down. Idle workers, stripped of wages, buy less; and the unhappy cycle worsens for all.

Thus the crux of industry's problem in the years ahead is to find ways to sell more goods. This is a basic problem in business.

I am overwhelmed by our material and materialistic culture . . . and its accomplishments. We have developed manufacturing and marketing techniques unsurpassed by any other country. The editors of *Fortune* magazine have observed, "The foreign visitor is drenched with sights and sounds and smells emanating from a man-made environment to which almost all Americans appear to give almost all their energies."

What are some of the factors that make us different from the rest of the world?

Our *standard of living* is considerably higher than that of any other nation. In fact, the American way of living is one in which an ever-increasing standard of living is considered our birthright. And with a high standard of living, we have not only great physical and material well-being but also an opportunity to expand our economy still further, especially in the last part of the twentieth century.

We devote more aggressive effort to the *advertising* and the *selling* of our products than any other nation. You become particularly aware of this when you see an almost complete lack of aggressive selling and advertising effort in most other countries.

We also have truly amazing methods for *manufacturing and producing* goods.

Our *high wage rate* is essential at present to our way of life. And our methods of *self-service* (almost two-thirds of all retail sales) . . . our huge *shopping centers* . . . our *discount houses* . . . our *supermarkets* are relatively unknown in other countries.

With our 57 million automobiles, we are a *nation on wheels*. In 1958, for the first time in history, the total production of automobiles in all other countries was greater than the production of automobiles in the United States. But we are still the leading nation in the production of automobiles ... and you and I just take it for granted that we will go every place on wheels.

This means *different shopping habits* for us as consumers as compared with those of most other people. In so many other nations, most people must shop every day of the week. After all, most of them are going on foot to buy and, because they are usually without refrigeration, must buy food every day.

And we use *credit and borrowing* on a tremendous scale. Without credit, our economy would collapse.

These are some of the factors responsible for our "American Way of Life." Key principles of our system are private property, freedom in buying and selling, profit and wage incentives, plenty of competition, and some government regulation.

One Britisher has written about us: "The roar of New York's traffic, the blaze in the sky over the steel mills of Pittsburgh, the clang of metal as the cars roll in endless streams off the lines in Detroit, the swish of the machines in the corn of Iowa ... —all these are signs of that restless energy which is so prominent a feature of life in the United States."

American observer A. W. Zelomek has well said: "America ... is truly a land of plenty. We measure our car ownership and our home ownership in millions, our population in hundred millions, our income and expenditures in billions. We travel fast and far, at home and abroad. We think of ourselves in superlative terms as the richest, the most highly industrialized, with the highest standard of living, the most powerful."

But a *marketing revolution* has been taking place within the last few years. That is, the problem of business used to be how to manufacture and produce goods; but the principal problem has now become how to market or sell goods.

Our nation developed the highest standard of living in the

world because we produced more goods and services in every hour we worked than any other people in the world. However, during the 1950s we moved more and more from a seller's market to a buyer's market. Thus, marketing became more critical in our economy than production.

"What do you mean by the word 'marketing'?" you ask. This term does not just mean going out and buying groceries for the family. Actually, *marketing is the performance of those business activities directly related to converting purchasing power into consumer demand.*

In other words, marketing involves the carrying out of those activities which eventually place goods in the hands of consumers. It is frequently called "distribution."

Marketing involves buying and selling activities, transportation and storage, standardization and grading, financing, risk taking, and fact finding. Marketing includes *advertising and selling and merchandising.* It is the function of marketing to try to keep the production lines rolling by selling the products produced.

To quote NBC commentator Alex Dreier: "You and I . . . the American consumers . . . are what keep the American marketer hopping . . . continually trying to find new ways to attract our attention and our dollars toward the products he is attempting to sell. And it is done in a great variety of ways . . . through marketing research . . . through scientific packaging and labeling, through artistic displays, through motivational research, through expert salesmanship. . . .

"The wanted product is made available, priced within your income range, packaged to your taste, and offered under the most favorable conditions possible. And then you either buy it . . . or you don't. It's as simple . . . for you . . . as that. If you buy it . . . the marketer can rest on his laurels . . . for about 28 seconds. But no longer, for he knows that other marketers are working furiously hard and fast to do the same job he has done, and to do it better.

"But if you don't buy it . . . the marketer has purchased for

himself a king-sized headache. *Why* didn't you buy it? Perhaps
you didn't like the color or design of the product? Or was it
too heavy... or too light? Or was the package in some way
offensive to you? Did the label connote something unpleasant
to you? Was the display inconvenient... or confusing... or
inaccessible? Was the product over-priced, or under-priced?
Those last questions are among the most interesting in the
whole marketing complex. For it seems that you and I have
preconceived and very rigid notions on what something should
cost, even though we haven't the slightest concept of how much
is involved in its production and marketing... and Lord
help the marketer who can't produce that product at our price!"

Two years ago I had an opportunity to talk individually with
dozens of chief executives of "blue-chip" companies in Boston,
New York, Philadelphia, Pittsburgh, Detroit, Chicago, St. Louis,
Minneapolis, and Los Angeles. Again and again I was told by the
heads of the companies that they regard their principal job
today as being one of marketing. These men repeatedly said
something like this: "My job is to pull together all aspects of
our business. We have people who are competent in production, in accounting, in finance, and in legal matters; but the
main job we face is how to market goods, because the minute
we quit marketing and the minute we let our competition get
ahead of us, we are 'out of business.' We're not really out of
business completely, but we have not advanced; and, if we
haven't advanced, this is the same thing as going backward.
We're dead."

This does not imply that there is nothing more to be learned
about the manufacturing of products. There are tremendous
techniques still to be invented, I'm sure. *For the most part we
have the know-how to produce an infinite variety of goods and
products, but business has not yet developed all the ingenuity
necessary to market goods adequately.*

2. Dependence on You!

Most products today are manufactured by horsepower but
continue to be distributed by manpower! Therein lies a chal-

lenge to every business, to see if techniques can be developed to market goods more efficiently.

Andrew Heiskell, chairman of the board of Time, Inc., says that the major problem for American business is: "Will Americans spend enough to buy back what they produce at a constantly increasing rate of production?" If you and I continue to buy products and services at the same rate as in the past, we are helping to guarantee prosperity for our nation.

In his stimulating book, *The Standards We Raise*, investment banker Paul M. Mazur contends that the major economic problem facing the United States is not just the threat of foreign production, but rather the problem of finding enough markets in the United States to meet the production of American producers. "When purchasing power is not being converted into purchases at a rate equivalent to production, then the economy is headed for a period of hesitancy, recession, or even depression. . . ."

This means that consumers are all-important in our economy. Every business has to create customers.

Yes, the consumer has finally come into focus; and the psychological and sociological analyses of his behavior, his values, and his attitudes are being examined from all sides. The consumer wants to live in security, but with leisure and in luxury. And the consumer also has a new-found freedom, the power of income with which he can "vote" in the market place either YES or NO . . . to buy or not buy.

This freedom creates mobility. The consumer is on the go. And to go fast, he needs horsepower under the hood and woman-power plugged into the kitchen.

Publisher Henry R. Luce has aptly said that ". . . the consumer, who is everyman, is able to register what he wants, and we businessmen and entrepreneurs are forced in seeking our own gain to serve the public well."

Beardsley Ruml sagely commented: "No longer is last week's income a reliable guide to this week's spending; no longer does this week's spending tell the complete story on next week's consuming. . . . The consumer . . . may choose in some significant measure what, when, and where he will buy; and after that, how much he will pay for quality, design, and services which he can get along without if it so pleases him."

Take the contrast between the production of goods and the marketing of these goods. Although *production of goods* has been the great American economic achievement, the *marketing of these goods* is now the American challenge. While we have learned to control manufacturing costs down to the fifth decimal, we do not always know marketing costs to the nearest tenth dollar.

It is no wonder that marketing men are beginning to listen seriously to the sociologists and psychologists, the students of people. Perhaps some businessmen have wearied a bit of the sterility of some economists who push the dollars of wealth up and down their graphed charts. And most businessmen realize full well that the curves of the dollar sign are not the only causal factor in our society.

In the U.S.A. today, more than in any other place in the world, the consumer gets what he wants. This word "consumer" means you and me, and a lot of other people like us who buy goods and services.

After all, people are markets. Just remember that the word "market" means people . . . consumers . . . human beings.

The wants that you and I have and develop help to determine what sorts of things will be made and how many of them will be manufactured. Increasingly, the problem of the manufacturer is one of trying to predict what we, the consumers, want to spend our money for . . . and this is tough. At no time in the world's history have so many people had so much . . . as well as the opportunity to decide what else they want or don't want to spend their money for. *Companies revolve around us consumers, not the other way around.*

6

Spend Your Money and Take Your Choice

1. Let the Seller Beware!

The United States consumes almost 50 per cent of the consumer goods the world uses every year . . . and we do it with only 6 per cent of the world's population.

How are we able to do this? Our industries spend billions of dollars every year just moving their products out to consumers, and promoting their purchase.

As consumers, do we have any effect on this system with its myriad of goods? Of course we do, in a multitude of ways. We spend our money on anything and everything. No wonder, because most of us have a good deal of money to spend.

And we are willing to spend for things we don't really *need*, for things we don't have to have; we feel that if we can afford it, we must spend for things we *want*.

We are willing to take a chance in our spending as never before. After all, for most "convenience" purchases, such as toothpaste, cigarettes, cosmetics, etc., what difference does it make if we get a brand or a product we don't like very much? We are "out" a few cents, or at the most a few dollars.

And no matter what we buy these days, it is pretty good. The days of being fooled by shoddy merchandise or false packaging or mislabeling are no more. Or at least when such practices do occasionally occur, they are clamped down on pretty fast by the local Better Business Bureau or even the Federal Trade Commission.

The days of *caveat emptor*—"let the buyer beware"—no longer exist ... at least in buying most products in the United States. Even for the big-ticket items—a washing machine or an automobile—you rarely get a "lemon."

We consumers have demanded perfection in what we spend our money for ... and manufacturers have wanted to give us this perfection. As Adman David Ogilvy says, "The consumer is not a moron. She's your wife."

You and I and all consumers continue to spend our money throughout the year for hundreds of products just on faith, when basically we really don't know much about the product itself. We have confidence in the brand name, or we know that we bought the product before, or we believe it is what we want, and we know from experience that it is very unusual to buy a really inferior product.

After all, how much do most of us really know about the workings of an automobile or a washing machine—or, for that matter, about the actual ingredients of toothpaste or clothing? And as to the price of products, we just are not in a position to *know* how they should be priced—that is, "what is fair." We rely on comparative shopping to feel that we are getting a good buy or a bargain.

Even though we don't know the details of the manufacturing process for most products, we do have access to a lot of information if we want to use it. And that is one of the wonderful things about our economy.

Even if we could examine all the information about how a product was produced, packaged, and priced, most of us would not do very much with the information. We just are not that *rational* as human beings. Even if we had all of the knowledge about quality, price, and quantity of products produced, we probably would not act very differently in order to get the best price.

And there would not be enough hours in the day to absorb all the information necessary. So it is fortunate that we have other means of knowing something about the products for which we spend our money.

First of all, there is advertising. It can be of invaluable use to us as consumers. In addition to the "come-on" of most advertising—to which various writers have pointed with pride and which others have viewed with alarm—a lot of advertising contains facts and information we can use. We can learn something about the product, the packaging, and the pricing.

Second, in our great land of self-service we have an opportunity to know more about the product than in former years. In shopping, we can handle the product before we ever buy— and a lot of others, too, for comparison—and if we are so inclined, we can learn about the product by looking at it, reading the label, hefting it, listening to it, smelling it, tasting it, dropping it, thumping it, kicking it, squeezing it, rubbing it, etc.

Third, we have an opportunity—if we wish—to face hundreds, or even thousands, of buying situations per year. We are not limited to a state-supported store or commissary. We can shop freely and make comparisons from one store to another. We can even go from one shopping center or one community to another. This means a huge reservoir of experience for us as consumers.

We also have the advantage of "word-of-mouth" advertising. There is a "web of communication" from one consumer to another which helps us in our purchasing. I tell you about how good something is I have bought, or about its slight flaws . . . and you do the same for me. Here is another source of information for us.

Then, too, there are several private organizations whose information we can use if we'll take the trouble. We can subscribe to the services of Consumers Research, Inc., or Consumers Union. We can look for seals of approval by the *Good Housekeeping* Institute, by *Parents' Magazine,* and by *McCall's.* We can obtain information from such professional organizations as the American Medical Association and the American Dental Association. Most of us won't bother ... but lots of information is available if we want to use it.

Various branches of the government also assist us as consumers. There are a great many agencies of each of the 50 states which protect us as to fair weights ... as to proper grading ... as to sanitary conditions, etc. We also have the Federal services of the Public Health Service, the Bureau of Standards, the Federal Trade Commission, the Food and Drug Administration, the Bureau of Home Economics, and dozens of other agencies to protect us from fraudulent and improper products.

But probably the greatest protection of all for us as consumers is what the manufacturers do for us. This idea surprises some consumers who naively believe that "business" is trying to gyp the consumer every time possible.

Recent business history demonstrates that the reverse is true. No product that is in any way a dud for the consumer can survive very long in today's highly competitive economy. There are just too many other better products which the consumer can buy elsewhere. If a manufacturer's cash register does not ring for a certain product, it is because you and I as consumers have elected to buy from his competitors.

Actually we have less need than ever for *caveat emptor*— "let the buyer beware"—because of the constant competitive struggle among manufacturers for our money. We might even turn *caveat emptor* around, and make it *caveat vendor*—"let the seller beware"—beware of the consumer's power to choose freely from among the tremendous number of competing products.

2. Fads and Fashions

The modern manufacturer has to worry about us as consumers because of our ever-changing fads and fashions. True, manufacturers often promote fads and fashions ... but it is pretty difficult to know which ones will catch on and which ones will not. It is likewise difficult to predict *how* new ideas will be used.

Who could have foreseen the overwhelming success of hula hoops, and the mediocre reception given to flying-saucer sleds? Who would have guessed that the plastic air mattress would not be a best seller in beach equipment—but would end up under the sleeping bag of even the most experienced camper? Who could possibly have forecast the skyrocketing sales of eye make-up when Brigitte Bardot made fashion of the old saying, "The eyes have IT." ... which in turn caught the lipstick manufacturers off balance, for the female populace was then clamoring for nothing but "shocking pink" to set off their "black" eyes!

Fads and fashions are practically synonymous, although a rough distinction is that fads are likely to be more unstable and short-lived than fashions. I use the term "likely" because fads can grow into fashions in terms of greater popularity, or length of popularity; they may even become part of our culture.

For example, prior to World War I, men's wrist watches were looked upon as effeminate, until taken up by various military men, engineers, and other outdoor men. Stop lights on automobiles were simply fads in the 1920s but have since become a legally necessary part of our culture. Eyelash curlers were originally classed as a fad, yet they became fashion and have now been integrated into our culture. Many diets were just fads during the gay twenties; today it's often fashionable to be on a diet. However, such fads and fashions as peewee golf, jigsaw puzzles, and riddles have come and gone—mostly gone.

Consider the kinds of clothing worn for recreation and sports today as contrasted with yesteryear. Observe yourself and other adults at play. It is almost essential that a man wear shorts on the tennis courts, and no longer the white-duck, bell-bottomed trousers so popular thirty years ago; and on the golf course, slacks and not what were once called "plus fours."

You now put on one kind of costume to ride a horse, another kind of costume to engage in bowling, and still another if you are going square dancing. As to what is called "formal dancing," men put on a special garb consisting of Tuxedo, white shirt, and black bow tie—which caused me on one occasion to make the mistake of shaking hands with one of the waiters, because he and I were dressed identically!

Changes in fashion affect the egos of people enormously and, therefore, affect the spending pattern of all of us. In the case of women's fashions, changes have become almost automatic —it's the fashion to change fashion! One of the fads in women's clothing was the "sack dress"—the epitome of fashion in the spring of 1958. But the sack was deflated by the time of the 1958 New Year's Eve dance. Yes, in a few short months, the sack was being refashioned into a shortened, curved-to-fit-the-body silhouette. But such fads are fun to experience—and delightful to reminisce on—although not so delightful for the pocketbook.

Do you by any chance remember that some years ago it was unthinkable for a woman to let others know that she liked to smoke . . . and when it was out of the question for a boss to remember his secretary at Christmas with some nice perfume? . . . Speaking of Christmas, do you recall a time when just everyone had *green* Christmas trees? Gone, too, are the days when only the rich man's son drove convertibles—today thousands of fresh-air fiends can be seen cruising around in open cars.

And when the suave sophisticates (fashionable term today) of the superhighways arrive home, they automatically turn on the hi-fi. These new-fangled sounds are quite a change from the gramophone (Caruso's records were sensational), which was replaced by the "Victrola."

The fashion of bare legs for females is quite a different idea in our society than bare legs among primitive women in Asia and Africa. And the number of inches of leg exposed—either bare or nylon clad—affects not only men but also the styles of shoes, skirts, dresses, hats, jewelry, suits, coats. . . .

There are definite fashions in entertainment, too. Both radio and television once were jammed full of quiz programs (remember when?) . . . and "who-done-it's?" . . . and "westerns." Next year, who knows??? Perhaps there'll be more "school" on TV, and maybe classical music will reach the heights of fashion.

Home Sweet Home has had some fashionable changes, too— we no longer make ourselves comfortable in a rocking chair by the wood-burning stove in a large, homey kitchen; now we're more likely to have an efficient-sized kitchen with an adjoining, large family room filled with contour chairs, hassocks, and driftwood lamps, and warmed with a Presto Log fireplace.

Fashions exist not only among the socially elite but also among sharecroppers, clerks, children, and members of all strata of society. What is fashionable for upper-class, upper-status people, though, may not be nearly so fashionable with lower-status men and women. Compare golf and the country club with the pool hall. Compare polo matches with horse races. This doesn't imply that upper-status men don't play pool or go to the races, but such activities are much more popular with lower-status men.

As people move from a lower social status to a higher social status, they begin to take on the attributes of the higher-status group, and this affects their buying habits. As a man moves up the business ladder and hence the social ladder, he may find it more and more important to play golf, whether he enjoys it or not. This almost becomes a "must"—it is the thing to do.

Sometimes, however, fashion transcends all ages and social strata. For instance, think of the "trench" coat, worn by dad or lad, dowager or damsel, bricklayer or banker. Tennis shoes usually have been popular with the collegiates, but now they are worn on occasion by all ages and in all "circles." Flat shoes were a tremendous hit with high school girls a few years back —now they have become a part of *every* woman's wardrobe.

Let's follow the antics of the hula hoop which "circled" the U.S.A. in 1958. This innovation didn't become a fad just because youngsters wanted to play with hula hoops. Actually a tremendous TV spot campaign was used to cover most major markets in the United States. Along with the TV campaign, a person-to-person publicity campaign got under way with a whole corps of men traveling throughout the United States to demonstrate the hula hoop in stores, schools, playgrounds, on street corners, and just about anywhere else. Of course, the hula-hoop craze was news and, therefore, was aided tremendously by magazine and newspaper stories. Amazingly, millions of parents—the very same parents who were objecting to the hip swinging, wiggles, and belly gyrations of Elvis Presley—were encouraging their own children to engage in navel maneuvers with hula hoops.

How can you ever predict what people are likely to do, what's going to be important to them? It's hard to do. If you had been a retailer during 1958 and had seen the hula-hoop fad developing, you would have been bright to buy up all the hula hoops you could get early in the year, sell them real fast, and get rid of your stock, because this fad was not likely to survive on a big scale. One of the most poignant ads of 1959 appeared in *The New York Times* classified section in late summer: "Thousands of hula hoops ready for immediate delivery. No reasonable offer refused." I wonder if sometime we'll see in an antique shop a hula hoop, a sack dress, and even a TV "isolation booth."

The fad which represented a kind of emancipation for women was that of "bobbed" hair. This fad was so practical for many women that it became fashion and is now a characteristic of American feminine culture. Today hair fads are based not on the fact that the hair is short, but on the various styles and colors into which short hair may be coiffeured. The "ducktail" haircut is out of date—now the hair is combed and then effectively mussed up with the hand (another Bardot influence). But if you really want to be in style, it must be the "latest."

Fashions can reverse themselves. In my grandmother's day, if a woman had a sunburned face it might have suggested to a lot of people that she worked in the fields or out of doors, when what the woman wanted was for everyone to know she was a pale, delicate lady of leisure. Today ladies of leisure acquire golden tan to show to everyone that they not only have time to lie on the beach, but that they are physically more attractive than their paler sisters.

At one time, females not earning a living with their hands promoted the idea of long fingernails, which subconsciously communicated to other people that they were among the "leisure class." Today, however, the fashion is accepted on the basis that long fingernails are attractive and feminine.

Years ago, Thorstein Veblen in his famous book, *The Theory of the Leisure Class,* called attention to the need of many people to express themselves—express their egos—by engaging in *conspicuous consumption*. This meant spending their money or their time doing things which differentiated them from other people and which were prestigeful. "Without reflection or analysis, we feel that what is inexpensive is unworthy."

Conspicuous consumption accounts for a great deal of our spending. Supposedly a former manager of Chicago's famed and expensive Pump Room restaurant said jokingly about the people who have their meat served on flaming swords, "They seem to enjoy this, and it doesn't seem to hurt the meat very much."

Historically, it has been possible for the *nouveau riche* to buy new things, flashy things, which demonstrate that they have "arrived." Today there are other ways people can engage in conspicuous consumption and call attention to themselves: new-style houses or cars, exotic vacations, ownership of a boat, and so on. As Veblen said, "We readily, and for the most part with utter sincerity, find those things pleasing that are in vogue."

However, since the bulk of the population is now well fed, well clothed, well housed, and "well automobiled," it is possible that some people, instead of engaging in conspicuous consumption to call attention to themselves, may even engage in underconsumption. They "make-do" with less expensive things, by *not* buying the latest styles and by continuing to drive older cars. This might lightly be termed "Veblen's disease" —conspicuous consumption in reverse!

One mother carried the idea of simplicity so far that her little girl came home from dinner at a friend's house and reported: "Mommie, they didn't give us regular napkins. Instead, we had to use pieces of linen!"

Sociologist David Riesman of Harvard University thinks that "there is a tendency for people, once they are accustomed to upper-middle class norms, to lose zest for bounteous spending on consumer goods." This results in *in*conspicuous consumption.

How about Ford Motor Company's luxurious $10,000 Continental? Efforts to sell these supermobiles to people known to have substantial amounts of money were not very successful at first. The Continental did not become the "social car" or even the mark of social status. So the sales strategy was changed, to reach the all-American live-it-up kind of people . . . the mink coat and yacht buyers. The best prospect for the early Continental turned out to be the man who had "come up the hard way," had a good income, and was a good spender —perhaps a gravel-pit operator or an owner of a successful pizzeria.

Each of us, in dozens of different ways, is trying to express his own unique personality. This may not even be on the conscious level, and usually isn't talked about. But, to quote Pierre Martineau, director of research and marketing of the *Chicago Tribune:* "In our gestures, in our jewelry, in our patterns of speech and dress, in a thousand subtle mannerisms, we are trying to convey to others and to ourselves exactly what we are. We don't want anyone to be mistaken about us. One woman conveys her accentuated femininity with a smart coiffure, much costume jewelry, cosmetics, and exotic cigarettes. Her next-door neighbor wears no make-up and a dowdy haircut, but refuses to smoke. One garbs herself in pirate's costumes and pixie pants, even for her housework; the other restricts herself to drab house dresses."

The psychology of fads and fashions shows how easily we fall into irrational ways of behavior. Why do we? One reason is that we want new experiences, adventures, and thrills. We tire of doing the same old things day in and day out. We crave new experiences. Adoption of fads and fashions is one means of releasing our tensions and escaping from some of our inhibitions.

3. The Consumer Be Pleased!

Ours is a constantly changing consumer market . . . more dynamic than any in history. It is increasingly difficult to predict what people will spend their money for. We are living and will continue to live in an era of great flux. Because the consumer is king, we shall live in an era of greater and greater competition among manufacturers.

Prof. Robert Ferber of the University of Illinois says in *Business Horizons* magazine: "Had anyone predicted ten years ago that the mainstay of postwar prosperity was to be consumer spending, he would have been ridiculed. Traditionally, business investment in plant and equipment and in inventories had been the spark plug, as well as the foretoken, of business conditions; it helped determine consumer income, which then led to a more or less predetermined level of consumer expenditures."

The point is that with the great changes in our income patterns, our population, our spending, and our credit patterns, there is *a greater and greater amount of competition for your dollar and mine.*

There has been a tremendous increase in the proportion of middle-income families; and, with both political parties dedicated to a full-employment economy, this trend will continue. There is also a great homogeneity as to percentages of total income spent by people on various kinds of items. Within a few percentage points, high-income households distribute their expenditures percentagewise in much the same way as do low-income households. In other words, richer or poorer, most of us spend our money for about the same kind of things and in about the same *percentages*.

There are, of course, some significant differences in buying behavior by classes, but this is more in terms of the quality of the products than their price. The great uniformity in spending habits is certainly a paradox—for we tend to act more and more like one another, when actually we have the greatest opportunity in history to act differently.

Higher-status people tend to have the same kinds of buying habits as other higher-status people; and lower-status people tend to have the same kinds of buying patterns as other lower-status people. And the differences in buying habits of different status groups are no longer very great: both the laborer and the lawyer, the plumber and the plutocrat may drive a Cadillac and vacation at the same ritzy hotel in the Bahamas.

Still, for certain kinds of products, there may be what might be called "personality types." That is, there are some differences in buying behavior by classes. Products such as sausage and beer are typed as lower class, and one of the problems in selling sausage and beer is to get higher-status people to buy them in quantity. It has been shown that the 38 per cent of our population who are "blue-collar" workers consume about 52 per cent of all the beer sold.

A "reverse" kind of problem for business is to persuade lower-status people to drink frozen orange juice, so popular with higher-status people. And there are the savings-and-loan associations, so popular with lower-status families, but not with upper-status families.

We have lots of blue-collar people, but we are becoming increasingly a white-collar nation. The most significant fact about "labor" in the 1950s had nothing to do with strikes or Jimmy Hoffa, but was an event that occurred in 1956 and was scarcely mentioned in the newspapers. The event was that in 1956, for the first time in our history, *the number of white-collar workers became greater than the number of blue-collar workers.* In a sense, this was an historic milestone in our economy. The forecasts for the 1960s indicate a continuation of this trend.

We are also getting more suburban and more educated. The number of youngsters of school age is now at its highest point in our history. And we are developing a population that is older than ever before, yet paradoxically with more children.

There is also growing sophistication as to *kinds* of things we are willing to spend our money for. No wonder, because we have more money to spend than ever before. Our backlog of savings in the United States is the greatest of any nation that has ever existed. There has been nothing comparable in history. Savings deposits of individuals rose from $232 per capita in 1936 . . . to $771 in 1946 . . . to $1,077 in 1956! Today they are about $1,600.

Furthermore, we have a tremendous expansion of consumer credit, so that buying can take place on a greater scale than ever before in history.

Because as consumers we can buy with such confidence, we should be relatively happy. But not so the manufacturer—his life is by no means an easy one. In fact, a manufacturing career, especially in bringing out new or untried products, is a tremendous gamble.

In the nineteenth century Commodore Vanderbilt is supposed to have said, "The public be damned." On the other hand, today's modern businessman has no choice but to say, "The public be pleased!"

Even though a business tries to give the consumer what he wants, consider how wrong business judgment can be and, therefore, what risks must be taken. You and I—and other consumers—sharp-eyed, wary rascals that we are—seem to lie in wait for the manufacturer to make a mistake. And then he ends up with one of the thousands of products that doesn't sell.

A manufacturer of cake mixes thought that his principal market would consist of working women who had very little time to spend in the kitchen. But the facts turned out that his principal market consisted of housewives with big families, and the marketing plans had to be changed.

Another example—a small company that made dog food in a certain city decided that the product would be promoted primarily to people in the suburbs because people in the cities did not have so many dogs. But the facts turned out to be for the particular city that only one-third of the dogs for the metropolitan area were in the suburbs and that two-thirds of the dogs were in the city!

A company producing floor wax tried primarily to reach families of lower income, having in mind the kinds of people who might use the wax on the linoleum floors of their living rooms and dining rooms. But the facts turned out to be that the wax was bought mainly by families with above-average income.

How on earth can business properly assess what we as consumers are likely to do? We are fickle . . . and we are demanding. Charles G. Mortimer, chairman of General Foods Corporation, has listed 10 different kinds of *convenience* which you and I expect almost as a matter of course:

1. *Form Convenience:* Wide choice of fresh, frozen, canned, various powdered, flaked, solid, cake, bar, paste, cream, or liquid food products
2. *Quantity or Unit Convenience:* Numerous sizes of packages of a single product; large versus compact or small cars
3. *Time Convenience:* Retail stores staying open evenings and odd hours for shoppers' convenience
4. *Place Convenience:* Shopping centers for one-stop shopping; telephone booths everywhere
5. *Packaging Convenience:* Packages that protect contents, that are easy to find, store, carry, open, use, and dispose of
6. *Combination Convenience:* Matched luggage; silverware and china place settings; complete-unit laundries and kitchens
7. *Automation Convenience:* Automatic dishwashers, laundry equipment, clock-radios; automatic gear shifts in cars
8. *Consumer Credit Convenience:* Homes, automobiles, appli-

ances, or vacations paid for out of income yet to be earned
9. *Selection Convenience:* Wide range of forms, units, patterns, models, colors, flavors, styles, and prices in just about everything consumers buy
10. *Readiness Convenience:* Such ready-to-cook convenience foods as cake mixes, heat-and-serve dinners

Not only do you and I insist on all these different forms of convenience—we expect them and take them for granted. If we don't get what we want . . . we let the manufacturer (not the consumer) be damned!

Our demands for convenience account to a considerable extent for the cost of what we buy. But because we have money and want to buy, we are willing to pay more in order to get just what we want.

And then consider all the differences in our demands, *according to the locality in which we live.*

Take men's hats, for instance. Men's hat brims tend to get wider as you go from the East to the Middle West and then to the Southwest. You may be reasonably sure that a lot of men in New York's Manhattan will have hat brims less than 2½ inches wide . . . in Kansas probably 2½ inches . . . and in the Southwest 2¾ to 2⅞ or 3 inches. What a headache for the manufacturer!

Then, think how inconsistent we are in our color preferences. Go into the hot sunny climates of the South, and there is a greater tendency for women to want bright, warm colors than in the colder regions of, say, Minnesota or New England, where duller, "colder," colors are preferred. Shiny patent-leather bags have been known to sell much better in the South than in Northern climates. The reverse of this is the conservative navy-blue handbag, a fairly consistent best seller in Northern communities.

Even the use of facial cosmetics varies from one section of the United States to another. In the lead are New York and California, but at the other extreme, Vermont females in rural sections don't need as much "grease paint" as big-city ladies.

We even have locality differences in what we feed our dogs. Although the three basic kinds of dog food (canned, meal, and biscuits) are available almost everywhere, there are regional preferences. For example, dog biscuits are relatively more important in New England than in the Southwest; and the reverse is true for canned dog food in these areas.

And the sale of dog food is no small business. The Gaines Dog Research Center has estimated that the 26 million dogs in 18 million American homes are responsible for an annual sales volume of $500 million worth of prepared dog food. This is more than is spent in one year on baby foods!

Further, as to regional preferences, why are vanilla wafers so popular in the South but not in the North? Why will some Southerners eat only yellow cornmeal and other Southerners eat only white cornmeal? Why is a greater volume of candy sold per capita in Utah than in any other state? Why are luggage sales, on a per capita basis, so much better in Montana than in Mississippi? Why are more square feet of floor covering per home sold in Minneapolis than in Boston ... and why do people in Boston buy fewer shoes per family than in most other cities? Why is iced tea popular in the South, iced coffee in the Middle Atlantic States, and hot tea in New England? And why is chicory necessary in New Orleans?

Our individual preferences and foibles may be fun for us as consumers, but they are tough on manufacturers. At least for items like the ones mentioned, they make his manufacturing and marketing problems very difficult.

On the other hand, we should not exaggerate this point. We should recognize that there are thousands and thousands of items which are absolutely standard throughout the United States. Cecil D. Southard, for many years vice-president in charge of wholesaling for Butler Brothers, says that about 85 per cent of the items bought for their 2,500 Ben Franklin variety stores are controlled by a standard stock check list which is used by all stores throughout the country. Butler Brothers—franchised stores, such as Ben Franklin stores, are standardized. Butler Brothers buys the same work clothes, work gloves, work shirts, handkerchiefs, shoelaces, combs, scissors, brushes, notions, toiletries, hardware, et cetera, et cetera for its stores in Missouri and Minnesota, Connecticut and California. The great majority of items on the basic stock list are exactly the same, and there is little difference according to locality.

The same pattern, of course, is true for lots of products sold nationally through other kinds of outlets—everything from washing machines to automobiles.

The main point is that, as consumers, we do expect and demand a lot. And increasingly business is going to give us what we expect. The motto of the modern manufacturer has to be:

The consumer be pleased!

7

You Have the Money and the Time

1. Dollars and Discretion

Mystery always surrounds the consumer and his spending plans. There are millions of decisions every day . . . to buy now, to buy later, or not to buy at all. And these decisions in turn determine our economic destiny as a nation.

After all, no one of us is under any compulsion to part with his dollars. Yet most consumer income goes for "discretionary" purchases, for things we want but don't necessarily have to have—a clothes dryer, new furniture, a vacation trip. A considerable portion of our spending is also for impulse purchases, sometimes for products we didn't even dream of owning just a few years back.

In other words, consumer spending can be classified as either essential or discretionary (nonessential). And more money is available today for discretionary spending. To quote A. W. Zelomek, from his book, *A Changing America:* "In 1941 the typical middle-income family had an annual income of $1,458, spent $1,017 on basic living costs, paid $2 in federal income taxes, and had $439 left for discretionary spending. By 1958 the typical average income had risen to $5,235. Basic costs for the same standard of living had increased to $2,005, the federal government was taking $415 in taxes, but the family still had $2,815 left for discretionary spending."

It is true that the dollar was worth only half as much in 1958 as in 1941; but even taking this into account, it would mean $1,407.50 (in 1941 dollars) as contrasted with $439 in 1941.

At the June, 1959, meeting of the American Marketing Association, Dr. Grover W. Ensley, executive vice-president of the National Association of Mutual Savings Banks, said: "When the consumer wonders about making ends meet today, he has different ends in mind than did his forbears of not so long ago. Today's breadwinner is not worried about how to feed and clothe his family but rather how to budget the second car, the payments on his suburban house, his son's college expenses, the family's vacation trip, the orthodontist's bills, and the new outboard motor." Most of these represent discretionary spending.

When Mrs. Consumer goes shopping, she thinks about how to buy economically, so that she can have something left over for a permanent and also give her youngsters money for the movies or the school game, or a space-age toy.

Consumer spending has been on the rise for many years, and no halt is in sight. Personal disposable income reached the new height of $337 billion in 1959, and consumer expenditures the new high of about $314 billion.

How have American buying habits changed over the years? The story is dramatically told in a 1959 report of the U.S. Department of Labor. Back in 1900, scarcely one out of five workers' homes was owner-occupied, as contrasted with three out of five today. The average home then had no running water and no inside toilet; light was supplied by kerosene lamps; and cooking was done on a wood or coal stove.

Compare this with today—electricity, running hot and cold water, at least one fully equipped bathroom, central heating, a vacuum cleaner, a washing machine, a telephone, a television set, at least one radio, a gas or electric cooking stove, a refrigerator. And most families, if they wish, can buy electric blankets, air conditioners, fans, mixers, a dishwasher, a garbage-disposal unit.

As of 1910, almost half of the steelworkers in the United States were earning less than 18 cents an hour; and there were deductions from pay for ice water, disablement funds, medical fees, identification badges, and credit advanced by company-owned stores. This is quite a contrast to today's average $3 an hour for steelworkers, with numerous fringe benefits, and also premium pay for overtime.

In 1929, the average annual salary for all wage earners in industry was $1,405 (with the work week 50 hours or more). By 1953, the figure was $3,590 annually.

Most middle-class families of today have an income that to the frugal farm families of the nineteenth century would have implied great wealth. Those families followed the Benjamin Franklin maxim: "Spare and have is better than spend and save."

Trends toward spending have gone so far that many people "look down their noses" at prudent, self-denying thrift, so respected by earlier generations. The 1900 values of "work and save" have given way among many people to the 1960s belief in "be happy and be fulfilled." People used to say, "A penny saved is a penny earned." Today some people say, "You've got to spend money to make money."

What about the relationship between spending and saving? Even before we decide whether to buy one kind of product or another (a vacuum cleaner instead of a power lawn mower), or one brand instead of another (Hoover instead of Electrolux), we have to make a decision to *spend*. We can make another choice instead . . . to *save*. We can decide not to buy at all, if we wish. After we have put our money on the line for food, clothing, shelter, the automobile, and taxes, we have many dollars left to do with what we want. These are our true *discretionary dollars* . . . to use as our own discretion tells us.

Even with all the living beyond our incomes, due to more

and more consumer credit, savings are on the upgrade. Remember that "saving" means more than money in the bank; it includes the cash value of insurance policies, the equity in your home, any investments you may have. In 1949 the savings of the American people were over 4 per cent of their disposable income, but by 1959 were almost 7 per cent, some $23 billion.

But, as the *Wall Street Journal* said on October 7, 1958: "When savers deposit money in a savings and loan association, they are in effect postponing spending. The association then lends their money to others who use it, in most cases, to buy houses. The net effect on spending is nil. One group has postponed its spending; another, by borrowing, has accelerated its outlays. The same is true for funds placed in savings banks and life insurance companies."

Even though *as a nation* we are saving a lot more than we ever have before, *as individuals* we are saving less. That is, we are letting Uncle Sam and the pension funds do the bigger part of our saving for us. And since our income is larger and we are *saving less* as individuals, we must be *spending more*. And we are!

The total personal consumption expenditures of our nation skyrocketed from $79 billion in 1929, to $172 billion in 1940, to $194 billion in 1950 . . . and to a total of $291 billion in 1958. Pretty big spenders, aren't we?

On a per capita basis, this means that we spent about $637 per person per year in 1929, approximately $1,284 in 1950, and nearly $1,600 in 1958.

Where in the world do we spend all this money? I'm sure that this is a question all of us ask ourselves privately . . . and it is too bad that no one answer can suffice for everybody. Nondurable goods (such as food and clothing) accounted for about a constant 50 per cent of this total spending in 1958; services, 37½ per cent; and durable products (like refrigerators, furniture, automobiles, and jewelry), 12½ per cent.

But it is significant that the greatest percentage gains over

the years fall into the realm of "durables." This means that
we are spending more money on things that last a while; and
so, in a sense, we are "saving" as we spend.

In 1959, the *Wall Street Journal* further confirmed this
theory by reporting the views of some economists: "The switch
of millions from paying rent to paying on mortgages actually
means no dangerous new burden, say unworried economists. It's
just a change, they say, from one type of payment to another.

"And they carry this reasoning further. Money that formerly
paid the laundryman has merely been switched to installment
payments on the washing machine, they say. Yesterday's ice
money pays on the refrigerator. Cash that once went for bus,
trolley, and train fares now helps meet payments on the family
car."

We are rich and getting richer. The average annual family
income today is over $6,000 . . . and the average for families and
single individuals is over $5,000. Around 7 million families
have incomes of over $10,000 . . . and over 2½ million families
have incomes over $15,000 annually. Three-fourths of us have
liquid assets, such as money in a checking or savings account,
savings and loan association shares, U.S. savings bonds . . . and
no wonder, since there are so many opportunities for others
to pay us well for the use of our dollars. One out of every eight
American adults owns stock in a public corporation, with
about half of all stockholders in the $5,000 to $10,000 income
bracket. Over 110 million Americans have insurance policies.

Your financial way of life has startingly little resemblance
to that of your parents . . . and it may be different for young
people in their twenties as compared with people in their
thirties.

Lots of people can rattle off their monthly payments almost
down to a penny, says William H. Whyte, Jr., in *The Organization Man,* although this doesn't necessarily mean that they keep
formal budgets. "Quite the contrary; the beauty of budgetism
is that one doesn't have to keep a budget at all. It's done automatically. In the new-class rhythm of life, obligations are

homogenized, for the overriding aim is to have oneself pre-committed to regular, unvarying monthly payments on all the major items."

The American consumer is a complex individual, with a voracious appetite for new and better products. His decisions to spend, or not to spend, have a lot to do with our continued prosperity.

2. Time on Your Hands

In the United States we work less and earn more than people in any other country in the world. We have more time of our own, and more money to spend. And, because of increases in productivity, the trend is to even more money and more free time.

In 1800, the average work week was 84 hours! By the end of the Civil War it was down to 70 hours ... and men began to find an hour now and then for the new game of baseball, for circuses, carnivals, and an occasional fling at the trotters. By 1900 the 60-hour week prevailed; and by the time Herbert Hoover went to the White House in 1929, it was down to 50 hours or so ... with Saturday afternoon off for sports, shopping, or (for some) the speakeasy.

And now, just as we are getting used to the 40-hour week, we find that even it is slipping into history. A 1958 survey by the U.S. Department of Labor indicated that 45 per cent of office workers put in fewer than 40 hours a week. In that same year, the United Auto Workers were asking for a 32-hour week, and the International Association of Machinists voted unanimously to press for a 30-hour schedule. Fewer than 40 hours per week seems to be the trend for most workers today. The trend also indicates more interest in having longer vacations and more frequent paid holidays instead of just getting a shorter work week. In fact, people are more interested in overtime pay to finance their growing number of wants, and more time off for their many activities.

Traditionally the man who worked did not have time for

leisure, but this is no longer true. It used to be that a man worked from dawn to dusk and beyond, in order to provide food, clothing, and shelter for his family ... but these requirements can be paid for today by working only about half as many hours.

Here are some of the ways leisure time has been acquired: *Shorter hours:* The average work week of the industrial worker has declined by one-third since 1890 ... and mechanized farm equipment has also cut the farmer's work week. *Longer weekends:* We have gone from a 6-day week to a 5½ week to a 5-day week during this same period. *Paid vacations:* Over 42 million wage and salaried workers are now eligible for paid vacation time. *Retirement:* Almost all labor contracts now contain some type of retirement provision. And don't forget the *coffee break.*

Our leisure hours now outnumber our working hours! With about 56 hours a week of sleep, the average worker spends about 40 hours on his job, but has a leisure week of 46 hours —with 26 hours for transportation, eating, and grooming. The focal point of his life may be his leisure hours instead of his working hours ... especially if his job does not require too much skill. Many jobs have become so highly mechanized and repetitive that they give a man or woman almost no opportunity to express his individuality while at work.

Leisure seems to be a term which everyone talks about but which few people can readily define. Most people think of leisure as "nothing to do," and recreation as "fun." Certainly it implies absence of work and, therefore, more time on our hands.

But what activities are for fun, and what are not for fun? If a man has a bottle of beer at a friendly neighborhood tavern, most of us would call that recreation. However, if he has some of this malt beverage with his lunch, is that the same as having a cup of coffee, or is he "having fun" while he eats his noonday meal? Ordinarily clothing is not thought of as a recreational expenditure ... but how about a ski outfit or bathing suit?

Most of us would agree that money spent for radios, TV sets, phonographs, spectator fees, games and toys, sports goods, photographic equipment, and pet foods is definitely for recreation. As a nation, we like to have "fun," and we are willing to spend money for it.

Leisure time is not only spending time but also consuming time. This is the time when you can wear out your furniture, blow out your picture tube, scratch your stereo records, break your camera, dent your fenders, lose your golf balls, run your boat on the rocks, or run out of charcoal briquettes. Oh, yes ... and have your name posted on the overdue list at the club. All of this is consuming, of the first order.

Another effect of leisure time is the increased time we have for charity drives, hospital work, boys' clubs, church activities, and similar laudable works. These activities also have effects on our social status. As our social status changes, so does our way of living and thus our pattern of consuming. The furniture is replaced ... another car is purchased ... new clothes are bought for the whole family. The spreading of the luxury of leisure in our dynamic society thus adds to our consumption.

So the question, "What shall I do in my spare time?" becomes, "When will I ever have enough time to do all the things I want to do?"

Fortune magazine has observed how ironical it is that the "workers," not the "bosses," constitute the new leisure class in the United States. Professional and managerial groups cannot dream of even a 40-hour week, and most need 50 or maybe 60 hours to accomplish their nonautomated jobs. Furthermore, the number of people for whom this is true is on the increase; the number of men in managerial, professional, and technical occupations is rising faster than the expansion of the male labor force as a whole.

Probably the biggest change in our leisure time has occurred in the home, where we spend about 70 per cent of our time. We now have all sorts of things that save us time—dishwashers, clothes washers, clothes dryers, stoves that turn on and off automatically, electric coffee makers ... and more time than ever to turn our eyes to the big box—TV. We even have time to take 500 million baths a week.

We are now looking forward to more home gadgets. Do you have a small refrigerator in your bedroom yet? Well, you probably will, in time. And designers and engineers are dreaming up lots of new devices for us: a special closet in which clothes might be dry-cleaned overnight by ultrasonic waves ... a 5-in-1 laundry machine that washes, dries, sanitizes, presses, and folds shirts and linens ... a gadget that scrubs, rinses, and dries the floor without being touched by Mrs. Housewife.

What are most people doing with their increased leisure? As A. W. Zelomek indicates, three things are taking place: We are becoming more active—participants rather than merely spectators. Many of the recreational activities once limited to the rich are now becoming available to middle-income and even lower-income groups. The mass movement to the suburbs is causing a changing pattern in our recreation habits.

We spend over $40 billion a year on recreation. This boom in the leisure-time market has surpassed all expectations. Why? The boom is due to a combination of things: the rapid expansion of the middle-income group during the fifties ... the explosion of the sprawling cities into the suburbs ... an increase in the use of credit, even for pleasure activities ... technological improvements in leisure products ... more labor-saving devices in the home ... shorter work weeks ... faster transportation to "get away from it all" ... increased emphasis on having fun.

A special report by *Printer's Ink* gives some figures for annual spending on recreation that would have staggered our forefathers: $0.3 billion on hi-fi and stereo components ... $0.6 billion on swimming pools ... $2.1 billion on photography ... a like amount on boating ... $2.3 billion on overseas

travel . . . $3.5 billion on gardening equipment . . . $16.8 billion
over-all on recreation and domestic travel.

The quickening pace in participation sports is extending to
almost all fields. We are doing more boating, skating, water
skiing, bowling, golfing, and fishing than ever before. From
playing cards to swimming in pools, Americans have never
spent as much on leisure-time products as now. We are pitch-
ing more tents, whacking at more golf balls, and using up more
film than ever.

However, Prof. David Riesman has called attention to
some different patterns of leisure in different kinds of social
classes. Radio and TV listening are the top two activities for
both upper- and lower-prestige groups . . . but lower-prestige
group members spend more time just driving around or in
taverns and may be contrasted with the upper groups who go
out to parties more, as opposed to just "dropping in."

Recreation is no longer so much along family-wide participation lines as formerly—instead, it is designed for individuals
or couples, suited to special interests of different age and sex
groups. This is brought out in Dr. Arnold W. Green's textbook
on sociology, where other changes in traditional family functions are also discussed—home is no longer the center of
economic activity, and work within the home is curtailed as
much as possible.

As once it was wrong to play so much that it might affect
your work, now it is wrong to work so much that it may affect
your family life. Anthropologist Margaret Mead believes that
work hours, length of vacation, and amount of overtime tend
more and more to be evaluated in terms of their possible
effect on family life.

However, some of us—especially many older people—do not
seem to be capable of completely enjoying our leisure. Dr.
Theodore Levitt of the Harvard Graduate School of Business
Administration writes: "We pride ourselves on not having had
a vacation in ten years and think that one of the most com-

mendatory things that can be said of a man is that 'he died with his boots on.' Max Lerner says that the outstanding characteristic of American civilization is that it is a success. But we're uncomfortable about it."

No doubt Professor Levitt exaggerated a bit, to make his point. But there is little question that our puritanical traditions have caused some of us to shun too much play. Back in 1792 the Methodist Discipline, outlining the policy of Cokesbury College toward recreation, said: "We prohibit play in the strongest terms . . . the students shall be indulged in nothing that the world calls play. Let this rule be observed with the strictest nicety; for those who play when they are young will play when they are old."

In the 1850s a leading department store included the following in the set of rules for employees: "Men employees are given one evening a week for courting, and two if they go to prayer meeting. After 14 hours of work in the store, the leisure hours should be spent mostly in reading."

Although such statements seem extreme to modern Americans, there still is some feeling that not too much time or money should be spent on recreational activities. The late Sumner Slichter, professor of economics at Harvard University, moralized that "most men are not prepared to make good use of large and sudden additions to their leisure." And the American love of leisure and material things has been blamed for lag in our economic growth. At a 1959 National Industrial Conference Board forum, certain economists took the position that overemphasis on material things had dragged the nation's economic growth almost to the bottom of the list of major nations.

Surprisingly enough, though, we are spending money for leisure and recreation in just about the same *percentages* as we did back in the 1920s. This is in spite of the fact that the work week is now so much shorter. Since 1929, we have spent approximately 5 per cent of our income for recreational activities and equipment.

There are more of us to spend money on recreation, but

most of us spend most of our money on nonrecreational pursuits. Of over $336 billion which we had in after-tax income for 1959, only one-fourth, $84 billion, was left after we had spent our money for food, clothing, housing, and transportation. Of this $84 billion, about $24 billion went into some form of saving (by individuals and by their employers); $19 billion paid for medical care; $17 billion was for "personal business" (such as bank service charges, brokerage costs, interest on loans); $4 billion was toward education ... which left only $16 billion (about 5 per cent of the $336 billion) for recreation and "fun."

It is true that our teen-agers "hot-rod" around, buy cha-cha records, and eat "elephant" sundaes ... but as adults they settle down to the age-old pattern of bringing up families. Most of us Americans spend most of our money in remarkably sober fashion.

8

Who Spends for What?

1. The *Life* Study of Consumer Expenditures

Behind all the figures and facts on spending is society—consumers. Beyond the field of economics is the living, moving profile of the consumer U.S.A.

In poor English, but with good logic, more of us ought to ask, "Who is people anyhow?"

In order to answer such a question, *Life* magazine undertook its now famed Study of Consumer Expenditures—a 15-month, 10,000-family "safari into darkest marketing." This project was not just a walk on the beach. It was a scientifically planned walk into 10,000 U.S. households, at a cost of almost $2 million.

The study covered virtually the entire spectrum of consumer expenditures. The over-all purpose of the survey, conducted for *Life* by Alfred Politz Research, Inc., was to describe the markets for each of the various goods and services which consumers buy. "Who spends how much on what?"—this is answered by measuring how much of the total expenditures in each of the consumer markets was accounted for by various types of households. A household, according to the U.S. Census Bureau and as used by *Life*, comprises all persons who occupy a dwelling unit.

Two different types of interviewing techniques were used.

Some of the information was obtained by a recall method—by asking people to remember major purchases, such as an automobile or a refrigerator. The other method was a family record or diary in which daily purchases by members of the household were recorded; this diary listed the items, the price paid for each, and the kind of store where each purchase was made.

The L.S.C.E. (*Life* Study of Consumer Expenditures) is a detailed profile of America drawn from the ringing of 140,000 doorbells and 90,000 interviews by 280 trained interviewers working every day for 15 months (October, 1955, through December, 1956) to secure 8 hours of interviews of the behavior patterns of each of the 10,000 households.

Recorded, coded, and tabulated on over 1 million IBM cards is a vast deposit of human values. Here are delineated the attitudes of U.S. consumers, as expressed by $200 billion worth of their spending decisions. And behind all these millions of tabulated facts, and behind the ½ million diary-recorded purchases of products, by day, by seasons, by city or suburbs or region, by age, by education, by income, by family composition—is the spending profile of the U.S. consumer.

Although the results from the *Life* study were first published in 1957, it will be useful if we describe all results *in the present tense.*

There are 34 per cent of the households with $5,000 or more in their annual wallets. And over 60 per cent of the heads of households have high school or more in their heads. U.S. consumers—the "people of plenty" in the market place—spend an annual household average of 4,108 dollar bills for all consumer goods and services.

The basic statistic presented is average annual dollar expenditures per household. Because these averages are computed from a representative (probability-selected) sample of all households, the findings have been projected to the aggregate dollars spent by *all* households in the United States.

Total current expenditures are divided among eight major types of expenditure:

1. Food, beverages, and tobacco
2. Clothing and accessories
3. Home operation and improvement
4. Home furnishings, equipment, and appliances
5. Medical and personal care
6. Automotive
7. Recreation and recreation equipment
8. Other goods and services

More detailed expenditure categories are then shown within each of these eight major groups, such as baby foods and prepared mixes under food, men's and boys' footwear under clothing, and tires under automotive.

Expenditures are analyzed by seven household characteristics:

1. Household income (from all sources before taxes)
2. Age of the household head
3. Occupation of the household head
4. Education of the household head
5. Stage of the household in the life cycle (young single persons or young married persons without children, households with children, etc.)
6. Geographic region (with metropolitan areas separated from nonmetropolitan areas within each region)
7. Market location (within different metropolitan market sizes, inside central-city areas separated from the balance of the metropolitan market areas and the nonmetropolitan market areas)

Another household characteristic related to its consumption is its size; and the average number of persons per household is reported for the households in each classification.

In addition to average dollar expenditures per household, "budget-type" figures were computed which show what shares of all the money spent by all households in a given classification go for food, for clothing, etc.

2. Some Patterns of Spending

What has come out of this big, complex, massive national survey? The first impression is one of great stability and order.

In a very broad sense, we can almost say that there are no great "class markets" in the United States any more. The American family distributes its budget roughly in the same proportions among all the major consumer goods, whatever its income—or whatever its occupation, location, education, and family structure. Even the senior citizens, people over sixty-five, buy pretty much the same *type* of goods and in the same *proportions* as everybody else buys them.

It seems to be a conservative market in its wants and appetites. Only one major expenditure group has been added to the old trinity of food, clothing, and shelter: the automobile. And, since two-thirds of all people depend on it to get to work, it is a necessity despite the chromium, color, and luxury which Detroit has built into Henry Ford's black box on wheels.

The picture of the American people dissolves into turbulent, dynamic complexity as soon as the figures in the study are subjected to closer analysis. How to explain that the college-educated spend so much more money on liquor than anyone else? How to explain that the well-to-do with incomes over $10,000 a year splurge on rugs—spending almost as much on them as they do on major appliances? (Has wall-to-wall carpeting become a symbol of status?)

But there are other findings from the L.S.C.E. that seem common sense. Families with children are the best market for frozen juices, vegetables, and fruit. The higher people's educational level, the more they buy things that get the woman out of the kitchen. Suburbia spends a good deal less on spectator entertainment and sports, and a good deal more on homemade recreation, than city citizens.

Of all families in the United States, about half (all those earning less than $5,000 before taxes) seem to spend all they earn, or more. The interviewers who ran the survey in the field reported that family after family, after seeing for the first time every penny of their spending recorded in black and white, asked, "And where does all this money come from?" There were other unanswered questions ... about the money available to give children the education needed in today's industrial society ... about reserves for the cost of serious illness ... about what the reactions of exuberant consumers would be to even a mild economic setback.

But a lot of questions were answered.

As a beginning, let's see how consumer spending changed over the twenty-year period from 1936 to 1956. Consumers spent 36 per cent of their dollars on food in 1936, but only 29 per cent in 1956 for food, beverages, and tobacco. Rent and home operation took 30 per cent of consumers' dollars in 1936, but only 19 per cent in 1956.

But expenditures for clothing went from 10 to 12 per cent twenty years later, and automotive expenditures doubled —from 7 to 14 per cent. This 14 per cent is one out of every seven dollars in our wallet!

The *Life* study examined households in five "stages" of the life cycle:

1. The young, single or married household with no children (3.7 million at the time of the *Life* study)

2. Infants or young children in the household, with or without teen-agers in addition (almost 20 million)

3. Only teen-age children in the household (8 million)

4. Older married couple, but no children present in the household (11.3 million)

5. Household headed by an older single person (6.5 million)

It is group 2 that spends the most money. These millions of households—40 per cent of all households—account for 45 per cent of all the expenditures.

Probably the most amazing thing about the results is that they demonstrate that U.S. consumers are a surprisingly homogeneous market. Regardless of income, families tend to spend their money in pretty much the same way . . . and this sameness extends to practically everything the family buys except food! The accompanying table shows how households of various incomes distribute their spending.

Distribution of Annual Household Expenditures in U.S.A. by Annual Household Income

Item	All households, per cent	Annual household income					
		(1) Under $2,000	(2) $2,000– $2,999	(3) $3,000– $3,999	(4) $4,000– $4,999	(5) $5,000– $6,999	(6) $7,000 or more
Percentage of U.S. households	100	18	14	15	19	20	14
All goods and services—total	100	9	10	14	20	24	23
Food, beverages, and tobacco	100	10	12	15	20	23	20
Clothing and accessories ...	100	8	9	15	20	23	25
Medical and personal care ..	100	11	10	14	19	24	22
Home operation and improvement	100	7	11	14	21	24	23
Home furnishings and equipment	100	7	10	13	19	26	24
Recreation and recreation equipment	100	8	9	14	20	24	25
Automotive	100	7	9	14	20	26	24
Other goods and services ...	100	8	8	13	20	23	28

For example, look at column 4, for households with annual incomes from $4,000 to $4,999. They represent 19 per cent of all U.S. households. Note how these households, which account for 20 per cent of expenditures for all goods and services, likewise account for expenditures hovering around this 20 per cent in the eight separate classifications. They account for 20 per cent of the purchases of food, beverages, and tobacco; 20 per cent of the money spent for clothing; 19 per cent for medical and personal care; 21 per cent for home operation and improvement; 19 per cent, home furnishings and equipment; 20 per cent, recreation and recreation equipment; 20 per cent automotive; and 20 per cent, other goods and services.

Now, note similarly the columns to the left and to the right of column 4, and how the percentages for each of the eight categories come close to the percentage figures second from the top of each column, for *all* goods and services.

As you might expect, columns 1 and 2 show that lower-income groups do not spend in proportion to their numbers ...and columns 5 and 6 show that upper-income groups spend out of proportion to their numbers. Thus, the one-seventh of U.S. households with $7,000 or more annually account for one-fourth of all consumer spending.

But even at the extremes of lower income and of higher income, the *ratio* of spending in each classification tends to be the same, and similar to what is spent for all goods and services by all groups.

You might think that the upper-income homes represent the cream of the market. But the *bulk* of the market lies elsewhere, with the middle-income groups ($3,000 to $7,000 annually).

To illustrate, let's group these middle-income households (columns 3, 4, and 5). We find that they represent 54 per cent of all U.S. households and account for 58 per cent of all consumer expenditures. And by categories they spend:

	Percentage
For food, beverages, and tobacco	58
For clothing and accessories	58
For medical and personal care	57
For home operation and improvement	59
For home furnishings and equipment	58
For recreation and recreation equipment	58
For automotive	60
For other goods and services	56

Pretty obviously, here is where the greatest volume of sales is made. It is this *middle-majority group* that represents the big mass market.

This pattern is equally evident when we focus on specific products within the largest major category—food, beverages, and tobacco. The 14 per cent of U.S. homes with annual incomes of $7,000 and over account for the 20 to 24 per cent expenditures for such products as meat, fowl, and seafood; meat sauces; frozen vegetables, fruits, and juices; desserts and ice cream; confections and nuts. But the middle-income households ($3,000 to $7,000) account for *most* of these sales: 58 to 61 per cent of the expenditures for these products.

There is, of course, some selectivity by income, and by education. For instance, the study indicates that the better-educated households have a great affinity (and available money) for frozen foods. Households headed by persons with some college education spend almost three times as much on frozen items as those headed by someone with only a grade school education.

The big market for most food products, of course, comes from families with children. Where the children are under 10, the average family spends $1,379 annually on food, beverages, and tobacco, 15 per cent above the average for all families. But as these children—and their appetites—get larger, we find that households with adults and teen-agers spend $1,442 annually, 20 per cent above the average.

This is not simply a result of higher incomes among teen-age households. For the three *broad* income levels—incomes under $3,000; $3,000 to $7,000; and $7,000 or over—per capita spending for food and beverages in households with older children exceeds spending in households with younger children.

The *Life* study has some interesting surprises as to food expenditures. As you would expect, over half the cereal market is in the households with children under ten. But, as you might not expect, slightly over one-fourth of this market is accounted for by households with *no children* and headed by someone *over forty years of age*. And 7 per cent of the baby-food market comes from households with no children and headed by someone over forty!

Households headed by craftsmen, foremen, operatives, and nonfarm laborers comprise 38 per cent of all households, and make 42 per cent of all food purchases ... but their gullets are moistened by 52 per cent of all the beer and ale sold, and they burn 45 per cent of the tobacco (by value).

The frothing nectar from the brewer's vats finds special favor in childless households at whose summit sit persons under forty years of age. At the same time, hard liquor and vinous potables are most warmly received farther along in the life cycle—among childless households with married heads who are over forty.

As to age, it was found that dried fruits and vegetables—culinarily speaking, a survival of an earlier culture—are used relatively heavily in households with older heads. And the households at late stages of the life cycle also use coffee out of proportion, in expenditures, with their expenditures for food generally.

As to region, households located in the Northeastern part of the United States not only spend more for food on the average, but a larger proportion of their food budget goes for meat, fowl, and seafood.

As a nation, we like to eat well, and we are willing to spend money for it.

3. Diplomas and Dollars

Certain products show a special sensitivity to household characteristics, such as income or education. But even for products which are most sensitive to these characteristics, the *majority of expenditures* come in every case from the vast *middle majority of the market*.

One of the more extreme examples of responses to income is the product category, removable floor coverings, which includes carpets, rugs, and linoleum. The study clearly demonstrates that the "hard core" of the floor-covering market has the money to buy quality—about 26 per cent of all carpeting, rugs, and linoleum is purchased by the 5 per cent of U.S. homes with annual incomes of $10,000 or more.

Of even greater importance, this hard core of the floor-covering market has the educational attainment to understand the difference between the junk and the jewel. Approximately 77 per cent of carpet, rug, and linoleum purchases are made in households where the head of the household has had at least some high school education or beyond.

In fact, the L.S.C.E. shows that expenditures for every major product category are responsive to education. By 1965, as younger households become older, it is estimated that there will be an increase of 7½ million household heads who will at least have graduated from high school. The *Life* study shows that items particularly sensitive to education face an even greater market potential than products which do not respond to more schooling.

As of the beginning of 1957, there were 19.6 million households with children under ten . . . and this helps to explain the boom in the 1950s in the appliance industry. These relatively young households were acquiring refrigerators, washing machines, vacuum cleaners, and other (to them necessary) appliances on a huge scale.

Education is becoming an increasingly important factor with respect to patterns of buying. Almost needless to say, income and occupation are closely related . . . but since income has been discussed, let's turn to education.

Since 1930 we have had a consistent growth in the number of households headed by a high school graduate. And the educated earn more, in general. Of households earning $7,000 and over, 64 per cent have at least graduated from high school, and 24 per cent have attended college. In the middle-income bracket ($3,000 to $7,000 per household) only 47 per cent are high school graduates; and in the under-$3,000 group, only 22 per cent.

An interesting thing about the better-educated is that *they spend more.* Even when income is held constant, the person who has attended college tends to outspend the lesser-educated for all goods and services.

Another remarkable factor about the better-educated households is their *leadership status*—here are the experimenters and innovators. They respond strongly to the new and convenient, and especially the convenient. They use their income to "buy" time . . . a power lawn mower, a quick frozen food, the washer loaded once or twice a day.

For both air conditioners and clothes dryers, as examples, the better-educated are "faster with a buck." Households headed by a high school graduate represent 42 per cent of all households in the *Life* study, but account for 67 per cent of the sales of air conditioners and 66 per cent of the sales of dryers.

Amount of education is increasingly important in estimating future demand for products. Our young adults today have had much more of a formal education in school than our older adults.

As to the 42 per cent of U.S. households headed by someone who at least finished high school, where the household head is under thirty years old, 59 per cent of these homes are headed by a high school graduate. Between ages thirty and thirty-nine, the figure is 54 per cent, and then the percentages decline sharply, indicating that higher education primarily is a post-World-War-II phenomenon.

New diplomas go along with higher incomes, and also with increased spending behavior in lots of places . . . such as in the frozen-food section of the supermarket . . . at the hardware store . . . with the telephone company. We now have so many cameras and so much camera equipment that if we blew all at one time the billion flash bulbs that we buy each year, it would make Times Square look like a dark alley.

Many purchases, of course, may be but educated expressions of adjustment to a faster pace and a higher standard of living. Perhaps some of us use our "education" to help us to exhibit to others how "cultured" we are. This may even affect what we drink—up the social ladder from wine and beer . . . to blended whisky and ginger ale . . . to Scotch on the rocks, gin 'n tonic, or a vodka martini (very dry, please).

Certainly with greater education go more luxurious tastes. And our society has overwhelmingly accepted the proposition that higher education is very desirable. College enrollments jumped from 1.35 million in 1938 to over 3.25 million in 1958.

As we continue to insist upon higher education for our youngsters, we are assured of a more demanding and larger-spending adult population than ever before.

4. Profile of the U.S. Consumer

An equally interesting study might be one of how people spend their lives . . . their time. Says A. Edward Miller, publisher of *McCall's:* "The determination for the spending of money is guided basically by how you want to spend your *time,* what it is worth."

A study on a scientific basis of how consumers spend their lives would be a formidable but extremely useful study, probably of some years' duration. But until such work is carried out, the most accurate information as to who spends for what is found in the *Life* Study of Consumer Expenditures.

This study is a gigantic but complex X ray of the profile of the U.S. consumer. The question is—with infinite possible combinations and permutations of the 1 million IBM cards— who can possibly interpret *all* the data from them? The digital computing technician? That would be like asking an electrician to interpret your cardiogram.

Perhaps the magnitude of just the tabulation job alone can be grasped from the fact that a fast IBM machine requires over two days of working time for just one run-through of all 1 million cards. Yet somehow the data have been made to fall into place in interesting and even unexpected ways.

For a profile of the U.S. consumer, the "pie" chart on page 99 shows how the average U.S. family divides its dollars for consumer goods and services. Note that the average household income (as of the time of the study) is $4,108. The highest share of these dollars, 25 per cent, goes for food. The second largest outlay is for home operation and improvement, 19 per cent. The home on wheels—the automobile—and its upkeep claim third place, with 14 per cent of the dollars. These three categories total 58 per cent.

Next come clothing and accessories, 12 per cent; home furnishings, equipment, and appliances, 9 per cent; miscellaneous, 7 per cent; medical and personal care, 5 per cent; recreation, 5 per cent; tobacco, 3 per cent; alcoholic beverages, 1 per cent.

These are average figures. But we are concerned with more than just the "average" family. After all, an average may be misleading unless we also take into account the variations above and below the average. (There is the story of the man who drowned in a creek which had an *average* depth of only 8 inches; but he had the misfortune to drown in that part of the creek which had a depth of 6 feet.)

Nevertheless, in order to present a fairly typical picture of what U.S. consumers are like in their spending habits, we do have to rely on average figures. Here are some facts which may give you some additional insights into how consumers spend their money; and, as previously, the statements are given in the present tense.

1. *There is a remarkable homogeneity in the way the U.S. public spends its money.* The great mass market is made up of the 63 per cent of U.S. families earning from $3,000 to $10,000 a year, and accounting for 72 per cent of total consumer-product expenditures.

And within this broad grouping everyone appears to spend in similar fashion—the richer and the less rich alike. Except in the case of food, beverages, and tobacco, the various income levels spend approximately the same *share* of their total outlay in each of the major consumer-goods classifications . . . though differing, of course, in actual total *dollars* spent.

2. *The desire to own and consume goods exceeds the ability*

to earn, for a substantial segment of Americans. In households with incomes of $4,000 a year or less, 47 per cent of all U.S. households, the typical family spends more than it earns. Part of this excess represents debts to be paid out of future earnings or out of savings. Another part represents spending by retired persons living on savings.

How the Average U.S. Family Divided Its Dollars for Consumer Goods and Services in 1956.

THE AVERAGE HOUSEHOLD: TOTAL EXPENDITURE $4,110

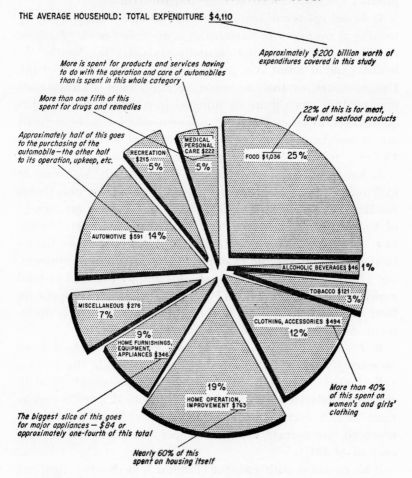

Approximately $200 billion worth of expenditures covered in this study

More is spent for products and services having to do with the operation and care of automobiles than is spent in this whole category

More than one fifth of this spent for drugs and remedies

Approximately half of this goes to the purchasing of the automobile—the other half to its operation, upkeep, etc.

22% of this is for meat, fowl and seafood products

MEDICAL PERSONAL CARE $222   5%

RECREATION $215   5%

FOOD $1,036   25%

AUTOMOTIVE $591   14%

ALCOHOLIC BEVERAGES $46   1%

TOBACCO $121   3%

MISCELLANEOUS $276   7%

CLOTHING, ACCESSORIES $494   12%

HOME FURNISHINGS, EQUIPMENT, APPLIANCES $346   9%

HOME OPERATION, IMPROVEMENT $763   19%

More than 40% of this spent on women's and girls' clothing

The biggest slice of this goes for major appliances — $84 or approximately one-fourth of this total

Nearly 60% of this spent on housing itself

SOURCE: The Life Study of Consumer Expenditures, Time, Inc., 1957

And it should be noted that 18 per cent of all households live on less than $2,000 a year, and 32 per cent on less than $3,000.

3. *Expenditures by different occupation groups, in general, run in proportion to each group's proportion in the population.* As an example, the craftsman-foreman-operative categories make 39 per cent of all expenditures on all goods and services, and they also account for 38 per cent of U.S. families. There are some notable variations, as pointed out earlier, for certain product categories, such as beer and tobacco.

4. *Broad economic regions are not so meaningful a way of looking at consumer characteristics as are other market-location characteristics.* We cannot factually say that "the South," in broad, general terms is a poorer market than the rest of the United States, or that it should be considered a second-class market. It is much more meaningful to compare specific types of markets; as an example, 18 per cent of all U.S. households are in Southern nonmetropolitan areas, yet account for only 13 per cent of total U.S. expenditures.

5. *Suburban living is related to an unusually high rate of expenditure in most product categories.* Suburban households residing outside of cities of 500,000 or more spend an average of $5,381 per year, 31 per cent more than the United States as a whole, and 13 per cent more than household expenditures in the cities. As specific examples, suburban areas—representing 27 per cent of all U.S. households and 31 per cent of total expenditures—account for 47 per cent of all dollars spent on floor coverings, 45 per cent of the expenditures on sports equipment, and 40 per cent of the pet-foods spending.

6. *Presence or absence of children in the household is an increasingly significant factor in spending.* While the average U.S. household spends $4,108, the average household with children under ten spends $4,607, which is 12 per cent more than the U.S. average. In households with children from ten to nineteen, the average expenditure per household rises 19 per cent to $4,881.

This contrasts with younger childless households who spend

an average of $4,332, and older childless homes where the expenditures are $3,639 if the household head is married, and only $2,350 if single.

7. *Education is increasingly important in understanding the forces and characteristics behind the pattern of expenditures.* Those households whose head has had some college education spend, on the average, nearly twice as much over-all as those whose head has not finished grade school. They also spend twice as much on housing; almost three times as much on frozen fruits, vegetables, and juices; and 2½ times as much on photographic equipment.

No study of the magnitude of the *Life* study has ever been undertaken by any other business organization. While there have been other studies by individual companies to determine consumer markets for specific products, the resulting information is not likely to be made available to other people or organizations.

Thus, the study provides data where little or none previously existed. It gives us more information on who buys what than can be obtained any place else.

9

Vive la Product Différence!

1. Discernible Differences

The second largest food chain in the United States, Safeway, reports that the men who do their buying are offered approximately 6,000 NEW items each year. This is at the rate of about 20 each business day . . . or about 120 a week.

In the last decade, the food industry has undergone a revolution. But women still have the same problem of cooking everything so that it is done at the same time. It's a marvel to me how they can coordinate "instant" potatoes, rolls, and pudding with "minute" steaks and with frozen vegetables which take about 6 minutes to prepare. Apparently a woman hardly has time to toss a salad before it's time to set the table.

Yes, there are lots of new, new things to make it quick and easy for the little woman—but perhaps the trend went a little too far, for she felt that producers were not flattering her talents as a mother and housewife. She wanted products which greatly simplified her cooking but didn't instantize it completely. So there was a new trend and correspondingly lots of new products which were easy to use but made her feel creative.

In all industries, new products are springing up galore. In 1957, Procter & Gamble reported, "More than half of our

102

volume today is coming from products that didn't exist in 1945." For General Foods, the figure was 36 per cent; and for the St. Regis Paper Company, 25 per cent.

In that same year David Sarnoff, chairman of the board of R.C.A., said that "80 per cent of the products we are now selling did not exist ten years ago." It is said that General Foods expects 70 per cent of its successful new products to be obsolete in ten years.

At the twenty-first annual convention of the Super Market Institute in 1958, Lee S. Bickmore, president of the National Biscuit Company, pointed out that 75 per cent of food volume at that time was in products which did *not* exist twelve years before.

To show how fast things are moving, *Life* magazine reported in two different issues of 1959 that ten years before one out of every four products advertised in that particular issue of *Life* was little more than an idea or project in an experimental laboratory.

All this proves that producers are giving us consumers what we want and are also giving their stockholders dividends, but they are giving themselves problems of the nature that up the sales of Bufferin. Their biggest problem seems to be one of expansion.

One of the best ways for business to expand is to offer us new products. Businesses must grow—there is a saying that if your business does not grow, you are practically dead. Almost all businesses are offering us so many new products, in fact, that now the problem is not one of just growing, but of individualizing their products. Each new product must have some *discernible difference* from other products, if you and I are going to become interested in buying it.

It is not always the product that is best or cheapest that is appealing, but the one that is *different* that catches our attention. Difference (or differences) in the *product* itself may be in the way it is *packaged,* or in the *advertising and promotion* which give you an "image" of the product as being different.

But in any case, the seller's objective is for you to *discern* a difference, or feel that you discern a difference.

If, for example, it is possible for chemists to develop a floor wax better than the ones previously made, it is not sufficient for the advertiser simply to tell you, the consumer, that one wax is better than another. You must also be able to discern from experience that the wax actually is better.

A brilliant example of discernible difference was in the new Parkay margarine brought out by Kraft Foods a few years back. Parkay margarine had been on the market for many years when it was discovered that this product could have some new features introduced. Chemists in the Kraft laboratories finally developed a method whereby margarine could be taken out of the refrigerator ice cold and then spread smoothly on a piece of bread, without tearing the bread.

Undoubtedly you have had the experience of taking butter out of the refrigerator, and when you spread it on the bread, the bread has broken or torn in your hand and the butter has not spread very smoothly. Obviously Kraft had a real product advantage over butter, and over other margarines. So this was a very closely guarded secret until advertising announced on a national scale that Kraft had a product which SPREADS SMOOTH EVEN WHEN ICE COLD. And the following summer, the advertising added KEEPS FORM WHEN WARM—referring to the fact that Parkay margarine also had the advantage of not "running off" the plate in the summertime, as some spreads have the habit of doing. With its genuine product advantages supported by dramatic advertising, Parkay sales skyrocketed.

An opposite kind of example is one where the product difference was not discernible to the consumer. Some years ago a company produced a high-quality liquid starch, called Brisk. There was no question that Brisk was much better than its competitors. This could be demonstrated technically in the laboratory, but women did not continue to buy Brisk because they had to pay about 20 cents more for this product than for other starches. It was *not discernible* to the consumer that Brisk was that much better, and the product no longer exists.

People don't necessarily buy unless they can discern an advantage. The manufacturer may know the advantages, but the consumer may not discern them; so price may become the deciding factor.

Imagine a bedding manufacturer trying to promote a new type of mattress. The discernible differences in mattresses are hard to detect in a store—it is extremely difficult for most consumers to judge their quality, comfort, and durability. Even if we could examine inside the mattress and look at the coils, padding, etc., most of us have had no special background of experience to evaluate what we see or feel. And so the price and the brand name become the most discernible differences.

Even if there is no physical difference, *if people believe things to be true, then they are true—for them!* If consumers like a product, they develop definite attitudes about that product.

What are the real differences between one cigarette and another? What are the real differences from one soap to another? The discernible difference may be in what you have begun to "feel" about your particular brand. In spite of all the blindfold tests in the world, you know that if you are a Camel smoker, you are not very likely to smoke Salem cigarettes. If you use Dial soap, you are probably not going to use Lifebuoy.

Psychologically speaking, a sale often depends on whether or not you and I, the potential customers, believe the product will raise our own evaluation of ourselves. Although advertising is not going to make us continue to buy a product we don't want, advertising and sales promotion may suggest to us a difference between one product and another. How many males are "thinking men" and smoke Viceroys? How many females are intrigued by a perfume "to leave alone unless you can meet its challenge"? Have you heard of the young lady who looked at all the perfumes with names like Indiscrete, Intoxication,

My Sin, Passion, Shocking, and Surrender, and asked the clerk if she didn't have some other perfume for beginners.

Perhaps we can't even tell the difference in a blindfold test between a good grade of instant coffee and regular coffee ... but chances are we are willing to pay a little more money for the latter. And certainly for many such products there are very noticeable differences: contrast Camel with Kool or Kent, and contrast Lifebuoy with Cashmere Bouquet.

The successful manufacturer must search constantly for something new, something different. Provided the product is all right, this difference may be successfully promoted through advertising, so that you come to feel that the brand you choose is the best. If a product is not "right" for you, however, then no amount of advertising and promotion of any kind can make you buy it again and again.

Many people naively assume that advertising and promotion alone can "make" a product. This is not true. We might say instead that the product makes the advertising. Not only can no amount of advertising cause people to buy again and again a product that they do not feel is their "kind of product," but they will not buy even a second time a product which is faulty. *Advertising and promotion efforts alone cannot substitute for quality or utility in the product itself.*

The Morton Salt Company once got interested in the possibility of producing a salt toothpaste. Officers of the company said that this was a great product; they said they liked it themselves; their wives and families liked it; and employees said it was a great product. But it seemed a good idea to find out also whether or not other consumers—not Morton people—liked the toothpaste.

Accordingly, tubes of salt toothpaste were put in the homes of different families, and then call-backs were made in order to get their reactions. And these reactions may be characterized by such statements as: "You told me this was salty, but my God!" "If you had been around the first time I tried that salty stuff, I'd have wrung your neck!" "The first time I tried to use that product I wanted to vomit."

The salty product difference certainly was discernible! But this was not the sort of difference consumers liked, and so the toothpaste was sent back to the laboratory for further refinement. Some months later, with a product developed that tasted less salty but was excellent for cleaning teeth, Morton toothpaste was advertised and sold on a test basis in several Middle Western communities. But the new difference from other toothpastes still was not what consumers wanted, and the product was permanently withdrawn from the market.

It is apparent that development of a new product with differences is a pretty complicated process these days—and it's expensive. There are at least four phases to new-product development: exploration of new ideas; screening of the ideas; consideration of various proposals; selection of certain products which the manufacturer takes a chance on, for actual manufacture and promotion.

Pledge—which waxes as you dust—is a good example of a new product which achieved immediate and continuing success. It represented a useful new idea in furniture care. Johnson's Wax was able to interest housewives who ordinarily did not use a furniture polish, and the sales of furniture polish doubled in a very short time. This was almost entirely due to the advent of Pledge.

This is a success story based on very careful planning; but for every success story there are scores of instances where the new product is unsuccessful.

Obviously what we spend our money for depends on both ourselves and the producer. But, in general, we don't buy or continue to buy a product unless we feel that there is a discernible advantage to us. We like to be able to say to ourselves, "Here is something different . . . and I like that difference."

2. America's Silent Salesmen

Ancient Confucius said, "One *picture* is worth 10,000 words." A modern Confucius would say, "One *package* is worth 10,000 words."

Packages and containers have become America's "silent salesmen." Today, most products have good quality and so must often compete on the basis of packaging. Yes, packaging can become the discernible advantage in many instances.

Fred R. Messner, vice-president of the G. M. Basford Company, tells of a consumer research study where each woman in a selected group of housewives was given three different packages. Although the women didn't know it, each of the three packages contained exactly the same product—a certain brand of instant coffee. "One of the packages was specially designed. The others were merely a stock glass jar and a can. The women were asked to compare the contents and report any preference.

". . . At the end of three weeks of actually using coffee from each of the containers, 95% of the women said they liked the coffee in the specially designed container better than the 'other two.' " The special packaging produced the conviction of special product.

You can think of examples of this phenomenon in your own buying—the Cheer detergent box, the Log Cabin syrup container that used to look like a log cabin, the whiskey in the special decanter.

On the shelves of our stores are thousands upon thousands of different kinds of packages and containers, each of which it is hoped by its producer is crying out to us, "Take me home . . . take me home!" Store shelves are jammed and crowded. But one product seems more attractive than another—perhaps because of the way it is packaged, or it may be just the colors of the package or the label.

More and more, the package has replaced the vanishing salesman in our stores, which are becoming more and more self-service. The package has become one of the most vital links between producer and consumer.

In a year's time the average housewife opens approximately 1,700 different packages of all kinds. So it makes a lot of difference how the products are packaged. The job of a package is to protect the product, because it gets a good deal of handling . . . and also to increase the chances of your buying the product.

For most of us, the selection time in buying products is not great. The next time you are buying groceries, just notice how little time you take to decide on each purchase—just a few seconds. And note, too, how many of the items you buy on impulse.

After checking over 5,000 shoppers in 250 supermarkets, Du Pont researchers found that 63 per cent went into the supermarket without a shopping list, and that 7 out of 10 purchases were made on impulse. Other studies have confirmed what we might call "Du Pont's law," and have also shown that women in supermarkets buy more products that are not on their shopping lists than are on such lists.

The package is very often the discernible advantage—the sale-clinching factor.

A product called "Off," an insect repellent, has two kinds of labels on the package. In the South, it says on the label "ROACH and Ant Killer." In the North, the words on the label are "Roach and ANT Killer." It is the same product, but the package has a different sales emphasis.

Almost every cereal has coupons for toys or games, or cutouts for children. ReaLemon (lemon concentrate) looks like a real lemon, and it squirts lemon juice when squeezed; the lemon juice is the same, but the similarity of the container to a lemon makes the contents taste "better" than the product of bottled competitors. Revlon has stick mascara in a "pen" container; but Merle Norman has the same product with an eyelash comb in the "pen" container, making the discernible difference.

Dial shampoo has a high-quality product which competes with other equivalent products because of a discernible difference: a nonbreakable, spillproof squeeze container in an odd color. Detergents come in a variety of colors. Cake mixes were so similar that Aunt Jemima included a plastic bag for mixing the ingredients, and even a throw-away-without-washing cake pan.

What are the features that you and I, as consumers, want in a package or container?

Most of all, we want something that holds and protects the

product, but one also that we can open easily. Hence, tear strips on packages ... string pulls ... pouring spouts ... "push-ins" on cardboard containers. We appreciate pop-ups, and crack-opens.

We hope for containers that will open almost at the flip of the little finger, but that will close and keep the product just as it was before we moved that little finger. We like plastic bags for cookies ... and for cashmere sweaters.

We like containers that don't slip out of our hands. A friend tells me that after slipping in the shower and falling on a glass bottle of shampoo, smashing it completely, he now buys shampoo only in a tube or a plastic bottle. These days plastic tubes are squirting everything from sun-tan cream to machine oil, to glue, to toothpaste, to ketchup, and whipped cream. We also want aerosols that spray everything from shoe polish, to insecticide, to perfume, to toothpaste.

We like realistic pictures of foods on containers, date-marked baked goods, and even cook-in packs that cook food in the original container. While we may treasure pretty stationery boxes and candy boxes, we may be happy with a cake mix that is boxed in a throw-away-without-washing cake pan. We like tops on bottles that hold a measured quantity, and with labels that say so. We even like measuring marks on some containers. Some of us like our soft drinks in cans, and others like them in bottles ... but apparently many people prefer to intoxicate their friends from the contents of bottles.

For powder 'n paint, ladies like containers that are "purs-able" for their cosmetics—eye shadow now comes in a tube and cologne in a stick.

For the most part we are willing to spend more for special packaging features. Quaker Oats was willing to invest time and money in a bread mix that was packaged in a new type of box that boosted the retail price of the product almost 20 per cent, but which cut the time for preparing the bread from about 20 minutes to less than 1 minute. And consumers bought the product.

Some of the packages and containers we get are so fancy that we hate to part with them. A lady I know tells me that for over ten years she has saved a "gift box" from Nieman-Marcus of Dallas—just can't bear to part with it. Most of us, though, don't acquire such habits of collecting and hoarding packages— instead we put so many beautiful boxes and labels into our trash cans that they begin to take on the appearance of what Thorstein Veblen might have called the "conspicuous waste-basket."

Interviews with housewives have given some clues as to what they do and don't like about various kinds of packages. In one study, difficulty in opening cans of evaporated milk was the cause of some consternation; one woman reported: "I think it took me 15 minutes to get the can of evaporated milk open. I didn't have an ice pick to punch a hole in it. I tried a can opener, the kind you use for beer, but I couldn't get enough leverage to make a dent in the can. Finally, I called in my fourteen-year-old boy to see what he could do, and we tried a screw driver but it was too large. So, we finally took the beer-can opener and poked two tiny holes into the can and got a thin trickle of milk."

Another example concerns cardboard cartons for fresh orange juice. The housewives considered the carton convenient, and the taste was good—but only for the first day! And there were objections to spoilage and leakage.

Here are some quotations about other kinds of products. As to cake mixes: "One label I saw on a Duncan Hines package today was Scotch plaid, orange and yellow. It was very distinc-tive among the other brands just because it was so different. It automatically caught your eye, whereas the other ones look about the same and it gets monotonous." For hair sprays: "When she went to the store to buy a hair spray, the very first one that caught her eye was the Revlon, and she looked at it, and thought it would look real good on her dressing table, and she bought it just on account of that." As to cereals: "You know what I think is a good package? The way the Quaker

Oats come. You flip that box top, and you just take it off, and you pour it out, and to me that's terrific."

Dr. Ernest Dichter, president of the Institute for Motivational Research, Inc., lists the following standards of good packaging which the consumer expects:

- *Convenience:* Does the package hold enough of the product to satisfy your needs without being too bulky or too heavy?
- *Adaptability:* How well does the package fit into your freezer, cupboard, glove compartment, or dresser drawer?
- *Security:* Do you feel assured of quality? Does the package make you feel it?
- *Status or Prestige:* Do you feel that by buying the package you are expressing something about yourself?
- *Dependability:* Does the package let you feel that you can rely upon the manufacturer?
- *Esthetic Satisfaction:* Are you pleased and satisfied by the impact of the design, color, and shape of the package?

Dr. Dichter goes on to say: "Product personality consists of two parts that we can only isolate on paper. One is the *physical image,* the other is the *personality image.*

"Physically a bar of soap is round, square, or octagonal; but in its personality image it may appear boldly masculine or softly feminine, modern or old-hat, or high status or low, light and delicate, or heavy and coarse.

"Although we have separated the two images here, the consumer never does so. He sees a unified image of the product's personality. And, significant for the package designer, any negative features of either image will affect the total picture in the consumer's head.

"For example, some men might reject a bar of soap that was ovoid-shaped, strongly scented, and packaged in a frilly box. Too effeminate, they would say. But they might accept the same soap if it were brick-shaped."

The big companies—soapers, cigaretters, and breakfast fooders—have spent millions of dollars trying to design the kinds of packages that will have the greatest consumer appeal.

In fact, all firms that sell their products in packages have devoted time, effort, and money to this problem.

They want to know about such things as:

- *Visual Acuity:* Does the package stand out on the shelves among other packages? To increase visual acuity, many producers develop "family resemblance" of their products. Kellogg's is a good example.
- *Color:* How does the package compare with other packages? Think of Campbell's soups, which also have "family resemblance."
- *Legibility:* At what distance can you first read the brand name? JELL-O is a wonderful example.
- *"Angle" Vision:* Can you "spot" the package and recognize the brand when it is not right in front of you? The product SOS can be so spotted.
- *"Dark" Acuity:* Can you see and recognize the brand even in a poorly lighted section of a store? Ivory soap is easily visible with its bright blue-on-white package.

No wonder that manufacturers are increasingly interested in testing of packages from a psychological standpoint. The Leo Burnett Company advertising agency of Chicago has pioneered in the development of a special consumer-reaction laboratory, which is providing psychological information for advertisers about various products and packages. After all, if a busy housewife cannot find a particular brand quickly, she is likely to pick up another brand instead.

A number of psychological instruments have been developed in the Burnett agency to evaluate packages and package designs. These are not just fancy gimmicks, gadgets, and gauges to look impressive, but rather specially designed equipment adapted from psychological laboratories ... and all developed to help make packages more appealing to consumers. An angle meter indicates how easily the printed messages on packages can be identified at different angles or positions. A distance meter measures the distance at which a shopper can identify products on the store shelf. A size meter determines which of similar-size packages appears larger. There are other devices also, such as a camera for photographing eye movements . . . a blur meter which makes packages look somewhat fuzzy, as they do to the 35 million or so women who go shopping without wearing their glasses . . . specially designed meters to indicate emotional reactions . . . all used to obtain practical results for manufacturers and eventually for consumers.

The Pillsbury Company asked the Burnett agency whether or not the location of the flavor designation in a new package would confuse the consumer by taking her eyes away from the illustration of the cake. It was found that the new design did not have this weakness, and the package was adopted.

The Kellogg Company wondered about the relative visibility to the consumer of two versions of a package with gold foil wrappers. The two packages were identical except for the color of the product name "Concentrate"—on one package the color was blue, and on the other white. The research showed that the blue name had greater visibility in most situations. It also demonstrated that in using foil packages under good lighting conditions, a "dazzle" effect is present. In a normally lighted supermarket the light comes from many angles and would create numerous highlights on the foil wrapper at nearly every line of regard. For the blue name this was no problem, as it tended to absorb light, thus providing a good contrast with the shiny gold foil.

Another example: Three proposed versions of the Campfire Marshmallow package design were tested in the Burnett laboratory. The research showed that the brand name was equally visible on all three versions of the design, but that consumers had decidedly different feelings about the designs. Design A seemed to denote quality and sophistication that would probably have great appeal for adults. Design B was felt to be "cold looking" and harsh and mechanical looking. Design C, with a variety of flowing lines and colors, was considered interesting and exciting, so that it would probably appeal more to children as a "fun" package.

The Container Corporation of America has its own perceptual laboratories, to test the effectiveness of various designs and labels. Specializing in the scientific testing of package designs is Visual Research, Inc., of Chicago, headed by Dr. Edmund W. J. Faison, experimental psychologist.

The manufacturer wants his product packaged in such a way that we consumers will find it more attractive than the "fellow" sitting on the shelf next to it, or above or below, and that we'll buy his product.

True, the *discernible difference* is often in the product itself—so that we, the consumers, can actually see that the shine on the floor does last a long time, or that teeth do get whiter from the toothpaste, or that the electric shaver does give a closer shave (and not just of a peach). These are the kinds of rewards we consumers are looking for.

But just as we often judge a book by its cover, *the discernible differences can well be in the packaging.* And these differences do cost money.

After all this, it is evident that the manufacturer must have a very substantial financial interest in the packages for his products, whether grocery products or something else. As a matter of fact, the percentage of his selling price represented by packaging may run as much as 35 per cent for cosmetics and toiletries, 24 per cent for a great many foods, 15 per cent for wax polishes, and 5 per cent for liquor.

According to the *Wall Street Journal,* we American consumers were spending in 1959 a record *$13 billion* for the containers in which our food, clothes, and other products were packaged. This was about $5 billion more than a decade earlier. By the way, this $13 billion was equivalent to about one-sixth of the Federal government's budget for that same year.

The *Wall Street Journal* also indicated that the 2¾ per cent of total expenditures on goods and services then going for packaging would probably climb about 4 per cent within five years. America's "silent salesmen" are becoming more and more significant.

10

Are They Tops or Flops?

1. Products and People

Most new products fail! There are various estimates on this. Some observers think that as many as 90 per cent of new products fail. Others talk about only a slightly lower percentage.

Only about 8 per cent of the new products introduced each year in the United States are really successful, according to Thomas B. McCabe, Jr., director of marketing services of the Scott Paper Company.

Frank Armour, Jr., president of the H. J. Heinz Company (57 varieties) tells me that he expects 24 out of 25 new food products not to succeed, that is, not to have continued success over a period of years. This does not necessarily mean completely new products, but at least product improvements— something new.

Most consumers assume that simply because something is new it will be bought—it will be "gobbled up." Too many believe that, "if a man can . . . make a better mousetrap than his neighbor, though he build his house in the woods, the world will make a beaten path to his door." This sounds fine, but it's just not true in business. It doesn't work like that.

There are very few products which people have rushed out to

116

buy just because they were new. It takes things like Polaroid cameras or, when they first came out, radios or television sets, or toasters—products of this sort—to catch on. For hordes of new products, people simply do not rush out to buy them. It takes years of persistent promotion.

Even those products which do get to the top have a hard time staying at the top. Often, what was one year's great product leader is no longer a product leader a few years later.

Compare the life of a product and the life of a person. A human being goes through the following stages: gestation, birth, childhood, adolescence, maturity, adulthood, old age, and death. It is the same for the life of a product.

First, a period of gestation . . . although as compared with human life, there is considerably more emphasis on planned parenthood. After the agonizing period of gestation, finally the product is born. But there is considerable infant mortality— to such an extent that most products, if they do not die aborning, do not live very long. Those that do get into childhood and finally reach maturity and adulthood have to have things done to them to keep them going: a new package, a new slogan, a new design, new ingredients, in order to look attractive in company with the many "younger" products since born.

How many products can you find today that were on the market ten years ago? *What were once tops, today may be flops.*

The A. C. Nielsen Company, world's largest marketing-research organization, found out that of 100 leading grocery brands heading their respective categories, 30 had lost their leadership only six years later . . . and after another five years, 30 per cent of the *new* 30 leaders had lost their thrones.

The Grey advertising agency says that 80 to 90 per cent of new products never even reach the market . . . and of those which do, only 4 per cent last as long as two years!

After all, we consumers don't always behave as logically and rationally as you might expect. For example, some people insist on buying white eggs instead of brown-colored eggs, whereas others prefer the brown ones. The eggs taste exactly the same, but there are these kinds of preference. Another example is that beef with yellow fat actually should be more expensive because this is better for us, but most consumers prefer to pay more for beef with white fat.

But remember, all of us are entitled to behave in lots of irrational ways, and this is fun. I should like to suggest that you count up and find out how little of your time is really spent in such concentrated activities as reading, studying, and real "brain work," and how much of your time is spent in fantasies, day dreams, play activities, and the like. This is by no means an attack on consumer rationality. It does point up the fact that the consumer is a "baffler" at times.

This is one of the pitfalls of many companies and their products. Oftentimes producers and sellers believe that they have the best products and so should have no trouble in selling them. They fail to realize that you and I are not always logical and rational in how and what we buy.

There is an enormous sale of soft drinks in the United States, particularly cola-flavored drinks ... and gelatin desserts are also quite popular. But when a manufacturer produced a cola-flavored gelatin dessert, consumers didn't buy. Logic would suggest that they would buy, but taste and experience showed that they would not.

Alfred Politz found that drivers who reported difficulty in pressing the accelerator pedal down in their cars believed that their automobiles did not have good pickup, whereas those who found it easy to press the pedal down thought that their cars had a good pickup. The remedy was relatively simple: Less tension in the spring controlling the accelerator pedal.

Another example has to do with vending machines. It is possible through electronic methods for hot dogs and hamburgers to be cooked in a vending machine in less than a minute after you put your coin in—hot and ready to eat. But the consumer couldn't *see* anything happen to the hot dog or hamburger in the machine, and so didn't believe that the food was well cooked. The solution was to install some orange-red lights in the machine—they had nothing to do with the cooking—but when the consumer put his coin in the machine, those lights went on with a nice glow, and customers were satisfied that the machine was working!

Professor Harry W. Hepner of Syracuse University gives the following example: "A manufacturer of small firearms decided to go into the production of forged-steel tools. This was a new line for the company and yet it went ahead with the engineering of the product without full knowledge of user preferences, customs, and practices. The tools were well-designed and were given rust-proofing treatment which left a dull finish rather than the popular shiny steel finish common in such tools. The company was certain that sales would go well and undertook a full-scale development and marketing program, but the tools did not move from the dealers' shelves. Building craftsmen would not buy them because they didn't like the dull finish."

So, you will probably say, "Why not ask people what they will do . . . what products they will buy?" Well, this poses some problems, too. George Romney, president of American Motors, couldn't be sure that people wanted a compact car, just by counting noses; but he was convinced that these cars served a need. Clarence Birdseye was a man who simply believed that frozen foods served a real need; but it took several years before many consumers agreed with him by buying many Birds Eye products.

When you ask people what it is they will buy, they may try to tell you what they honestly believe at that time . . . but what they *say* they will do does not always square with what they *actually* do later on. And the things which some of us think we don't want may turn out to be very important to us at a later date. In an article in the *Journal of Marketing*, Dr. Jean Namias reports that most of the purchases in her study of household durable goods were made by those consumers who previously had said that they did *not* plan to buy.

BBDO advertising agency found from a study conducted over a period of five years that in any given year three-fourths of all electric-appliance sales and four-fifths of all automobile sales are made to those people who at the beginning of the year said they were "uncertain about buying" or were "definite that they would not buy." Furthermore, this same study showed that from one-third to three-fifths of all buyers actually purchase a *different brand or make* from the one initially considered!

Like products, we consumers are also "unstable" in the sense that our desires seem to vary a bit with how much money we have on hand. Our spending behavior varies at different times in our lives, and even at different seasons of the year, and with some of us even according to the time of the week or time of the month. It is little wonder that producers have such difficulty in trying to predict the actions of us "fickle" consumers . . . in trying to determine whether a proposed product will be tops or flops.

2. Failures and Successes

Suppose that a manufacturer has decided on his product and its packaging, and he sincerely believes that he has an important new product, or an important development for an old product. How is he going to know whether it is going to "catch on" with consumers?

He has one big unanswered question—will my product sell, or will I get hurt?

The answer is that the business gamble is tremendous, and the manufacturer just has to take a chance. He makes a decision and prays he is right. He must engage in an enormous amount of investment spending. Perhaps he doesn't make money on the product in the first year or even in the second year. And even if the product becomes profitable in the third year, these profits have to compensate for losses built up in the first year or two.

Add to these years of getting himself in a good profit situation, the years of work which he has put into the development of the new product—the planning, tooling up, manufacturing, arranging to get the product into the warehouse of the wholesaler, to get it on the shelf of the retailer, to help to get it off the shelf to the consumer—add all this up, and the total investment is huge. The hopeful attitude is that the result will be profitable, but the manufacturer may end up with a failure.

Here is an interesting example. Breathes there a man (or woman) who has never sworn softly under his breath (or even over his breath) about the difficulty of getting ketchup out of the bottle? You know, you shake and nothing happens ... and then everything happens! The ketchup all comes out at once. Over the years the H. J. Heinz Co. received loads of suggestions from consumers: Why don't you do something about this?

So the Heinz Company did, and in 1955 produced a different kind of container—one with a large opening that was easy-pouring, or from which, if you preferred, you could spoon the ketchup out. But the new container went off the market at the end of 1955, having incurred losses of hundreds of thousands of dollars.

Why was this a failure? People *said* they wanted this kind of container, but they didn't buy it. Was the answer in the lack of promotion and the lack of advertising? Yes, this was one of the factors. There was not enough advertising support to call to the attention of Mrs. Consumer that there was a new kind of bottle available, and what it would do.

A second factor was that this new kind of container *looked* as if it held less ketchup than the former bottle. Actually, this was not true, but psychologically it was true. And, as I have said elsewhere, *if people believe things are true, then they are true ... for them.* If the container looks as if it contains less, people respond accordingly.

The new container also had to be priced a little bit higher, per ounce of ketchup, than the old one. The thinking had been that the physical advantages of the new container would offset its slightly higher cost. But it didn't happen that way. Instead, the higher price appeared to join forces psychologically with the seemingly smaller size.

And finally, and this was a real problem, the ketchup now became discolored. The container's mouth had been made twice as wide and the air poured into the open bottle several times faster than previously; and thus the ketchup, exposed to so much oxygen, turned slightly brown.

Over-all, probably the main thing was that most consumers, as well as most retailers, were just *used* to ketchup coming in tall bottles.

An even more dramatic example: Before the Edsel automobile had ever been manufactured ... before it was even off the drawing boards ... in fact, before it had ever been named ... it had already cost the Ford Motor Company $250 million. No, not $2.5 million, or $25 million but $250 million! *Before* the car ever existed, except in imagination. And after this initial investment, and millions more, the car turned out not to be "right" so far as Mr. and Mrs. Consumer were concerned.

On the other hand, here are two stories with fairly happy endings. One concerns Nieson ("Wishbone") Harris, the man who founded the Toni Company. In 1946 I saw a report written by a New York advertising agency executive who had visited Wishbone Harris in order to make some investigations about his then new product, the Toni Home Permanent. The question was whether this would be a useful product for an advertising agency to take on and advertise. Would it likely be a successful product? (After all, an advertising agency does not like to be associated with an unsuccessful product.) People in advertising agencies (believe it or not) know that "all the advertising in the world" is not going to cause people to buy and continue to buy a faulty product. But this report said that the Toni idea wasn't new and that the product would probably not be successful.

That was in January, 1946. Yet in January, 1948, Mr. Harris and his brother sold the Toni business—original investment only a few thousand dollars—to the Gillette Company for $20 million!

Another story: About ten years ago into the office of Earle Ludgin, chairman of the board of Earle Ludgin Company advertising agency in Chicago, walked a man, Dr. Jules Montenier. Dr. Montenier had with him a formula for a new deodorant. Mr. Ludgin came to the conclusion that this had real possibilities, and a product called Stopette was born, and with it a television show sponsored by Stopette—"What's My Line?" On this show for many years were some memorable commercials about, "POOF—THERE GOES PERSPIRATION!" For many years Stopette was the leader in its product field ... and sales were stupendous.

In recent years, Stopette has not been so successful, because there are other people who also can manufacture deodorants and put them out in a variety of ways, such as Bristol-Myers, which manufactures a product called Ban ... and so a lot of people have been sold on rolling a little ball around in their armpits instead of "poofing" to get rid of perspiration.

As I have said previously, however, it does not take long, even with a new product, to have competitors catch up with it and pass it by. Every product lives in the shadow of possible obsolescence.

Any successful product must be of good quality to be "right"; and it should be different and appealing. The competitive problem is then that when a manufacturer makes a new product that is good, somebody else usually catches up with him and makes a similar product very quickly. Five years or ten years don't have to go by before somebody else has essentially the same idea.

Take the product which has come into being in the last few years—known as mixes. There are over 100 different cake mixes and pie mixes being sold by three companies alone: Pillsbury, General Foods, and Duncan Hines. The problem for each of these manufacturers is how to get all of his mixes on the shelves of the grocer. There just isn't room enough for all of them.

And the consumer can't really have a choice of all of these mixes unless she shops around at a dozen different retail outlets. Even at the store where she usually shops, she still has the problem of making a choice between all these different kinds of mixes.

The same sort of choice is just as difficult—maybe more so —for clothes, household equipment, home furnishings, and appliances. A washing-machine manufacturer—Whirlpool— developed a new idea: We have something special (a filter) in our washing machine that collects lint. And lots of sales were made. But all the other washing-machine makers were able to do the same thing.

One refrigerator manufacturer arranges his refrigerator in such a way that the deep-freeze compartment is on the bottom instead of on the top. Other refrigerator people then do the same thing.

A new idea is developed, and somebody else copies it. Products tend to grow more and more alike in this free-for-all competition. So, the Gargantuan task the producer and retailer face is to try to do something that will give them discernible advantages over their competition—and to keep on thinking of new discernible advantages.

Can something be made or something changed that will make us feel that we ought to buy? We consumers may simply *feel* that what we now have is out of date ... psychologically obsolete. Our old car or vacuum cleaner or washing machine or refrigerator may still work satisfactorily, but if we begin to feel that it is getting obsolete, then psychologically this is the case. *What people believe to be true is true ... for them.*

Most of us put great stress on having new things. In order to "keep up," we buy things that are new ... and often shiny. We *believe* our "old" model is no longer satisfactory.

It is not so prestigeful to buy a used car as a new car, even though the person who buys the new car knows (if he thinks about it) that in the very first year—whether he ever drives the car or not—he will lose one-third of the purchase price through depreciation. If he pays $3,000 for a new Ford and drives it just a few hundred miles, he can sell it a year later for only $2,000 or maybe less. It has cost him around $100 a month just in depreciation. Still, most of us would *prefer* to buy a new car because of the images we have of ourselves and the nagging worry, almost unconscious, of "what the neighbors might think."

We have interesting examples of "psychological obolescence" with automobiles. Year after year new models have come out, with only slightly different features; the general idea is that you, driving last year's model or one of the year before last, may not feel so "comfortable" because you feel that your old car is becoming obsolete. You may rationalize your purchase of a new car in a variety of ways: "Well, my old car is eating up a lot of oil at the present time." Logically, if you really added up the cost of the car's "eating up oil" over a year's time, it might amount to $20 or $30—hardly comparable to putting down a few hundred or a few thousand dollars for a new car, but we do rationalize this way.

Or we say, "My old car is getting a little shoddy. I'd better get a new one." The general pattern is that people replace their cars, on the average, at the end of about three years' ownership.

Psychological obsolescence is especially important for products which can be *seen* by other people. This helps to account for our interest in new gadgets on cars, new styles in clothing, new decorating schemes for our living rooms. "Conspicuous consumption" affects most of us.

For the kinds of products seen a good deal by others, a certain amount of "built-in" obsolescence helps to meet the emotional needs of the great majority of middle-class consumers. How many women want to buy a hat, a dress, or even a pair of shoes that will last for ten years? How many would like to buy dishes that would last a lifetime?

We get pretty much upset about products that break down, because of obsolescence, and we agonize about not being able to buy new parts. But "psychological obsolescence" is welcomed by lots of consumers in our affluent society for purchases that can be seen by neighbors and friends.

3. Counsel from Consumers

To avoid failure in school, and likewise to achieve success, a student must harness his changeable mind and study the subject at hand. So it is in marketing a product—it must pass the test of the consumer. To do this, manufacturers are placing more and more emphasis on thorough study of the markets—of you, the consumer.

Why did people buy what they did for the prices paid? There are lots of unanswered questions affecting buying behavior, such as the differences between price and value ... the role of national brands versus private labels ... the influence of word-of-mouth recommendations ... the effect of store displays ... the position and location of merchandise within the store.

Life magazine has set up what it calls its "Marketing Laboratory" in order to explore the answers to such questions. There are units operating in several cities, with highly selected and trained housewives who serve as panelists. The panelists have gathered information on such diverse subjects as Christmas cards, cereals, air travel, evaporated milk, deodorants, hair sprays, appliances, cake mixes, dog food, cigarettes, coffee, toilet soaps, automobiles, soft drinks, frozen foods, candy, life insurance. In carrying out their assignments, these housewives provide four different types of information:

1. *Home Testing of Products.* The women report in writing on their experiences in their own homes (or on occasion those of friends and neighbors) in making use of the specific product, or kind of product, assigned.

2. *Retail-outlet Studies.* This has to do with in-store information regarding the sale of the product (or product category). Each panelist visits several previously selected stores each week to check on how the item is sold in these stores—pricing, packaging, location in store, display, number of packages, etc.

3. *Consumer Interviews.* Each panelist interviews from 10 to 20 consumers each week, the interviews lasting from 15 to 45 minutes. The interview questions are primarily directed along motivational and attitudinal lines—why they bought what they bought, the influence of price, attitudes about the advertising suggestions on the packaging, and similar factors.

4. *Panel Discussions.* After the previous three steps have been completed, the panelists gather in a conference room in each community where, under the guidance of a marketing specialist, they discuss their personal experiences and attitudes toward the products under investigation. Tape recordings are made of the entire sessions.

Obviously this Marketing Laboratory does not constitute a national cross section of attitudes and opinions. But it is a method for obtaining rather quickly a broad spectrum of opinion in various sections of the United States.

For instance, in an investigation of deodorants, results indicated that a majority of the women believed that, after a period of two or three months, they built up an "immunity" to a particular deodorant. And so a large proportion of women changed brands every few months. Curiously enough, many made this change with the full knowledge that most of the deodorants have substantially the same basic formula and ingredients. The changes were made for psychological, not logical, reasons. As I have said repeatedly, *if people believe things to be true, they are true . . . for them.*

Another project had to do with the "image" which women had regarding their electrical public utilities. Most did not understand how their electric bills are computed, and their overestimates of the cost of electricity were considerable. On the average, the panelists thought that it costs over 4 cents an hour to run a TV set, whereas it actually costs 0.6 cent. They estimated the cost of running a 100-watt bulb for three hours at 2.7 cents—the truth is less than 0.8 cent.

In another project the Laboratory investigated the use of shopping lists by housewives. Lists were copied before the customers entered the store, and shopping bags were checked as these same customers left the store. A comparison between the *buying intentions* and the *actual purchases* was thereby possible. It was found that the women generally bought more items and a greater variety of items than were on their shopping lists. Many of the brand names written on the shopping lists appeared to be generic rather than specific; for instance, "Kleenex" might appear on the shopping list, but the shopper might purchase some other brand of facial tissues, such as Scotties or Angel Soft.

Another organization that makes intensive studies of consumer purchasing is Gallup & Robinson, Inc., of Princeton, N.J. Personal interviews are taken with housewives in their homes, to find out why they bought what they did. Information is picked up on shopping habits, brands bought, influence of price, brand switching, and as many other factors as possible to determine what led up to specific purchases.

As an example, an interview with a housewife in Coahoma, Mississippi, revealed how this lady shopped by herself on Friday at a Kroger store, after looking through store ads in the *Clarksdale Press Register*. Her daughter had seen Stripe toothpaste advertised on television, and her mother bought Stripe on this shopping expedition and had bought it since, for the past nine months. "The kids love the colors, and I think it makes my mouth feel refreshed."

In Tennyson, Indiana, Gallup & Robinson report how a woman went shopping with her husband and bought Sanka instant coffee, and has been buying it since for about three years. "I just wanted to try it out. They said it was caffeine-free and claimed it makes you sleep better, but I just like the taste of it better. I tried Instant Maxwell from Rex Marshall, but it tasted like it was scorched."

Another housewife, shopping with her husband, bought Scott tissue on impulse because she had seen it advertised on television three months previously, and purchased it regularly ever since.

It is from studies of this kind that more and more information can be obtained about how and why we spend our money. Lots more information from consumers is needed, to find out whether products will be *tops* or *flops*.

The rallying cry of almost every manufacturer is: "Diversify or die." The feeling is that you must progress or perish . . . and so companies are feverishly searching for new products, or at least product innovations.

Often the fate of new products is determined within a few weeks or months. For those new products that do succeed, their life expectancy is continually being threatened by the advent of other new products of competitors. Many products don't even die, but, like old soldiers, just fade away.

11

What Do You Imagine?

1. The Priceless Ingredient

In the City of Bagdad lived Hakeem the Wise One, and many people went to him for counsel, which he gave freely to all, asking nothing in return.

There came to him a young man who had spent much but got little, and said, "Tell me, Wise One, what shall I do to receive the most for that which I spend?"

Hakeem answered, "A thing that is bought or sold has no value unless it contains that which cannot be bought or sold. Look for the Priceless Ingredient."

"But, what is this Priceless Ingredient?" queried the young man.

Spoke then the Wise One. "My son, the Priceless Ingredient of every product in the market place is the Honor and Integrity of him who makes it. Consider his name before you buy."

This story has been used for many years by E. R. Squibb and Sons in the promotion of their excellent products. It indicates that the priceless and unmeasurable ingredient reflected in today's market is the *brand name* of the product ... including the reputation of the brand, and peoples' feelings and attitudes toward it.

Remember that a *brand* is simply a word, mark, symbol, device, or combination thereof used to identify some product or service. The term *trade-mark* is the legal counterpart of brand, so that trade-mark and brand are almost synonymous.

A successful brand name means many advantages for you and me, the consumers, because:

Brands simplify your shopping. For instance, "Just look for the big red letters on the box." JELL-O has made it easy for you to select this product from the array on the shelves.

Brands help you in repeat buying. If Crisco has been purchased and liked, repurchase of Crisco is easy in stores of all types.

Brands mean constant quality. With few exceptions, when a manufacturer identifies a product by a brand name, this product becomes his "child" and he necessarily assumes responsibility for its character. Each product in a brand line becomes the calling card for all other products in the same or related lines. The producer must make a product of uniform good quality, or else you will lose faith in his brands.

Brands provide protection against substitution. A brand is a guarantee of quality. Without proper branding, you would have to depend on the word of a salesman as to product information and quality.

Brands help to stabilize prices. Jantzen bathing suits sell for essentially the same price in Washington, Wyoming, Wisconsin, and West Virginia...and throughout the United States. Smaller manufacturers of swim suits must watch Jantzen prices, and not have their own prices too much out of line with Jantzen and other national brands.

Brands help you to depend on new items. You have learned that, "You can be sure, if it's Westinghouse." Each of its new products has the advantage of a well-earned reputation for quality merchandise at a fair price.

Successfully branded names, which offer so many advantages

to the consumer, also mean increased profits for the producer. But these same brand names also involve serious responsibility on the part of the producer. Arthur B. Langlie, president of the McCall Corporation and former governor of the State of Washington, has proposed the following set of brand principles:

1. *Quality.* The symbol promises unique and distinctive quality that may be relied on through repeated purchases of the same brand.

2. *Value.* The symbol promises honest prices, competitive with and in the price range of the product it represents and equitable among consumers.

3. *Competition.* The symbol promises vigorous but fair competition.

4. *Advertising and Selling.* The symbol promises truthful and informative descriptions of the product to which it is related.

5. *Progress.* The symbol promises continuous market study to maintain the product abreast of the tastes and fashions prevailing among customers, and constant research embodying in the products the values of scientific progress.

I think you will agree that most national brand names live up to these principles: Armour, Westinghouse, Jantzen, Meadow Gold, Kodak, IBM, Bissell's, Abbott, Bayer, Breck, Maytag, Sanforized, Campbell's, Simmons, Arrow, Toni, Franco-American, Baldwin, Prince Matchabelli, Simoniz, Gillette, Kellogg, Kotex, Pond's, Lux, Canada Dry, Crosse & Blackwell, Salada, Wrigley's, Hoover, Hamilton, Talon, and hundreds of others.

And you immediately have confidence in the product when you see the pictures of the Quaker Oats man, the Dutch Cleanser maid, the White Rock fairy, the Morton Salt girl, or Elsie the cow.

Along with Borden's, Kraft, Chase & Sanborn, and thousands of other *national* food brands, don't overlook the importance of the *private* brands. The Jewel Tea Company's Bluebook brand

and Royal Jewel are private brands. So are National Tea's
Natco brand, and its Top Taste coffee. There are numerous
A & P private brands, such as Ann Page chile sauce, noodles,
and spaghetti; Nectar tea; Sunnyfield butter; Jane Parker
bread, rolls, and cakes; Bright Sail insect powder and floor wax.
There are Atlas tires of Standard Oil ... Craftsmen tools of
Sears.

Whether national brands or private brands, *most of us want
new things and lots of them.* And as we spend more dollars
on more things, brand names become our stand-by—our assurance that we have quality and fair price along with easy,
rapid selection.

This is increasingly true in our age of self-service. More
and more we are learning to depend on self-service not only
for groceries but even in buying household furnishings, household appliances, and automobiles.

The point is that *the product's brand name is critical in
affecting whether we buy or don't buy.*

Research conducted by the A. C. Nielsen Company on food
products shows that when housewives cannot obtain the brand
desired, 36 per cent go elsewhere to obtain it, and 20 per cent
temporarily do without. Not only does the manufacturer's selection of a name for a new product have a far-reaching effect on
the eventual success or failure of the product, but the problem
of finding a suitable name may be almost as complex as
developing the product itself. The names of the new compact
automobiles, Falcon and Valiant, were decided upon only
after intensive study.

Just try the following experiment. Imagine that you have
invented the newest and best deodorant ever. You need a name
for it. What on earth are you going to call it? Here are some of
the names already in existence: Five-Day, Ban, Mum, Quest,
Veto, Nullo, April Showers, Dixie Peach, Etiquet, Odo-Ro-No,
Revlon, Shulton, Yardley, Lander, Dainty, Fresh, Stopette,
Avon, Ever Dry, King's Men, Yodora, Jergens, Seaforth, Arrid,
Hush, Trig, Evening in Paris, Non-Spi, Secret. What *new*

name, not in this welter of names, are you going to think of that will make people remember your brand of deodorant? Pretty difficult, isn't it?

Brands are comparatively new to our civilization, but there has always been a driving desire for something new. Even Adam and Eve had everything, and still they wanted something more. But unlike Adam and Eve, we today have no limit— the more new things we want, the more new things we get ... new things that work better, or last longer, or are more attractive. Many times we are happier with these new things just because they are new.

In the grocery field, the A. C. Nielsen Company reports that a study made of 118 nationally advertised brands selected at random showed the importance of new, improved products. For the 53 brands that showed competitive gains, the principal reason in over a third of the cases was that the product was either new or improved. For the 65 brands which lost ground, nearly half the cases were because of competition of other brands which were new or improved.

Over the years every producer of a brand, whether national or private, has to decide whether to make any changes in the product, the package, the price ... or even the "imagery" of the product. Change in the imagery may cause millions of people to have drinks with "Schweppervescence." Change in price may influence which clothes you buy. Change in package may affect your breakfast-cereal habits. Change in product may cause you to buy something completely new, a small car instead of a big one—or two cars the size and price of one.

The producer constantly has to be on the lookout for possible changes that might intrigue the consumer. A new color ... a new package ... a new name ... a new form ... a new function ... a new gadget ... NEW ... NEW ... NEW! What will the consumer want? What will the consumer choose? Probably something new, if we have the money and feel venturesome. These are all components of the *priceless ingredient*.

Thus, both the producer and the consumer are very much concerned with brands . . . and with "brand loyalty."

From the producer's standpoint, his dream for our loyalty to his brand is threefold: he hopes, first, that we will immediately *recognize his brand* when we see it or hear about it . . . second, that we will *request his brand* or reach for it . . . and, third, that we will like it so much that we will *buy only this brand* and accept no substitutes.

From the consumer's standpoint, many of us do develop a certain amount of "brand loyalty" for various products, and buy the same brands over and over again. Some men smoke Camels and drink Schlitz, rather than mere cigarettes and beer . . . and some women don't stop to think about buying a detergent when they always use Tide.

Don't you yourself, for instance, nearly always buy a certain brand of soap or toothpaste or breakfast food, which you prefer to all others? Also, for gasolines many of us are pretty brand-loyal, although preference for a particular brand of gasoline may be more related to service-station characteristics than to the brand of gasoline itself.

A pioneering research project by Prof. Ross M. Cunningham of the Massachusetts Institute of Technology's School of Industrial Management reveals many instances where 90 per cent or more of a family's purchases have been concentrated on a single brand of a product over a period of three years. This brand loyalty, however, does not extend to all product classes —thus, those who are highly loyal to a brand of one product may have little loyalty to a brand of another product. Also, there is a good deal of "secondary loyalty," where purchasers are loyal in some degree to one brand of a product but also have a lesser degree of loyalty to another brand of the same product.

One of the main jobs of advertising is to get us to remember brand names. After all, advertising helps in the economical distribution of products, and may add value to the products. Here is a specific example. Some years back Simmons wanted to determine the value per mattress of their brand name. They requested that two mattresses be offered side by side, both of the mattresses actually a Simmons Beauty Rest. But one stack of mattresses was unlabeled, and the other labeled in the usual fashion. The salespeople told any customer who asked that the unlabeled mattress was a Simmons Beauty Rest, but without the label. Simmons discovered that people would pay $20 more to buy the product with the label. The brand name increased the value to that extent!

Are you willing to pay something for the name Bayer ... Texaco ... Yardley ... Gillette? The problem of getting us to remember brand names is infinitely more difficult today than ever before. How can *all* the new brand names possibly register with us? We just can't keep up with the brand parade.

And today's stream of new products may look like a mere trickle in a few years. In the drug field alone, products not yet available will probably produce 50 per cent of retail drug sales five years from now.

Remember, too, that every new product spurs duplication by competitors. Where is the limit on new products and brands? There isn't any, and the total number of new products you will be exposed to during the 1960s will be fabulous.

On the other hand, we ought to be thankful that there *are* brands, and that we, therefore, have some kind of psychological guide to what we are getting, and continuing assurance that it is a wise purchase. Most of us will continue to take pride in buying branded products for the assurance they give us. And the better-known, better-promoted brands are more likely to be bought than the lesser-known brands.

After all, the rewards of an intelligent purchase are many. For products that we use, we like to have confidence in what we buy. For products that we keep, there is real pride of possession for a quality product. The brand is the *priceless ingredient.*

2. Pictures in Our Heads

Have you ever seen children play Images? It is a game where one word or name is suggested to the opponent and then the opponent must immediately give a word or name which is closely associated with the original word. It goes something like this: black ... magic, blue ... sky, ice ... cold, Amos ... Andy.

Playing this game would be a snap for adults if we used advertising as the basis of the game: Lucky Strike ... fine tobacco, Pabst's ... Blue Ribbon, Ivory ... pure.

Think of the image which you have of a Cadillac, and of a Chevrolet. What about the image you have of a dress from Saks Fifth Avenue, and one from Gimbel's? One from I. Magnin and one from Hale's? What is the image you have of Brooks Brothers suits and Robert Hall suits? Consider the following and their probable imagery for you:

Macy's	bargains
Betty Crocker	good recipes
First National Bank ...	conservative, dignified, well-off
U.S. Steel	powerful

Note the imagery of gasoline products. You never really see the gasoline that goes into your car, and many people are aware of the fact that gasoline marketers exchange bulk supplies. Nonetheless, many people have rather clear beliefs about Standard or Gulf (dependable quality) as compared with Shell (hot, speedy, scientific).

Images may be defined as "pictures in our heads" ... which we have about products, companies, people, places. Once we begin to react to the image of a product, this may become even more important to us than what is "really" there, the product itself.

Most of our judgments about products are made pretty quickly, just as they are with people. Haven't you had the experience of meeting someone for the first time and having the unexpressed feeling, "I don't like you"? And you may not even be able to tell why. As the rhyme says:

> I do not love thee, Dr. Fell,
> The reason why I cannot tell;
> But this I know and know full well,
> I do not love thee, Dr. Fell.

The astonishing rapidity with which first judgments are made is amazing. Dr. Gordon W. Allport, Harvard psychology professor, suggests the following experiment: "While riding in a public conveyance close your eyes and turn your head toward some fellow passenger not previously observed, perhaps someone sitting obliquely opposite. Open your eyes for a brief glimpse lasting two or three seconds, and then with the eyes closed introspect upon the impressions as they arise. Here is a person, never before seen and completely unknown. With but the briefest visual perception, a complex mental process is aroused, resulting within a very short time, thirty seconds perhaps, in judgments of the sex, age, size, nationality, profession, and social caste of the stranger, together with some estimate of his temperament, his past suffering, his 'hardness,' his ascendance, friendliness, neatness, and even his trustworthiness and integrity."

Likewise, we make almost immediate judgments when we see a product for the very first time. These judgments are based on our past experience, true, but also on the product's imagery. The "pictures in our heads" help to decide which products will separate us from our money! Along with brand names, they help to determine our spending habits.

Just think of the great advertising slogans that build images of products. Miller's Highlife, "champagne of bottled beer." Winston, "tastes good like a cigarette should." Ivory soap, "it floats," and it's also "99 44/100% pure." Morton's salt, "when it rains it pours."

Advertising writer Donald David of the Campbell-Ewald Company of Detroit says that if you wanted to build a successful image, an acceptable "personality," for a line of women's high-style shoes, you might use such attributes as: avant-garde ... young ... daring ... sophisticated. "By contrast, a manufacturer of men's shoes might look well to men if his advertising gave the following impressions: proud ... quality-minded ... honest ... dependable."

Symbolism or imagery becomes part and parcel of a product's form (Lady Schick electric razor) ... its size (Renault) ... its color (Revlon lipstick) ... its "class" (Rolls-Royce) ... its beauty (Lux soap) ... its functions (Mr. Clean) ... its slogan ("Modess because") ... its picture (Green Giant peas).

The imagery of a name may be so effective that people call for the well-known brand name instead of the product they actually want. Did you ever ask for Kleenex when you really wanted Scotties, or for Band-Aids when you really wanted Curads? Have you ever heard someone talk about his Victrola, or the Laundromat? Such names have become generic, standing for all similar products. A General Electric serviceman tells of the number of phone calls he receives which open with, "I'd like to have you come and fix my Frigidaire ..."!

The image of a product is directly correlated with its brand name. But an image goes deeper than a brand name. While the brand and image can well represent the product, only the image represents the consumer. Most men and women think of Camels as a "masculine" cigarette—a man's cigarette!—whereas a Salem is more of a woman's cigarette.

The image of a product is often the reflection of an inner urge or desire on the part of the consumer. And producers are well aware that our urges and desires can be effectively stimulated by imagery.

Researcher Pierre Martineau has this in mind when he defines a product image as "the total set of attitudes, the halo of psychological meanings, the associations of feeling, the indelibly written aesthetic messages over and above the bare physical qualities."

He continues: "If this seems vague and too intangible, after all consider the human personality and how inexact it is. What is my 'self'—which I am absolutely certain that I have? I am only what other people think I am. I am the sum total of their attitudes. They see me as a physical body and also as a symbol to which they fasten many meanings.

"A product . . . similarly has such symbolic associations. I and millions of others will each in our own way see it as a symbol of something—it may be good or bad, dull or exciting."

In writing in the *Journal of Marketing*, creative advertising man William D. Tyler points out that there may be three kinds of images. There "is the one that gives you a *subjective feeling* about the brand. It is the one that makes you feel that this is *your* kind of product when you hear or see the name."

Another image is the *objective* kind. This is not so much self-identification as a mental picture of the *product* as appealing to you. "It is not a picture compounded of facts and figures, but of moods and rewards and values that surround it with desirable aura." Hamm's beer creates a certain mood with "The Land of Sky Blue Waters." Pepsi-Cola creates a young, gay mood. Ford is the car with fast pickup.

The third kind of imagery implants a *visual image* in your mind—a picture. The Lucky Strike bull's eye says Lucky Strike faster than the words on the package. The G.E. circle says General Electric faster than those words do. So does Prudential's Rock of Gibraltar, and the Cadillac V.

Blindfold tests on beer and cigarettes show that people can't really tell the difference between most brands . . . but many people also have rather clear and very different images of Budweiser as compared with Pabst, for example, or of Camels as compared with Chesterfields.

One of the great image-building campaigns of recent years has been Pepsi-Cola's. Once this brand stopped trying to be an economy cola and moved to establish a distinctive product image, sales soared. Pepsi-Cola developed the distinctive image of a light, refreshing, young-modern, sophisticated drink . . . all tied in with a low-calorie story.

A famous example of imagery is the man in the Hathaway shirt—with his eye patch. Is there any indication that the Hathaway shirt will look better, launder better, last longer, than, say, Arrow shirts? No, but an image was created here which helped to triple the sales of Hathaway shirts. Note, of course, that the basic product was good, and then a unique image about the shirt was created.

Ivory tends to be perceived as a family soap. Lifebuoy has a clear-cut image of being a man's soap. Lux and Camay share the image of being a woman's soap.

Some years ago the management of the Philip Morris Co., makers of Marlboro cigarettes, began to wonder if a bigger market could be had by changing the image of Marlboro. In terms of imagery, Marlboros were thought of as "feminine," more of a woman's cigarette than a man's. They were advertised as "Mild as May." As a result of an enormous amount of consumer research carried on by the Elmo Roper marketing-research organization and by the Home Testing Institute, plus almost infinite variations by Louis Cheskin of the kind of package that might be developed, it was determined by the end of 1954 that the former "feminine-looking" package of Marlboro would be abandoned, and instead a new package developed, one much more masculine in appeal.

A new advertising campaign was developed by the Leo Burnett Company advertising agency around the new Marlboro—with a tattoo on the back of a man's hand—but not just any man's—a virile-looking he-man who looked as if he was very succesful but had "come up the hard way."

This advertising had a romantic appeal, particularly in American culture, where so many men are concerned with whether they are thought of as virile or not. This seems of special concern to men in higher-status groups, who do not earn their living with their hands.

Incidentally, after the advertising campaign was started, it was discovered that Jack London had once written, "If you follow a man who has a tattoo, you'll find a story." The im-

plication is that he probably has had an adventurous and
romantic life.

The new advertising campaign was born in early 1955. It was
not until July, 1957, that the advertising headline appeared,
THE MARLBORO MAN, but he was already known as that. In
1958 the slogan became, WHERE THERE'S A MAN, THERE'S A MARL-
BORO. And a young woman was introduced into the picture,
looking coyly over her shoulder at a big he-man. Later came
the headline BETTER MAKIN'S. Always, though, the Marlboro
man had the tattoo. The success of this cigarette advertising
campaign was based primarily on *imagery*.

As another example, consider the importance of *imagery* in
selling automobiles. This does not imply that one buys an
automobile just because of its image. There are still the rational
problems of what you can afford to buy, how big your family is,
and even whether your garage is big enough! But there is
also the question of imagery. Following are the results of
some careful studies of automobile imagery made by the Leo
Burnett Company advertising agency.

A successful image of an automobile is based first and foremost on concrete product attributes. Cars are purchased as a
means of transportation, and the consumer's thinking about
cars is always affected by specific product qualities. Thus, some
of the basic ingredients of the Ford image are fast pickup,
general fleetness, and clean styling. The image of Chrysler
Corporation cars is that they are uniquely styled and well
engineered. The general imagery of General Motors cars (at
least until the 1959 models) was one of conservative styling.

A car is first and foremost a product, and its success or
failure will be viewed in terms of specific product qualities.
But the problem is one of how the consumer can intelligently
differentiate one from another. Most people can't differentiate,
except by such exterior and superficial criteria as color and
chrome, length, and lines. Most of us haven't the slightest
understanding of what goes on under the hood. The most im-

portant news in the fall of '59 about the soon-to-be-seen Buick was that it would have "sport ventiports," a new grille, and headlights placed side by side instead of on a slant!

Pierre Martineau writes: "We say with an air of finality that this car definitely is beautiful, that one is reasonably attractive, and another line will sell poorly because it doesn't have real beauty. . . . We are speaking of beauty as if it were an unchanging, eternal reality seen in the same likeness by everyone."

But all you need to do is to think of the last car you bought, and how you and your family said, "It's beautiful!" And your next-door neighbors probably bought a car of another make, and they used the same ecstatic words, "It's beautiful!" The image was "right" for each family, although the cars were different.

Certainly a man's image of himself and other people's images of him are in part determined by the kind of car he drives. To take an obvious example, a Cadillac is transportation for its owner, but it is also for lots of people an ego-building possession, one with which the owner identifies and one which helps other people tell "what kind of man he is." Perhaps we don't just buy a car, but we buy the kind of prestige which we think fits us.

Most of us even judge each other by the kinds of cars we drive. Dark-colored, four-door sedans suggest conservatism, dignity, reserve, maturity. Bright-colored, two-toned hardtops imply a greater tendency to showiness.

"Owner images" which are identified with each line of cars and which relate to the kind of people whom motorists associate with the car might be called anthropomorphic projections. The Greek word "anthropos" means "man," and the word "morphos" implies "in the image of."

This means that a line of cars is judged and evaluated in large part in terms of psychological projections such as: "What kind of a man would buy this car?" and "Is this car for me?" Every motorist asks himself these kinds of questions in deciding whether he wants to own a specific make of car. A positive or a negative evaluation of a car derives in large part, either consciously or subconsciously, from his answers.

These projections are based on both fact and fantasy. The image of the Ford owner as a young, stylish person, interested in speed and pickup rather than in smooth and solid roadability, applies to many Ford owners. Certainly Ford is stylish, youthful, speedy, and appeals to people who value these attributes. But these owner images are also fantasy projections; and the public picture of the owner of a given make may not always reflect the true characteristics of the owner.

In other words, when the image of a car is not solidly founded in a public awareness of specific and positive automobile qualities . . . when the public doesn't know for sure just what kind of a car this is and just what it can and can't do . . . then the owner profile is vague.

And some well-known automobiles disappear from the American scene. Remember the Packard? I can recall when the man who owned a Packard was the prestigeful man in my community, the way the Cadillac or Chrysler owner is today. But with both style and price changes downward over the years, Packard manufacturing breathed its last in 1959.

In 1957–1958, what happened to the new automobile called Edsel? After all of the advance rah-rah and hoop-la before the Edsel was "unveiled," everyone was expecting some kind of a super-duper something-or-other automobile, but when the wraps were taken off, what did you see? Just another car. It didn't look very different from other autos, except for a "horse-collar" grille. The image which was built up in advance wasn't lived up to by the product itself.

The Edsel was designed to be "all new" and "all different." To promote the car as new—really new—Ford decided not to link the Edsel even with the corporation's well-tried engine or with Ford's standing reputation for good performance. Instead, the Edsel was introduced and promoted as an *all-new* car. But specific discernible attributes were not played up—

such as dependability, durability, roadability, economy, etc. Just new. Even the name "Edsel" wasn't exciting.

The serious-minded automobile owner asked himself: "Why *would* a man buy an Edsel?" And more importantly, "Why should *I* buy an Edsel?"

In answering the first question, the typical motorist arrived at two possible answers. Either the Edsel buyer was altogether loyal to Ford and would buy *any* Ford product, or else he was the sort of person who would try anything new, and who bought his car without regard for the important qualities of performance, economy, and dependability.

The answer to the second question—"Why should I buy an Edsel?"—was pretty universally, "No reason." Thus, in the absence of specific performance and engineering attributes of this new car, the typical motorist filled the void with the image of an unthoughtful person. This owner image became in large part the image of the car . . . and the owner image in turn reflected back to the car itself. If this was the car for careless, unthinking buyers, there must be something wrong with the car itself. It must somehow be deficient in performance, quality, or workmanship.

Now, this does not imply that people logically went through all these steps. I am simply saying that these kinds of thinking did go through the minds of people. Finally, in November, 1959, the Ford Motor Company announced the death pangs of the Edsel. What was by now a $400-million dream came to an undramatic end.

Another important dimension in the image of a line of automobiles is the image of the *corporation* that makes the cars. This refers not just to the image of the car itself, but to the over-all "umbrella" of the big corporation. There are a few big automobile corporations today, as you know—General Motors, Chrysler, Ford, Studebaker-Packard, and American Motors—which make most of the automobiles in America. When you buy a car made by one of these companies, your image of the company affects to some extent, either consciously or unconsciously or both, the image you have of the specific automobile. The very size and public visibility of these corporations are important contributors to the images of their cars.

On the other hand, the image of the corporation may be unimportant and almost irrelevant in the purchase of various brands of packaged goods. As an example, when a woman buys a detergent, whether it is Joy or Lux or All or Vel or something else, she probably cares very little whether it is manufactured by Procter & Gamble, Lever Brothers, or Colgate.

In general, though, the name of the product and the name of the company means a great deal to us. *These names help us in deciding what to buy;* and they help to make up the "priceless ingredient" and the "pictures in our heads."

12

You Learn through Advertising

1. Advertising: Servant or Sinner?

For a successful manufacturer to try to do business without advertising or sales promotion is like a man winking at a girl in the dark—the man knows what he is doing, but nobody else does.

Yet you may feel that most advertising is bad. If you have such a "dogma," would you please curb it . . . just for a little while?

The basic reason so many people are against advertising is emotional. All forms of advertising and sales promotion are trying to get people to react—to do something they might not do just on their own. In a sense advertising must be "upsetting" to be effective . . . and we hate to be upset.

What is more, advertising tries to get us to *spend* money, whereas most of us from our earliest childhood have heard that it is better to save than to spend. It is considered more moral. So most advertising is asking us continually to do things we may feel emotionally are not quite right . . . and at a profit to the advertiser.

Advertising serves as a psychological "fall guy" for most consumers. That is, advertising takes the rap for what people don't like, according to the findings of Charles C. Lehman, senior analyst of Daniel Starch and Staff research firm. "What happens when Mr. and Mrs. Doe encounter advertising for a familiar, well-liked brand? Starch Reader Impression Studies consistently show that 'good' advertisements (ads which the reader personally likes) are implicitly attributed to the *manufacturer*. Readers frequently say, 'I always read this company's advertisements,' or, 'It is a good company,' 'I use the product,' 'Their ads are always informative.' In reader responses to a 'good' advertisement, thoughts and feelings about the people who created the ad are almost always absent. . . .

"But for ads thought to be 'bad,' it is not the manufacturers but rather the *advertising boys* who get clobbered. . . . 'It is just a misleading gimmick dreamed up by some advertising man.' "

As Prof. Edmund D. McGarry of the University of Buffalo has said: "Ever since advertising began to appear, moralists and critics have complained that it distorted people's natural desires, misinformed them as to the products they needed, played upon their emotions, and led to a waste of resources."

Since the total amount spent on advertising this year probably will exceed $12 billion, you may be sure that this money is being expended only because it reflects and answers the needs and wants not only of producers but of consumers. It is interesting that the addition of advertising to *Reader's Digest* has made possible a one-third increase in the number of articles and stories for the reader.

So why do so many people complain about advertising? The answers are simple, but not obvious.

We have millions of advertisers, sending information to millions of consumers through at least seven basic channels of communication—radio, TV, outdoor advertising, magazines, newspapers, direct mail, and point-of-purchase advertising. Consequently, people don't have too much choice as to when or where they will see or hear advertising. If they like it, fine; but if they don't, they may have to see or hear it anyhow. Advertising has to be endured, even when not endearing.

If we don't like a certain person, we can manage to avoid him and not invite him to our house; but advertising of all kinds comes to us, whether we invite it or not. It is to be expected, then, that we complain if we don't like certain advertising.

This is true of both *national advertising*, designed to win our preference for a particular make or brand of product ... and of *local or retail advertising*, produced to get us to buy at a certain store or retail outlet.

Perhaps the main thing that causes many people to be irritated by advertising is what comes over our radio, or especially through our television screen. It sometimes seems that almost every housewife shown in a commercial is an attractive blonde in her twenties, perfectly groomed and with a perfect build ... and that almost every husband is in his twenties or early thirties, with a short haircut and *never* wearing glasses, and also well built. Is that what most adults really look like? Henry Morgan wrote about TV advertising in the *Saturday Review:* "On the screen appear mindless teenagers who inhale, then turn and display their teeth to one another in transports of delight. ... Refrigerators have the power to make whole families quiver with pleasure at their enlarged freezer compartments, and gents bust out all over in smiles when shaving, looking at bottles of beer, and eating wonderful TV snacks made of pressed milk. Oh, the lip-smacking, the yum-yumming! The delighted tots cramming their tiny pusses with bowlfuls of Sawd Ust and plenty of cream and sugar! ... And the boob-faced girls chortling as they use superior hair sprays that—poof!!—cement their coiffures into lasting monuments!

"Smile at the bread that nourishes twelve ways; grin at the toothpaste containing DC-7B, the only ingredient made of real atoms; snigger along with happy 'dad' as he loses his vile headache with a compound that rips through his gastro-intestinal tract like an aspirin in orbit."

Apparently a lot of us feel the same way. And many of us object to loud, noisy commercials. However, most consumers have built up interesting defenses against advertising. Advertisers and advertising agencies have carried out research that finds that people turn away from their TV set when there is a dull commercial, or even leave the room. Some commercials are almost completely ignored, and researchers can find almost no trace of seeing or hearing the commercial. But other commercials that are worthy of the time and attention paid to them are heard ... and remembered.

When we turn the pages of a magazine, we also find stories and articles and advertising that we don't like. And it is good that we have the privilege in a democracy of reading the stories and articles and advertising that we want to, and that we don't have to read or like all of them. Think also of the number of books you have an opportunity to read and the number of movies you have an opportunity to see—in how many instances do you find shoddy books or movies?

When manufacturers try to reach consumers, they have so few ways of reaching their select audience that each must advertise to thousands or even millions in order to hit his limited market. Therefore, we as consumers must choose those ads of interest to us. When we purchase a shirt, we expect to have to select the one of interest to us ... and so it is with advertising. But a large percentage of today's advertising "is just plain dull," says Edward C. Bursk, editor of the *Harvard Business Review*.

Most of us see and hear so much advertising that we tend to "turn it off" from our minds a lot of the time. We can turn off the radio or television set by looking away or conversing with somebody else, or going to the refrigerator or the bathroom—sometimes the city water pressure suddenly goes down, when the TV commercials come up! And we can also "turn off" the advertising in a magazine or newspaper by rapidly turning the page. The amount of time most of us spend looking at an advertisement is usually only a few seconds. You cannot possibly try to read and digest every advertisement you see or hear, or you wouldn't have time to get anything else done.

There are several other specific and very pointed objections which some consumers have to advertising. Apparently advertising is the least understood industry in the United States; but a number of advertising agencies—especially the Leo Burnett Company, Benton and Bowles, and Young and Rubicam—have paid for advertising space to answer some of these criticisms.

1. The first criticism is: "Advertising makes people buy things they don't need!"

Yet, as one of the Benton and Bowles ads says: "If clothes are only for warmth and modesty, then all a lady really *needs* is one sensible dress. . . . If the automobile is only for transportation, then all a family really *needs* is a well-preserved 1928 Essex. . . . If washday is merely to scrub clothes, then all a housewife really *needs* is a bar of soap and a washboard."

And, according to Young and Rubicam: "Advertising *does* sell people things they don't need. Things like television sets, automobiles, catsup, mattresses, ranges, refrigerators, and so on and on. People really don't need these things. . . . All people really need is a cave, a piece of meat and possibly a fire."

Many people maintain that advertising makes other people buy things they don't need, partly because it makes them feel that they themselves are not extravagant. People of thirty-five or over can recall vividly when the *habit* was to be thrifty. Although our economy has changed considerably, people are not able so easily to change their values concerning thrift. Yet, with the desire for new items, they buy and satisfy their wants; then they may make advertising the scapegoat, by claiming that they were duped into buying something they didn't need.

2. A second objection is that advertising makes us buy, *without sufficient thought and deliberation.*

But what acts could be more deliberate than the slow and thoughtful responses which you and I make to advertising? To quote Prof. Edmund D. McGarry again: "Picture the consumer in his living room reading a magazine advertisement. He has had to choose the particular magazine, and pay for it;

he has had to select from among the hundreds of pages those he wishes to read, and he can either accept or reject the arguments presented. Assuming that he accepts them and resolves to make a purchase, he must still wait hours or even days before an opportune time arises to make the purchase. During the interval between the time he reads the advertisement and the time he undertakes the overt act of buying, he is entirely outside the influence of the message and may deliberate and search his soul to his heart's content either in private or in consultation with his friends. . . . He is a free agent and there is no possibility of coercion, duress, or constraint of any kind."

Obviously most of us *desire* other things and better things than what we have. And these desires of millions of us for a better way of life have helped to make the United States the most wealthy and most comfortable nation ever. Advertising is one of the principal factors in creating so much demand that mass production is possible . . . and so more goods can be sold to more people for less money. But advertising can't *make* us buy in a hurry, any more than education can *make* us learn in a hurry. We can shop at leisure with plenty of time to make up our minds.

Apparently those who fear advertising have faith in their own powers of resistance, but do not trust the resistance of other consumers of whom they are self-appointed guardians.

3. A third criticism some people make is: "Advertising makes things cost more!"

It would be absurd to say that advertising *never* makes *anything* cost a fraction of a per cent more. But the real question is: "How much would products cost *without* advertising?"

Let's suppose there were no advertising. Now, suppose you heard rumors about a new-fangled invention called a refrigerator, and you decided you might want one. But because very few other people knew about it, yours was practically a one-man or one-woman demand. You can imagine what the price tag might be. Without mass production and mass advertising, we might still be living in the icebox age.

Take a look at the following shopping list. Does it seem unusual?

2 cans frozen soup
pkg. brownie mix
instant rice
dietetic cereal
liquid detergent
crtn. filter cigs. (menthol)
pkg. aluminum freezer wrap
renew baby's antibiotic
hair spray
3 pr. stretch socks

This list may look quite commonplace ... but you couldn't have written this shopping list in the 1940s. Items like these and hundreds of others were at most hopeful ideas. Even after they existed as products, it took advertising, and lots of it, to make them household words. And because advertising is able to make them known to great numbers of people, manufacturers are willing to produce them in volume for you to buy, and at a price you can afford.

Even if you agree that advertising is necessary, you might say: "We spend about $16 billion a year on all primary and secondary school education, but the amount spent on advertising is about $12 billion a year. This is too much."

It may surprise you to know that advertising today is actually *much less expensive* than it used to be. In a study reported in the *Journal of Marketing* by Dr. Kenneth H. Myers of the Northwestern University School of Business, it was shown that advertising budgets for 1958 were only two-thirds of the level of the 1920s. That is, advertising's *share of national income* was actually lower than in any decade from the 1890s through the 1930s—and this is because advertising media have become more efficient.

But you then say: "We have lots more advertising than in the 1920s. How can this be?" The Myers study showed that physical volume of advertising per capita had expanded to over 2½ times the level of the 1920s. This expansion, of course, is due to the afore-mentioned efficiency and also to mass-media characteristics which now apply to advertising. So advertising is not only a necessary "middleman" between producer and consumer, but it is becoming less expensive.

In his volume, *The Economic Effects of Advertising*, Prof. Neil H. Borden of the Harvard Graduate School of Business Administration, concludes that advertising, although certainly not free from criticism, "is an economic asset and not a liability." He writes: "Advertising's chief task from a social standpoint is that of encouraging the development of new products." If you "don't believe in advertising," read Professor Borden's book.

Advertising is only one of the marketing tools used by a business. Every manufacturer of consumer products spends a lot of money on salesmen, sales-promotion techniques, and advertising. But for many manufacturers, advertising is their most important marketing tool.

4. Probably the greatest sources of consumer antagonism have to do with exaggerations and inanities in advertising.

A train of fallacious reasoning goes something like this:

> Some advertising is ridiculous.
> Most ridiculous advertising is dishonest.
> Therefore, all advertising is dishonest.

Instead of trying to analyze what is wrong with the above syllogism, we know that lots of consumers feel this way. Sometimes they fail even to make distinctions in kinds of advertising, and claim that all advertising is bad.

There are great differences in advertising of different kinds of products. Try to find distortions of truth in the advertising of most foods, appliances, household furnishings, clothing, rail and air services, insurance, and you'll have to search quite a while. On the other hand, a great deal of cigarette advertising leaves much to be desired—how can four different cigarettes all be lowest in nicotine and tar?—and claims for "miracle ingredients" in various pain killers and in some cosmetics may be so ludicrous that they leave us laughing, unless they are so irritatingly absurd that they draw our fire.

Hal Stebbins, president of Hal Stebbins, Inc., advertising agency says: "No one contends that advertising is lily-pure. This is a far-flung and ramified business. It calls for many skills on many fronts. As a result, it has its share of false prophets; of fast-bait-and-buck artists; of dimwits and bar-flies. But so has every other business—and possibly in greater degree."

Too much advertising has a special language all its own— most of us don't use such phrases as "anatomic styling," "cold, crisp taste," "fast, long-lasting safe relief," "volcano of fashion color." Leo Burnett, head of the advertising agency that bears his name, believes and puts into practice the idea that the American consumer is a human being, and appreciates being talked to like one, that he "hates stuffiness and dullness in advertising fully as much as he does in people." And Earl W. Kintner, chairman of the Federal Trade Commission, believes that "the level of sophistication of the American public is rising steadily."

The great majority of national advertising, if you will consider it objectively, is quite ethical. See if you can find anything objectionable or misleading in the advertising of the following companies and products: Allstate insurance, Allsweet margarine, Arrow shirts, Bell Telephone System, Campbell soups, B. F. Goodrich tires, Green Giant peas, Hoover vacuum cleaners, Jell-O, Life Savers, Maytag washing machines, Motorola television sets, Remington Rand, Santa Fe Railway, Star-Kist foods, Texaco, Tide, United Air Lines, Western Union, Westinghouse . . . and a host of similar products and companies.

You might also try thumbing through any important national publication, such as *Life, McCall's, Reader's Digest, Good Housekeeping,* or *Ladies' Home Journal,* and try to see if you can find any instances of unethical advertising. No one believes that all advertising is perfect ... but you'll have to look long and hard to find examples of objectionable advertising in such publications.

Advertising affects our lives in various ways. As has been well said: "It is pictures for children's enchantment. It is ideas for Mother's meal-planning. It is job security for Dad. It is the voice of better business for the grocer down the street, for the owner of the large department store downtown, and for producers everywhere."

5. Another complaint of some consumers is: *"Anybody* can see through advertising!"

That is really a very true statement—anybody can see through advertising, into it, and all around it because the advertiser puts his name up in big headlines or announces his name proudly over television and radio. To use an analogy, we might say that he puts his name up in klieg lights for the entire world to see. Everyone knows exactly what the advertiser is doing and what his motives are ... and what he wants us to do.

But the greatest advertising campaign in the world cannot turn a poor product into a good one any more than it can force somebody to buy something he doesn't want. What advertising can do—and does—is to create awareness about products and services. It seeks out and stimulates wants. It defines the differences between products. It demonstrates how things can be done better, more easily, more satisfyingly. In short, advertising presents us with the opportunity to desire, to select, and to buy if we wish ... and it gives us information we need in order to make our choices.

But some people insist, "Advertising never sold *me* anything!" Again, I have to say that the basic function of advertising is to inform ... to convey news about products, what they are, where to get them, and what they cost, and what their qualities are. There is certainly some question as to whether people who say so disdainfully, "Advertising never sold *me* anything!" really are that much immune to advertising.

Advertising is not one part psychiatry to two parts brainwashing, with a couple of dashes of henbane and dragonwort thrown in. Instead, effective advertising shows arresting pictures of products, and delivers fresh, interesting ideas about them.

6. A recent objection of consumers had to do with the erroneous belief that something called "subliminal advertising" has been or is being used on the radio and on television.

I am referring here to a technique that is *supposed* to deliver advertising messages so much below the level of consciousness that people do not even know the messages are being given. It is called "subliminal" because it is "sub" (below) the "limen" (threshold) of consciousness.

For many years psychologists have known about something called subliminal stimulation. This has been demonstrated in psychological laboratories over and over again. That is, it is possible for individuals to give *perceptual* responses to stimuli which they cannot even see or hear. It has not been demonstrated, however, by psychologists or anybody else that, because people receive subliminal stimuli, they will *behave* or act differently. And there is no evidence that subliminal stimuli will cause a person to do something that he does not want to do.

In late 1957, it was "claimed" by one man that while people were watching regular movie films in a motion-picture house in Fort Lee, New Jersey, subliminal messages were also projected on the screen at 5-second intervals at a $\frac{1}{3,000}$ of a second speed saying "Eat popcorn" or just the words "Coca-Cola," and that the sales in the lobby of the movie theater for popcorn and for Coca-Cola went up tremendously. Exactly how this took place is one of the best-kept secrets of 1957, because the people who engaged in this experimental work have never revealed the details. And yet millions of people apparently believe that this actually happened!

There is no national advertiser who will have anything to do with this idea. Likewise, every one of the networks in the United States and the Canadian Broadcasting Corporation has taken a firm position that it will not engage in attempts at subliminal advertising. The reasons are on both ethical and practical grounds.

From an ethical standpoint, no one likes attempts at thought control. Even attempts at subliminal advertising would produce feelings of real anxiety among radio and TV listeners and viewers.

From a purely practical standpoint, the question is whether or not it can be demonstrated that subliminal advertising would be more effective than "regular" advertising. And this has not been demonstrated! No one has even a shred of evidence that by advertising subliminally an advertiser could do a better job than he does in the regular way.

We can say that subliminal advertising is within the realm of possibility, as are lots of things; but a great deal of scientific work would have to be done to demonstrate whether or not it is effective. To modify the old phrase—"from the sublime to the ridiculous"—we might talk about moving from the ridiculous to the subliminal, except that subliminal advertising today seems ridiculous. Let's dismiss the subject by calling it the "ghost of subliminal advertising."

But in spite of all the gripes which consumers have about advertising, it is interesting that we buy to a greater extent those products which are advertised than those which are not! James O. Peckham, executive vice-president of the A. C. Nielsen Company, has pointed out that consumers favor advertised brands by about 3 to 1. Advertised brands of storage batteries account for somewhere between 50 to 60 per cent of the total market. In the case of tires, the advertised brands account for 75 to 80 per cent of the market. For drug store proprietary products, health and beauty aids, the advertised brands account for 70 per cent of the market. For food products and household needs, the figure is around 75 per cent. For gasoline, the figure is well over 80 per cent.

In other words, while we enjoy complaining about advertising, we have sufficient confidence in advertising that we go ahead and buy advertised products more than those which are not advertised. No one forces us to pay more for advertised brands, or even to search them out. In many stores which feature their own private-label brands, we may have to hunt for the nationally advertised products, and yet we'll still buy more of these than the nonadvertised brands. As Mr. Peckham says, "This freely expressed vote of the consumer—this *willingness* to pay more for an advertised brand—must mean that the consumer places a *value* on the advertised brand that the non-advertised brand just doesn't have."

Advertising has to do the job of promoting the product to the consumer. To do this well, the advertiser must also advertise the wants of the consumers to the producers. This means that *advertising is still the servant of both the producer and the consumer.*

2. Education through Advertising

The job of the manufacturer, unlike the hen, is *not* to "lay eggs." But, like the hen, he must remember to cackle about what he has produced—and the most useful means of cackling is to advertise effectively. Selling starts with advertising.

In a sense, advertising might be compared with personal selling ... in that something usually cannot be sold after only one try, but only after repeated tries. *Sales Management* magazine has reported that 80 per cent of sales are made after the *fifth* call. The figures are that 48 per cent of the salesmen reported on called once and quit; 25 per cent called twice and quit; 12 per cent called three times and quit; but the 10 per cent who kept calling made 80 per cent of the sales.

The need for the advertiser to "keep calling" is the same. That is why the same advertising message or a variation of it must be repeated over and over again. This is especially true of new products and innovations for already existing products. Describing new products as a "matter of survival," Pierre A. de Tarnowsky, executive vice-president of Warner-Lambert Pharmaceutical Co., says that a product cannot speak for itself and

that "people must be told and told and told" about the product
through advertising.

A report to stockholders of the Timken Roller Bearing Company once said: "Over the years advertising has helped keep the
public acceptance for Timken products at a very high level. We
expect to keep this preference but can never relax in our efforts
to let people know what we have to offer."

We consumers influence producers of goods to give us the
right product in the *right quantity and quality* and at the *right
price.* Very simply, we do this by choosing from among the thousands upon thousands of products available to us. And we are
schooled in these many choices *mostly through advertising,* because this is the fastest and best way for producers to tell us
about their products and services.

This means that modern advertising must be a unique blend
of economy, speed, control, and responsibility. As to economy,
advertising can deliver messages to a mass audience at a fraction
of a cent per person. As to speed, an advertiser can get a message to masses of people within hours, if necessary. As to control,
an advertiser decides what he wants to say, to whom he wants to
say it, and when he wants to say it. As to responsibility, an advertiser signs his message, becomes completely responsible for
it, and cannot disclaim it.

At the annual meeting of the stockholders in 1959 Charles G.
Mortimer, chairman of General Foods Corporation, told the
stockholders that advertising was necessary if the business and
the profits were to continue to grow. He said that General Food's
$96 million invested in advertising pays, "or we could not continue to pay dividends to stockholders, nor increase the volume
of present products and introduce new products to provide better profits and dividends in future years."

But Mr. Mortimer also pointed out that a business cannot
earn benefits for itself without first benefiting the consumers.
"This we do by holding down, insofar as possible, the price of
General Foods products often while improving their quality,
convenience, and utility."

While it is true that advertising, selling, sales promotion, and merchandising activities are designed to move us to action, they are also sources of information and news. Ask yourself: Without these sources of information, would I be able to buy as effectively as otherwise?

All of us, as consumers, face five decisions in buying. *What kinds* of products should we buy? *What quality? What quantity? Where* will we find the best sources of supply? *How* can we make our purchases most effectively?

The growth of advertising and sales-promotion activities is a result of giving consumers an opportunity to make more and more choices on the basis of what they can learn about the product rather than just on the basis of price. Also, with almost everybody having "dough" in his pocket in the 1960s, price alone is not so important a consideration as it was twenty or thirty years ago. There are even prestige values to many consumers in paying a little bit more for something.

What should be the principal characteristics or goals of advertising? There are five, according to Clarence E. Eldridge, former vice-president for marketing of the Campbell Soup Company: *truthfulness; believability; lack of unfair disparagement of competing products; effective presentation of sales points;* and *importance to the consumers of the sales points.*

Both from an ethical and a business standpoint, it is not very sensible to engage in *untruthful* advertising. If women are told that a hair spray will keep their hair in place and set for at least twelve hours, and then it turns out that this does not happen, not only do women resent the advertising, but they don't buy the product again!

But you say that there are misrepresentations in advertising. Yes, unfortunately there are, but not so many as you might think. The Federal Trade Commission, not noted for being in love with advertisers, examines thousands upon thousands of advertisements every year and finds only about 3 per cent that even require further study. In the mid-1950s, the FTC's annual number of formal complaints against advertisers was only about

125 a year, with cease-and-desist orders numbering only about 80.

Many people think that it is the Federal government alone which keeps most business clean and honest. Not so, says Lowell B. Mason, for many years a member of the Federal Trade Commission: "The most important deterrent to false advertising lies in the pervasiveness of competitors. The small number of federal agents scattered over the country encourages a deliberately false advertiser to regard the chances of getting caught by the government as very thin. But he realizes his competitors are ever present. In whatever market he trades, rivals are always close at hand to read his screed." Mr. Mason says that the greatest protection against false claims is the rivalry among merchants for the consumer's dollar.

Some people seem to believe that the purpose of advertising is to make you think you have longed all your life for something you have never heard of before. Many consumers get their dander up about advertising because they think it makes people do something they don't want to do. Strangely enough, people do not get quite so upset about personal selling, although there have been a great many more instances of real "gypping" in personal selling than ever have occurred in the history of advertising. One reason is that the sales transaction is usually a private transaction between buyer and seller. Advertising, on the other hand, is always out in the open. *Everybody* can see what advertising is and what it says—and the advertiser's name is in big letters for the world to view.

With the millions of advertising messages weekly, it is not surprising that there is some advertising—and there always will be—which is questionable from an ethical standpoint. This is no more surprising than to find that in the field of higher education there have been instances where basketball players have been dishonest, or that there has been gambling on athletic events. But this does not imply that all university basketball players are dishonest or that all college students are engaging in gambling.

And it is not surprising in business that there is a small percentage of advertising which is shoddy, unbelievable, exaggerated, or distorted. This is of great concern to most advertisers and hurts all advertising. Consumers are not alone in their concern about the ethics of advertising. This is also a matter of grave importance to all thoughtful advertising men. Leo Burnett has well said, "Every dollar spent for unbelievable advertising is money down the drain." Fairfax M. Cone, chairman of the executive committee of Foote, Cone, and Belding advertising agency says: "A single exaggerated claim in a newspaper or magazine or over the air contaminates every other advertisement to which the reader or the listener is subjected—for days or maybe weeks or months."

Believability may be more of a problem than untruthfulness. Here we have a situation where, even though an advertiser knows or believes that his statements are true, they may not seem true to the consumer. In that case, the consumer is likely to say, "It is untruthful." We want our toothpaste to clean our teeth as effectively as the ads say, and we want our food to have the yummy flavor claimed for it.

On the other hand, there are some kinds of advertising in which believability isn't important. As an example, an advertisement for Fisk tires has appeared for many decades which shows a little boy in pajamas with a candle and a big Fisk tire back of him, and the headline simply says "TIME TO RETIRE." Is there any problem of believability or any problem of untruthfulness? No. There are lots of instances of this kind where believability is not the key factor in the advertising: Jif peanut spread, "Jif is terrif!"; Budweiser, "Where there's life, there's Bud"; Modess, "Because."

A third characteristic of effective advertising is *lack of unfair disparagement of competitors, or competing products.* Certainly it is all right to suggest to the consumer that he make comparisons; and surely the advertiser wants the consumer to believe that his product is better than others. Most of us are proud of our products and our associates. Students at the University of

Michigan are convinced that it is better than the University of Wisconsin, and vice versa. In much the same way, the Westinghouse man believes his products are superior to those of General Electric, and vice versa; and the Procter & Gamble man believes his products are better than those of Lever Brothers, and vice versa; and so on. But *unfair* disparagement of competitors is not a sensible idea. It may backfire because of the average American's sense of fair play.

A fourth characteristic of good advertising is *effective registration of sales points*. This means that the *big ideas* should be got across. It means that information should be given. It means that the advertising goes in your ears or eyes, or both, and stays in. For example, an effective advertising slogan is simple to understand, easy to remember, and pleasant to repeat—"Fresh up with 7 Up," "Say it with flowers," "Good to the last drop."

Finally, the advertiser hopes that his sales points are also *important sales points for consumers*. One difficulty here is that many an advertiser is *manufacturer*-oriented rather than *consumer*-oriented. It is so easy to engage in brag-and-boast advertising that the advertiser may forget to talk about consumer benefits. Many an advertiser becomes so intrigued with seeing his company's name in print and on the TV screen that he may lose his public in a technical description of how the product is made (about which the consumer could not care less) and forgets to talk about how the product benefits the consumer.

There are many kinds of advertising. You may say, "Oh, no, there is only one kind—the kind to make a sale." This is true in a sense, because the objective either directly or indirectly is to get across selling points to potential buyers. But not all advertising is designed to make an *immediate* sale. There is also a second category of advertising with the purpose of creating *awareness on the part of consumers* (announcements of new models, or improvements). And there is a third category—advertising with the purpose of *creating* or *changing the image* or concept of a product or company. This is long-range advertising.

The first category of advertising—for immediate action—you find in a great deal of daily newspaper advertising. See most supermarket and department-store ads. You find it also where-ever any special deal is being promoted. You find it particularly where special prices are the incentive.

The second type of advertising—awareness on the part of consumers—you find in the announcement of a new model of an automobile, refrigerator, or washing machine. You may find it also in the advertising of a completely new product, for ex-ample, the Hoover electric floor washer brought out in 1959. Other examples relate to some improvements in products—a double filter on a cigarette, an old soap in a new color, a food product packaged differently. The advertiser is not necessarily expecting the consumer to rush out and buy immediately. But he does want consumers to know that something has happened; and he hopes that, after consumers have received enough ad-vertising messages and have had an opportunity to be sold in other ways, they will buy.

Third, there is an enormous amount of advertising which has as its main purpose to change the image or concept of a product. Look at the advertising by many national advertisers and you cannot help but be impressed with the fact that this is one of the basic ideas—to get people over a long period of time to de-velop a different idea, a different image, of the product. The avertiser wants us to think about his product differently: "Take tea and see" . . . "At 60 miles an hour the loudest noise in this new Rolls Royce comes from the electric clock" . . . "My, how they grow with Instant Vigoro."

No advertiser in the third category will be unhappy if some immediate action does result; but he will not complain if his advertising begins to show results only after a long period of time. *The over-all objective of advertising is to aid the selling process,* but it alone does not accomplish this. It is used along with other merchandising and sales-promotion efforts.

To quote Mark Huntington Wiseman about advertising: "The products it promotes are not just 'things'—they are symbols of status, taste, and intelligence; they contribute to comfort or health or pleasure; they satisfy longings for beauty or romance; they lessen labor or make it more fruitful."

Something other than logic tells a woman that a certain brand of soup is right for her family. She feels that a certain make of washing machine is right for her. Her husband believes that a certain brand of cigarette is right for him . . . and a certain make of car. Advertising is one of the reasons that they feel the way they do about products. Advertising will not make us buy a product we don't want, but it may be an important factor in persuading us to buy the product we have decided we want.

And remember, advertising doesn't sell an idea to many people in just one try—the idea has to be sold over and over and over again. So with over 1,800 daily newspapers, 8,000 weekly newspapers, 4,000 consumer and business magazines, 45 million TV households, 50 million radio households, an estimated 50 million car radios, thousands of billboards, and countless pieces of direct-mail and other forms of specialty advertising . . . every one of us is bound to be exposed to a whale of a lot of advertising. As a matter of fact, the average family in the United States probably is exposed to as many as 1,500 or more advertising messages in a single day; and this number is probably on the increase.

This growth in advertising and sales-promotion activities is a result of giving consumers an opportunity to make more and more choices on the basis of product information rather than just on the basis of price. Then, too, this growth in advertising is necessary for consumers to be good shoppers in a self-service era. So advertising has become the servant of both the manufacturer and the consumer—taking the place of the salesman by giving you advance information about products.

Not only is growth in advertising necessary for our immediate needs, but it actually encourages a higher standard of living. As a study by the Twentieth Century Fund points out, "A constant education of consumers to desire products they never heard of before is just as essential to the smooth functioning of our economy as are an adequate supply of electric energy and plentiful raw materials." This is why it is important for advertising not only to assist us as buyers but to encourage us to satisfy our wants and desires. In fostering consumer wants and desires, the growth of our economy is expanded and a higher standard of living is achieved.

Advertising, then, serves in a two-way education. It educates the manufacturer as to the needs and wants of the consumer . . . and helps to promote a higher standard of living. It educates the consumer as to the merits of different products . . . and helps the spender to spend more wisely.

13

Your Stores Have Personalities

1. Friend or Foe?

Warmth, friendliness, and style! These terms can be used to describe the personality of either your favorite friend or your favorite store.

"But can *stores* have personalities?" you ask. It is obvious that people have personalities . . . and that in a sense products have personalities. But also a given store may have a definite personality or image for you. The following story about a discount house illustrates this.

The executive vice-president of one of the largest advertising agencies in New York told me that he wanted to buy his daughter a present. He went to one of the city's biggest discount houses, but says that he sort of turned up his collar as he went in, afraid somebody would see him entering such a place. His image of himself, you see, was that he must buy only in a high-quality shop like Abercrombie & Fitch.

Samuel J. Sugerman, general manager of Kaufmann's department store in Pittsburgh, tells me that as Kaufmann's builds branches, one of the big jobs is to maintain the clearest image of the store. "There was a time at the turn of the century when the mere availability of merchandise was news to the prospective customer," he says. "Next came the availability of that merchandise under one roof, in a central location, in the hub of the city—the department store. Even that has long since ceased to be the prime reason for the public's patronage. Before the phrase 'store image' was coined, it was the store's character that attracted many purchasers. Currently the widespread establishment of branches poses the problem of maintaining a *store image* under greatly varied conditions of size, location, merchandising, and other factors."

What are the differences for us, the consumers, between shopping at a big department store or one of its branches, and at a discount house? Imagery is important. Most people feel they will get more courteous service in the department store, and that they are also getting prestige, convenience, greater selection of merchandise, delivery of their products, and option to return products if they don't like them, and so on.

But among all these factors (provided the product and price are satisfactory), the greatest are *friendliness* and *prestige*. Wherever you shop and whatever you buy, you hope to feel good about it. You like to cater to your own ego. And, after all, why not? It is your money.

You are much more comfortable shopping in certain stores than in others. Just as you enjoy certain personalities in people, you likewise enjoy certain store personalities.

Take as an example the supermarkets and grocery chains. In various studies it has been demonstrated that even though there is a variety of choices for the woman shopper—perhaps A & P, Safeway, Kroger, Jewel, National, and other supermarkets in her community—she will begin to buy at one place and probably stay with that choice. The primary reason will not be lower prices, better bargains, or greater savings. Instead, the great drawing power of the store where a woman shops is based on qualities indicated in these descriptions: "the store that is clean and neat," "the store where you see your friends," "the store with helpful personnel."

This is an interesting characteristic, the emphasis on the

personnel of the store, particularly in these times of self-service. It is not common for women to mention prices or bargains as the basis of shopping at one supermarket rather than another. Yet, strangely enough, if you will look at the grocery advertising in your local newspaper, especially during the middle of the week, you will find this is the big thing emphasized—the bargains you can get. But the important thing for most women seems to be the friendliness of the people in the store; and this may simply mean how she is treated by the stock boy when she asks him a question about where something is, or how she is greeted by the checkout girl.

In this connection, Franklin J. Lunding, chairman of the board of the Jewel Tea Company, says that the homemaker and purchasing agent for the American family are two people: Mrs. Customer-of-the-Head and Mrs. Customer-of-the-Heart. "But, in their efforts to attract her patronage, too many retail merchants make the mistake of appealing almost exclusively to Mrs. Customer's head by concentrating on *Price*. . . . They overlook the fact that Mrs. Customer's head is often overruled by her heart, using the term in its broadest sense."

In all shopping, customers like to feel they are *desired*. The need to feel wanted is great in all of us. If we can go into a store where we feel that the store personnel are taking a real interest in us, we go away with a warm feeling of acceptance. "It makes me feel good to go shopping there," is our attitude.

Contrast this with the situation where you did not get what you thought was the proper amount of attention from a salesperson, or you felt that the salesperson was rude. Most people will say, "I'll never go back to that store again." This may not be logical. It may not be rational. But for most people it is true.

The main question that you ask yourself, perhaps unconsciously, is whether the people in the store are *friendly*. But along with this are the questions, also unconsciously asked, concerning prestige: What is the status of this store? Is it high class, or low class, or what? Does it fit in with the image I have of myself?

Most shoppers seek out the stores which seem congruent with the images which they have of themselves. As Pierre Martineau, director of research and marketing of the *Chicago Tribune* says: "The upper-status woman cannot conceive of herself shopping in the subway store of a large department store. Regardless of bargains, she is repelled by the thought of odors, milling crowds, poorly educated clerks. Conversely, the wage-earner's wife is not going to expose herself to the possibility of humiliation by shopping in the quality store, whether it be Bonwit Teller or Nieman-Marcus or Lord & Taylor—even if she has the money to buy something there."

C. Virgil Martin, president of Carson, Pirie, Scott & Co. department store in Chicago, says: "It is high time we retailers recognize that we cannot be all things to all people. When we try to do that, we end up with no particular appeal for anybody. Each of us has his own individual niche in the market place."

What kind of people does a store want to appeal to? One Chicago retailer, when asked about his customers, said that the entire Chicago market was his oyster—people from all income brackets, sections of the city, surrounding areas, and social groups. But an analysis made of his sales tickets showed that nothing could be further from the truth. Although his store is located in downtown Chicago and, therefore, should attract customers from all parts of the Chicago area, analysis of his sales tickets showed that his customers come primarily from the south part of the city and southern suburbs.

Every store management must decide what kinds of customers it wants to attract. A Bonwit Teller or a Saks Fifth Avenue goes after one type of customer, and a Goldblatt's or a Macy's goes after another kind of customer. Each is extremely successful. Each has made the decision as to what kind of customers it wants. Therefore, each store can serve its customers more effectively and efficiently.

Contrast the kinds of people, in general, who shop at a Marshall Field with most of those who shop at a Sears, Roebuck. The general image or personality which Marshall Field has created not only for people in Chicago but throughout the United States is one of high quality and sophistication. Routine shopping is transferred into what might be termed an exotic adventure for many a bored housewife.

On the other hand, a Sears store is considered more comfortable, with lots of choices in appliances, household staples, paint, tires, and children's wear. As Pierre Martineau says: "Sears has created a public image of itself as a family store, both in the type of merchandise it carries and in such intangible meanings as warmth, comfort, friendliness, honesty, dependability, and even unselfishness. Whereas the wife is more apt to go shopping alone at Marshall Field, it is not uncommon for the Sears shopping trip to be a safari for the entire family.

"Sears, Roebuck and Marshall Field are the two largest department stores in Chicago, yet their store images are entirely different. The very merchandising strategies and personality aspects which are so successful for Sears are not uppermost for the Marshall Field audience, and vice versa. The upper-status woman expects a respect and a restraint from the salesclerk that would be interpreted by the wage earner's wife as formal and forbidding. On the other hand, the family atmosphere and the great emphasis on savings which attract the Sears customer are distasteful to the Marshall Field shopper."

Of great significance is the psychological identification with the store. As Mr. Martineau has said in another of his studies: "Two people in the same social class may want different stores. One may prefer a conservative store, one may want the most advanced styling. But neither will go to stores where they do not 'fit' . . ." He suggests that there are at least four factors which affect the personality of a store: (1) its layout and architecture; (2) its symbols and *décor;* (3) its advertising; and (4) its sales personnel.

Certainly the *layout and architecture* of the store "signal" to you immediately what kind of a place it is. This is not very different from entering someone's home and, almost unconsciously, learning from the furnishings what the family is like. You see lots of books displayed, or perhaps no books at all. You see linoleum on the floor, or perhaps wall-to-wall carpeting. You see art objects of a sophisticated sort, or maybe those of a very poor quality, if any. These things tell you immediately what the tastes of the people are in this home.

We get this same sort of information from other people, simply in the way they are clothed. The way a person is dressed tends to suggest to you immediately how you will respond to him.

In much the same way, when you go into a store where the architecture is very modern and up to date, as in a new shopping center, you get a different impression than if you go into one which is "arena-like," such as Robert Hall. In terms of layout, contrast the store which has wide aisles with the one with narrow aisles, or the store which has the merchandise displayed in attractive ways as contrasted with the one which has it piled up on shelves where everybody can paw over it. These factors identify different personalities, and they help us to establish store images.

Of course, stores can be too much alike. The architecture and layout can be so much alike from one store to another that the store personality is lost. Stanley Arnold, former supermarket operator and today president of Stanley Arnold and Associates, has been concerned with this problem in supermarkets. In an address to the Super Market Institute he said: "Truth be told, I'll bet I could take one of your best customers into one of your best stores—blindfolded beforehand—remove the blindfold, and defy her to tell me where she is. Is she in your store, or is she in your competitor's? Is she where she always shops, or is she where she never shops?"

Consider also the kinds of *color and lighting* that are used in displaying the merchandise. Even the colors on the walls of the store help to tell you something about the store's personality. The kinds of point-of-purchase displays (or the lack of them) also suggest to you what the store personality is.

The *advertising* which you see for a Marshall Field as contrasted with the advertising for a Sears is going to tell you a great deal about the character of the store, even if you have never been in either one. High-style art and conservative typography suggest that a store is expensive and formal. Newspaper advertisements filled with jumbled type faces imply that a store is cluttered and has a volume-turnover philosophy.

Of course, the mass-appeal store does not try to run the more elegant advertising of the quality department store. And a store in one section of a town does not necessarily use the same appeals as another in a different section. To be effective, the symbolic meaning of the advertising must mirror the personality of the store itself.

Sometimes it is not possible to separate the influence on the shopper of the store and of the brand. As one shopper said: "Well, you can tell it's a good store by its reputation—by what brands they advertise in their ads. If they advertise a lot of well-known brands, it's usually a pretty good place to shop."

In this connection, consider the following quotation from anthropologist John J. Honigmann's book, *Culture and Personality:* "... If to attract followers a high ranking leader associates with persons of lower rank he may himself lose rank so that his chance of attracting followers is reduced. Up to a certain point the 'fraternization' passes unnoticed, but there is a point when increases in the number of such associations produce a decrease in rank and leadership."

And so it is with stores and brands. Products considered high in quality should be associated with stores of high quality. Most of us will consider products high in quality and continue to purchase, so long as a store reflects quality.

Finally, as has been indicated, most important of all is the *kind of sales personnel.* Are the people in the store friendly or indifferent? Are they cooperative or not? Do they seem interested in you, the shopper? These are the biggest factors in determining how people will feel about the store and its personality. *Your store is your friend ... not your foe.*

2. You and Your Shopping

As William A. Patterson, president of United Air Lines, has observed, high-sounding phrases and slogans about superior services are hollow unless they are actually backed up by courteous behavior.

For department stores, clerks are mentioned more often than any other image-building factor. A typical comment: "If the clerks are courteous and friendly, I enjoy shopping there." *Chicago Tribune* studies have shown that:

- Wives of blue-collar workers are concerned with *utility*. They value cleanliness and neatness, and seek these attributes in stores. They desire modernity and price plus an easier way of doing things.
- Wives of white-collar workers living in a new suburb are concerned with *others' opinions* of them. They are involved in community affairs, often dominated by their children, and are anxious that their shopping be done in a "socially acceptable" way. Their purchases tend to be made largely in terms of symbolic value.
- Wives of upper-middle class suburbanites believe that to make money and to achieve status, one must spend money. Much of their shopping is justified as "being for the children." And they are concerned about *taste* and seek prestige stores.

But all three groups—in fact, all shoppers—want recognition from salesclerks. Some typical statements:

"The employees make you feel either at home or uncomfortable in a store by their attitude when they wait on you. For some, if you decide not to buy, they can make you feel like a crumb sometimes and you'll never go back."

"I like to go into a store and feel like a *person*, not some undesirable creature or thing who happened to intrude on a salesclerk's privacy. When a clerk acts as if you are intruding or doing them a favor, or is too uppity, I never go back if I can avoid it."

"I was just browsing in the millinery department when a snippy saleswoman asked me not to handle the merchandise. That was enough for me—I'd never go back there again."

Most of us could probably be called "the shopper who never came back." Ordinarily we don't complain or even grumble at discourteous salesclerks, and we don't even go so far as to write a hot letter to the president of the store or company—we just never go back!

The true art of selling in the retail outlet has dwindled to a new low. This is of major concern to the heads of leading department stores. Walter W. Candy, president of Bullock's—one of the great department stores of the Los Angeles area—tells me that proper selection and training of retail sales personnel is his biggest single problem. Retailers in Denver, Dallas, Detroit, and everywhere else agree that this is their greatest problem, too.

One retailer says that salesclerks are now being recruited as wrap-up artists instead of sellers. And perhaps you, too, have found this true. I can recall how in a big Chicago department store I received no information regarding a relatively simple product, a raincoat, from what I thought was a salesman. So, I went to the floor manager to ask for some information, and he asked me, "Why didn't you get the information from the salesman?" I replied, "I asked and couldn't get it." He then asked me to point out which salesman; and when I did the floor manager volunteered: "Isn't that amazing? He won a special prize last week for being the best salesman in the whole store!"

Looking back over the factors just discussed, what most shoppers want are:

- A desirable relationship with the salesclerk
- Store of same "class" as the shopper
- Store with good selection
- Merchandise attractively arranged, and clean
- Store that "stands back of" its merchandise

- Extra services without charge
- Price customer wishes to pay

But the personalities of the salespeople almost "make" the store for many shoppers. Perhaps this is in line with what sociologist David Riesman in his book, *The Lonely Crowd*, calls "other-directedness"—including a heightened awareness of other people. After all, more and more of us are concerned with what our friends and acquaintances think of us—more perhaps than with what our families think of us—and are genuinely concerned over the reactions of those with whom we deal in a shopping expedition.

In many shopping situations we are not sure of ourselves, and we like to have a salesperson who can be of genuine help. A research project by psychologist Robert N. McMurry revealed a number of doubts common to prospective women purchasers of major appliances:

- Should she spend the money for a stove rather than a television set or some other item?
- Among so many conflicting claims and makes, how can she decide which make to buy?
- How can she tell whether the standard or the deluxe model is the better value?
- Maybe she can buy it cheaper elsewhere.
- What will friends and neighbors think?
- All these special mechanical features look good, but maybe they won't work right.
- Maybe this model won't hold up.
- How can she get the *real* facts on what's the best buy?
- What if she happened to buy a "lemon"?
- What does her husband *really* think?

A successful salesman sympathizes—even empathizes—with the person who has these nagging doubts. He tries to relieve them by helpful information and friendliness. And if he is astute, he may even follow up the sale by a phone call or letter to the purchaser of a costly item, just to help relieve what I call "postpurchase anxiety." Do you know about postpurchase anxiety? You certainly do, if you will recall the *first* TV set, automobile, set of furniture, or washing machine you ever bought. After you bought it, you worried for fear you had done the wrong thing: "Oh my, maybe I should have bought a different product . . . or perhaps I shouldn't have made the purchase at all."

When you spend your hard-earned money, you want someone to take a genuine interest in what you get for your money. No matter how much or how little you spend, you also *want to shop some place that mirrors your own personality*. After all, human nature is very prevalent.

14

How About Price?

1. Prices on Trial

Today's prices are of real concern to all of us . . . producer and consumer alike. The producer knows that if his price is not right, he will lose his market and his invested capital. And you and I as consumers are always worried about prices being too high.

On the surface, both consumer and producer have reason for concern, because the dollar which bought 100 cents of goods and services twenty years ago buys less than 50 cents' worth today. In 1940, a loaf of bread cost about 8 cents . . . today, about 20 cents. Round steak, then 36 cents, is now about 80 cents a pound.

But we also know that increased productivity has done something to our deflated dollar. Prime example of this is in the field of electricity. The cost of electricity in 1900 was 17 cents per kilowatt-hour; by 1954 it had dropped to 2.69 cents.

Let's take a look at other "prices" in terms of the amount of work involved. The table on p. 180 shows how much labor an average factory worker had to do to earn some typical products in 1914, compared with how much it took to earn similar or better products in 1955.

Product	1914	1955
Electric light bulb	1 hr. 42 min.	6 min.
Pound of butter	1 hr. 37 min.	23 min.
Women's shoes	20 hr. 48 min.	4 hr. 51 min.
Ton of soft coal	24 hr. 29 min.	10 hr. 59 min.

To continue the contrast: Thirty years ago an hour of labor in a factory would buy 6 or 7 loaves of bread ... today it will buy 12 loaves of bread. Thirty years ago an hour of labor would buy a pound of butter ... today it will buy almost 3 pounds. Thirty years ago an hour of work would buy about 4 quarts of fresh milk ... today it will buy 9 quarts of milk.

It is now apparent that, when increased productivity is averaged in with the deflated dollar, the dollar does buy *more* than it did thirty years ago. So the consumer not living on a fixed income is comparatively better off today than during any previous economic period.

But the consumer's counterpart, the producer, still has an acute problem—proper pricing. Provided the product itself is satisfactory, to a large degree sales success is dependent upon proper pricing. As has been previously emphasized, a combination of selling and advertising, plus sales promotion, will not cause people to buy and continue to buy a product which they think is inferior, or which they feel has no product differentiation or advantage ... *or which is not priced right.*

There was a product, for example, tested in a few cities by the Campbell Soup Company. This product, called FR-8, was a premium-priced blend of eight fruit juices. The flavor accent was on grapefruit, and the price was about 20 cents higher than for a can of grapefruit juice. Consumers did not find sufficient distinctiveness in flavor to pay the higher price ... and the product was withdrawn from the market by the producer.

Many a businessman is faced with the crucial problem of deciding for a product, *what price will consumers be willing to pay?* A decision has to be made—a judgment influenced by facts. How does he decide on a price?

Businessmen are constantly trying to find out what their competitors are doing and expect to do. This does not imply spying on one another, but it does suggest trying to get intelligent information as to what other people are likely to do. Information is obtained from many sources—salesmen, wholesalers, distributors, manufacturers' agents, sales agents, retailers, and consumers.

In establishing or changing price, part of the necessary information may be obtained on a formalized marketing-research basis. But a lot of information is still secured on a hit-or-miss basis, and the old theory of charging "what the traffic will bear" is not always borne out in practice.

According to famed managerial economist Joel Dean, how to price a product is "too often solved by cost-theology and hunch." Writing in the *Harvard Business Review,* Dr. Dean has suggested instead several considerations for estimating demand and price.

First, is there an active demand for the product, or a latent demand that can be made active or created? A good deal of research is done by many companies to try to explore the preferences of us consumers and to explore our "educability." Can we be persuaded to want a product, so that it meets our requirements?

A second step in trying to find out whether we consumers will buy is to get into the range of price which might make the product economically attractive. This is very difficult to do, because at most times we consumers do not know what we would buy. And if we don't know what we will buy, then it's very hard to say what we would pay for a product which we have never seen. Even if it is described to us as a variation of a present product, it's still difficult for us to know what we might be willing to pay for it.

Given the price range, a third consideration is what sales volume might be expected at various points of this range. This is the most difficult type of sales forecasting. A series of different hypothetical prices is set up and then for each a "guesstimate" is made of what sales volume might be obtained at each price. Test marketing—that is, controlled experiments with different prices in this range—sometimes can improve these estimates.

A fourth point has to do with the possibility of price cutting by competitors. Every business has to be ready at any time to change its pricing policy because of competition. "Nonprice" competition through better quality and better service is, for pricing purposes, often the economic equivalent of price competition. Hence, this kind of reaction must be taken into account. Moreover, old-fashioned price cutting still does exist.

Joel Dean mentions other important factors which enter into the problem of establishing a price on a product. The producer must determine his "market targets." In other words, what share of the market does the producer want? The producer must also determine how this new product fits into his family of other products. Can this new product use the established channels of distribution and methods of production? Is a new promotion strategy required? If so, what kind?

It becomes vividly evident to us consumers that *the producer has a Herculean task in finding the right combination of costs for producing and marketing, so as to come up with a price which is pleasing to the consumer, meets the competition, and makes a satisfactory profit for himself.*

Dr. Dean suggests two alternative initial strategies for pricing a new product. A brief discussion of these two policies will enable us to understand better when and how to get what we pay for. It should be understood that either of these two strategies may be used in its extreme or in any modification with the other. The price the consumer pays depends upon which extreme or combination of the methods is used by the producer. Of course, there are many other classifications for pricing policy, but these two are of particular interest to us.

The *skim-the-cream price policy* involves high initial prices for the product when it is first put on the market—here the manufacturer hopes he can skim the cream of demand. Suppose, for example, a novel product has been developed such as an electric blanket; do you remember when the electric blanket was new? It was not immediately accepted as part of the expenditure pattern, and consumers did not have any way of comparing prices—of knowing what was high, low, or medium for this new product. In 1936 you would have had to pay $89.95 for an electric blanket. Today you have a choice of many different prices, even as low as $19.95.

Again, suppose you have an opportunity to buy an "electric gutter cleaner." Do you have any way of knowing what this should be priced at, or what you would be willing to spend for it? Well, if there were such a product, the question of how much to ask for it would be somewhat like the early pricing problem for electric blankets. How do you know what you should pay for it? Or how much would you pay for self-cleaning windows? Or for drinking glasses that would remain permanently sterilized?

In cases like these, a manufacturer might price the product fairly high when it first comes out, and then drop the price a bit later to meet the competition. This was true of the first ball-point pens. The initial high price serves to reach the "cream of the market," those consumers not so much interested in price. They feel that they can afford convenience and new items at almost any time. Such consumers may buy the $100 limited autographed personal editions (with each copy numbered from 1 to 250) of new publications ... the first color television ... solar heating systems.

The skimming-price policy may seem relatively safe for a manufacturer of a really new product, whether a new type of refrigerator or a new type of dishware. The high initial price may serve two purposes: market exploration and safety, and market segmentation. After all, some sales at this high price can be expected. This should result in a profit; but the manufacturer cannot expect a large volume of sales at the high price. Thus, he may elect the good, but restricted, profit over the possible, but not certain, large volume. However, in today's fast-moving world, with thousands of new products coming out, a producer may not be able to keep to a skimming-price policy very long.

At the opposite end of the scale is the *penetration-price method*. Here the product is introduced with very low prices in order to penetrate the mass markets. The sales objective is to get there "firstest with the mostest." This method would lead the producer to get in early and sell hard, especially on the basis of low price. For instance, bargain-rate coach fares of scheduled airlines were adopted at first apparently to meet the cut rates of nonscheduled airlines.

The penetration-pricing policy is often used in the maturity stage of a product's life cycle. In the case of new books or publications, the second stage after limited personal edition would be the $5.50 book in hard covers for thousands of buyers, and the most mature stage of the product would be the 35-cent Pocket Book. Reissues as 35-cent Pocket Books of classics, such as Shakespeare and Chaucer, have reached new markets.

Initial low prices are indicated when reductions in price bring more sales, when there is evidence that consumers do not think a product "cheap" just because it is inexpensive, when there are important cost savings from large-scale production, and often when there are threats of price cutting by competitors. Sometimes during the testing of a new product, you may be able to buy it at quite a reasonable price. If the quality is there, you have the feeling that you "got in on the ground floor."

On the other hand, when sales seem to be comparatively unresponsive to price but quite responsive to promotion, higher prices may be the general rule; but neither policy is *the* answer. And there are hundreds of other considerations.

It must now be obvious that if price is an important element in our spending, sometimes we may wait quite a while after the initial presentation of a product to the market before we buy. Many of us are now patiently waiting for a more favorable price on color television ... air-conditioning units ... radiant heating.

A serious problem for the consumer may arise from "reduced

pricing." We should be aware of the fictitious-price evil, illustrated by the seller who offers a price and says that it is a reduced price, when actually it is not. It is exemplified by an artificial markup in the price of a product before it is marked down. Millions of consumers seem to get irritated by "hard-sell" advertising. What they should really get angry about has to do with pricing. About one-third of the Federal Trade Commission's false-advertising cases deal wholly or in part with phony price claims. It is best to beware of the local "I can get it for you wholesale" chap who seems so well meaning.

The *Reader's Digest* tells how in 1958 the Chicago Better Business Bureau investigated "bargains" in appliances, such as washers, gas ranges, refrigerators. Of 23 so-called bargains, if a family had bought one of each, the advertised "savings" would have totaled over $2,000. But it was found out that actually a family would have spent about $50 more by taking the bargain than by buying exactly the same item at honest stores. Some saving!

Another example—a distributor offered to preticket watches for retailers at any price they wanted. He offered resale tags, with the price printed at $16.95, $19.95, $24.95, $29.95, $39.95, or $49.95. Cost to the retailer was from $9.50 to $14.50!

What can we consumers do about this kind of pricing? One thing, of course, is to buy well-known brands of merchandise. This is one of the reasons that people are willing to shop around a little bit more for nationally advertised products.

A second thing we can do is to realize that the test of value of an article is not what the price tag says it formerly cost, but what it costs today in other stores. This means some shopping around . . . a little searching to find out what kinds of prices are available.

A third thing we could do, of course, is to report any such instances of gypping to the Better Business Bureau in our community so that appropriate action can be taken.

Fortunately, only a tiny percentage of businesses resort to shoddy practices, and thereby make life difficult for others who are running their businesses in a normal, honest way. Practically all businesses are run on honest, ethical principles.

For all businesses, it needs to be emphasized: *Prices are always on trial.* A business firm may have decided on what seems a sensible price to attract buyers, but if not enough customers buy, then the price may be wrong. So the price may have to be changed . . . but this in turn may be confusing to consumers.

But before making a price change, a firm should try to be sure that it is the *price* that is at fault and not something else, such as the product or its sales promotion.

Consumers may vote a product in or out of the market. Hence, our votes at the cash register, coupled with competition and regulating agencies, prompt many businessmen to adhere to fair pricing. But we must realize that price is not the only test of quality. Whatever you buy, you also judge it by its purpose and what it means to you.

As a result, business rivalry has also channeled into another area of competition, namely, "nonprice" competition. This means greater emphasis on *quality of the product* and on *greater service* for consumers.

To producers, this results in higher costs because of greater investment of time, money, and talents. To us consumers, nonprice competition results in some upping of prices, but also in more services and conveniences.

2. Getting Your Money's Worth

Many a warm-blooded American male might be somewhat chagrined if he realized that the little woman is paying out his hard-earned money for such things as warmth, friendliness, and new ideas!

With fairly standard prices and guaranteed quality of merchandise, the frau is learning the pleasures of buying on a nonprice basis. And with a little introspection, that same American male also should realize that he himself enjoys reading the newspaper while an orthodox repairman fixes the refrigerator which, of course, has a "free-service guarantee" included in the purchase price.

To get us to spend our money, the product has to be priced "right" . . . for us. The saying is, "You get what you pay for." But other factors than price are becoming more and more important—*quality* of the product, *service* rendered, and *credit* extended.

Our society does not put as much emphasis on buying things cheap as on conspicuous consumption. And more people than ever have a good deal of money to spend. Also, cut prices suggest to many buyers that a product is shoddy or inferior in some way. Such factors help to explain why both manufacturers and retailers continue to put more and more emphasis on quality of products, service features, and easy credit, as well as on warmth and friendliness.

Take service, for example. We consumers expect more of it than ever before. This is because service becomes increasingly essential in our complicated, technological world. It just is not possible to have the know-how to repair all the appliances that operate in our homes.

A typical comment of a typical housewife: "I always seem to have a repairman coming about something. One came yesterday, one came today, there'll probably be one tomorrow. It almost seems as if the repairman is a member of the family."

So we want to buy products which we know we can get serviced well rather than those we might not. For instance, when the Necchi sewing machine first came on the American market, people were very slow to buy—for the simple but good reason that the company did not provide service. Today repair service and parts are conveniently available, so that buyers give this machine equal consideration with American machines.

Service is by no means limited to the more technical products, which might break down and need to be repaired. Service also includes all sorts of additional benefits in connection with the very simplest purchase.

You just take it for granted that when you buy groceries they should be put in a large paper bag—if it's a really good store, they'll use two, one inside the other. You may even expect them in turn to put the bag or bags in a large cardboard box. In any country other than the United States, one of the most utilitarian items in the home is the market basket, into which go chicken, eggs, fruit, bakery goods, sausage, cheese, and none of it in its own private container.

If you've been in some other countries, you may at first think that people never buy flowers in a florist shop. This is because in most countries you are simply handed the flowers, and you carry them in your hand. No moss, no green waxed paper, no plastic bag, no box, no ribbon, and no outside bag for easy carrying.

Another example of service is found in U.S. department stores. Remember way back when it was so difficult to select a wedding gift for friends? Today in many department stores you step up to a desk in the china department, mention the name of the bride, and within a few seconds you are told exactly what the bride would like and the extent to which these likes have been fulfilled. (Checks are even made between department stores, so that each store has an up-to-date listing of gifts.) It is then a simple problem of how much money you decide to spend. After your gift is "selected," you pay your money and the gift is sent out on the delivery truck to the prospective bride. It's so easy to spend your money these days!

Another example of service is found in filling stations. Today window washing is usually part of the regular service. And if you leave the car for additional service, you may even get driven to the bus or train stop or perhaps to your home.

These kinds of service, if you add up enough of them, make all products thus "serviced" cost just a little more. You don't get something for free. You don't get more paper wrapping and more windshields wiped, and so on, without paying something for it. But in our economy, we're perfectly willing to pay extra for these services—after all, the extra cost is "hidden" in what we pay for the products.

And we not only enjoy all these services, but most of us like to buy now and pay later. No longer do we believe the Shakespearean admonition, "Neither a borrower nor a lender be." As a matter of fact, in our dictionary Webster may one day soon include the word "chargit."

As Edwin B. George of Dun & Bradstreet has said, "Credit has proved to be the lubricant that facilitates the increased flow of goods in our economy." No business today can operate without substantial credit. The convenience of a charge account cannot be overestimated. Albert J. Wood has demonstrated that people prefer department stores where they have charge accounts over those where they do not have accounts by almost a 4 to 1 ratio. There is lots more consumer spending when the consumer can say, "Put it on my account."

Installment buying is a way of life accepted by most consumers. For young families this means buying things which would be impossible for years if it were first necessary to accumulate the capital for purchase. So most products of consequence are bought on credit today. Not only are most automobiles bought on credit, but approximately two-thirds of all furniture, electrical appliances, and floor coverings.

Some moralists are concerned over the fact that ours is a credit economy, and many older people worry over the fact that young people are willing to start out marriage and buy practically everything "on time." Many oldsters say, "I have always paid cash!"

But others ask why it is so demoralizing for someone to buy a product which can last as much as fifteen years and take two or three years to pay for it on an installment basis? Of course, the question is whether you can afford the carrying charges. The true costs of common types of installment credit are much higher than many people suppose. Costs for installment credit for home improvements may actually amount to 10 to 20 per cent; for electrical appliances, 18 per cent; for new cars, 16 per cent; and for used cars, 25 per cent; and in many cases the percentages may run even higher.

A related question is whether you actually do keep something fifteen years. Many things we buy—automobiles, appliances, furniture—certainly will last this long. But due to "psychological obsolescence," plus the fact that as we grow older many of us change our attitudes as to what is appropriate for "our station in life," we may trade in what we had and buy something new . . . and on credit.

There are many people who frown on such extensive credit —mainly because of abuses in the extension of credit during past years and to some extent today. Some people adhere to what *Chicago Daily News* columnist Jack Mabley calls the "Bohemian Easy Payment Plan"—you pay 100 per cent down and owe no more!

In general, however, *price, service, quality,* and *credit* are four important factors that the consumer is looking for. But let's not forget other intangibles that consumers also look for— friendliness, warmth, ideas, and prestige.

A research survey in some supermarkets showed that low prices alone are not sufficient to keep customers coming back. As the report said: "Supermarket shoppers are looking for other values—warmth, friendliness, social status. If competitive prices are also offered, the customer loyalty is, of course, reinforced."

Another way of saying this is that we are not buying statistics —we are buying food and a pleasant atmosphere.

One study of grocery advertising showed that while most women shoppers do read price listings for food items—or at least feel that they should—they follow prices for other reasons than to act on them. They want to keep informed, to get ideas for menus, to do some mental preshopping, and psychologically to reinforce their own ideas that their favorite store is the right store for them.

It may take skillful interviewing to find out, though, that

price is not *the* thing. We cannot always accept at face value
the statement that a woman shops at one store rather than
another across the street because the prices are less. Prices in
the two stores may be the same, but when through psychologically skillful questioning techniques you discover what is her
true image of the store across the street, you may find that it
is a threatening one. Instead of the store's beckoning her with
its luxurious atmosphere and flattering attentions, it may seem
to her a store for the upper-class women in the community
and may make her feel poor and defensive.

As I said in the previous chapter, we shoppers are looking
for values other than just price. Yes, we want to buy at a bargain—who doesn't?—but we find that we can do this in any
number of places. What most of us want is friendliness and
prestige.

The operator of a retail store can pep up his salespeople
(or order takers) by running contests, by working out bonus ar-
rangements, and by offering p.m. (push money) or "spiff" for
pushing certain products. *But the biggest assets of retailers are
friendliness and service.* Dudley J. Taw, vice-president of Mc-
Kesson & Robbins, Inc., says: "What is the big reason for sales
success? PEOPLE! . . . Customers today are shopping for nice people to do business with."

There are changes also in fads and fashions that affect what
we buy. Perhaps the words "fads and fashions" are too strong;
but at least there are differences in styling of products, differences in the ways they are colored or packaged, and the like.

Take soap, for example. In spite of the fact that when you
lather it, all soap ends up white, you can buy soap in a wide
variety of colors. For many years Dial soap, for instance, was
always yellow, but it is now offered in three different colors.

You and I take it for granted, for almost any product we
buy, that there will be a tremendous number of variations—in
style, color, texture, size, and so on—and we expect to have an
opportunity to choose among them. As I have pointed out before, this means higher prices. When we have lots of different

variations so that we can shop for all sorts of different sizes,
textures, colors, weights, and so on, the costs of manufacture
are increased ... the cost of warehousing ... the cost of
transportation ... and costs of the retailer ... and eventually
the costs for you and me, the consumers. But we are satisfied
with our spending behavior if we feel that we got our money's
worth.

15

Marketing Research Can Help

1. Under the Marketing Microscope

"Thirty-nine dollars and ninety-five cents, please." These are the words of the salesclerk as she looks up at you while writing out her sales ticket. This is the price of the new electric blanket you have just bought ... let's say it's a General Electric double-bed, dual-control electric blanket.

There is nothing very unusual about this experience—just a common, everyday occurrence. To be sure, it doesn't happen every day or even every year for you; but this very action does happen every day to consumers somewhere. Yet, if you stop to think about this experience, you will realize that it didn't just happen to take place. A great many things were necessary before you could make that purchase. Let's go back to the beginning.

The real beginning was back in 1936, the year in which General Electric sold its first electric blanket. But obviously the whole idea wasn't conceived and the final product made in that year; so you might say that the beginning was some years before 1936.

Anyhow, in 1936, there were 66 G.E. electric blankets sold. Even by 1940, only 3,532 electric blankets were sold during the year. Today, however, the number is in the hundreds of thousands. The story of this rise is in large part the story of how you were able to make your purchase at your store. It is a story of *marketing research* at work.

After developing the idea, G.E. continued to work to find new ways to improve the product. Do you remember how their first models had those lumpy thermostats throughout the blanket? Consumers weren't very much pleased with them, and so the company set out to find a new and better thermostat that would make a more comfortable blanket. By 1948 such a system had been developed, with the Sleep Guard wiring—no more lumps. General Electric created a better product for consumers—a safer product electrically and a more acceptable product, in an effort to improve the product's use for you and me, possible customers. Because of this and other attempts to satisfy our desires, you were able to buy the product you did.

But you didn't buy just any blanket . . . and not just a blanket at that. You bought a General Electric blanket, true—but more than that you bought the name General Electric and the warranty and service that goes with that name. How does it happen that the name G.E. is used rather than, say, Warm-sleep . . . that the warranty is for one year . . . that there are service centers for blanket repair in Atlanta, Baltimore, Boston, Chicago, Cleveland, Dallas, Detroit, Kansas City, Los Angeles, New York, Newington, Philadelphia, San Francisco, and Seattle . . . that a certain trade-in policy is followed in regard to blankets beyond the warranty?

These are not matters of chance. They have been carefully decided in view of many factors. The brand name G.E. on the package is used because it is already known to you—it already has a "personality," representing strong character and progress and quality. Thus your decision was made easier. The warranty policy takes into account the service and price of competitors and the General Electric price. These have been balanced, to give you the best guarantee for the lowest price. The location of service centers is based on company facilities, but also on population distribution and climatic conditions.

But these are not the only areas where a combination of marketing research and fact finding, coupled with business judgment, have helped to make this particular purchasing experience easy for you. You bought a *green* blanket. How did it happen that green was in stock? Partly it was because of research which revealed the preferences of consumers. The warranty cards included in each box and returned to the company are in six colors to correspond to the color of the blanket bought. In this way G.E. has a fairly good idea of what colors to make in what quantity. It is known what colors are selling; and since the returns are a fairly constant percentage of total sales, there is information about total retail sales.

The box that the blanket came in—its color, design, and size, as well as the plastic bag around the blanket—were all designed with the consumer's wants and attitudes in mind . . . your wants and attitudes.

The display rack in the store and its poster, with material and color samples, didn't just happen either. They were purposely planned to make selection easier for you.

So far, no mention has been made of the store where you made your purchase—perhaps your favorite store in your community, which sells towels, bedding, table linens, and small appliances. How is it that this particular store, in addition to the department store down the street and several other stores in town, carry G.E. electric blankets? There are a lot of things involved here, for example, the climate, the population of the town or city and surrounding area, the type of store, its reputation, the kinds of people who buy electric blankets, etc. Such factors were all taken into account by General Electric to decide that certain distributors, both independent and G.E.-owned, would be used to sell the product to retail dealers, and to decide the number and kind of retailers that would be best for a given area.

And the advertising that you already knew about for G.E. electric blankets probably had some effect upon your decision, even upon your desire for the product. The slogan in the advertising, "Warmth without weight, comfort without care," was even pre-tested on consumers to determine their reactions.

This does not mean that every decision about G.E. blankets has been made as a result of research findings. The point is that in some areas research has been used to provide the manufacturer with information from which he could make more intelligent judgments than otherwise. And the research has involved the *product* itself ... the *brand* ... the *packaging* ... the *price* ... the *service* ... the *warranty* ... the *means of distribution* ... the *display* ... and the *advertising*.

Those with products to sell are vitally concerned with providing us with what we want. But, ironically, information concerning consumers' tastes is both more vital and much harder to acquire than in years gone by. Consider the barriers to communication between the manufacturer and the ultimate user of a product. A manufacturer of such a simple item as paper table napkins may sell napkins through his salesmen to grocery wholesalers who sell them to retailers who display them on their shelves, hoping that they will be selected by self-service shoppers whom they will never know personally.

As long ago as 1933, Alfred P. Sloan, then president of General Motors, said in his message to stockholders: "Modern industry with its large-scale operation tends to create a gulf between the consumer and those responsible for guiding the destiny of an institution. We can no longer depend upon casual contacts and personal impressions—our business is too big; our operations are too far flung."

As Profs. Harper W. Boyd, Jr., and Ralph Westfall of the Northwestern University School of Business have said in their book, *Marketing Research:* "It is obviously foolish for any corporation to spend advertising dollars talking to consumers about products and services in which they have no interest or to try to sell a product the quality of which is not up to the consumer's standard. . . . The executive who must make marketing decisions has practically no direct contact with his customers. Yet, if he is to make sound decisions, he must know who his customers are and what they want."

This requires increasing emphasis on information about consumers, obtained through research.

If I may oversimplify, it can be said that two types of research are used to find out about consumers. The first method, called *marketing research,* is largely descriptive. It attempts to find out *what, where, when,* and *how* we buy. The other type of research is called *motivation research.* This is an attempt to find out *why* we buy.

Marketing research differs from motivation research in that it deals mainly with our actions, whereas motivation research deals primarily with the reasons behind our actions. An example may be helpful in distinguishing the two. If a manufacturer attempts to determine whether we are buying his product, he is doing marketing research; but if he tries to find out why we like its color, shape, size, and so on, he is doing motivation research. And the two methods are often used in combination.

Actually, motivation research is part of marketing research but, for clarity, they are separated here. The next chapter is devoted to motivation research ... but the present chapter is mainly about marketing research. Note that it is market*ing* research rather than market research. These last three letters "ing" are important to what we are talking about.

Market research is a much narrower phase of marketing research. It deals with methods of measuring what and how much we buy. For instance, a study might be made of the market characteristics of the Chicago metropolitan area, of downtown New Haven, or of the Ozark Mountain region.

Marketing research, however, includes market research or market analysis. It includes lots of other things, too, such as consumer surveys, attitude and opinion research—the sort of thing that you are familiar with from knowing about public-opinion polls—analysis of advertising, and so on.

The Grey Advertising Agency of New York has pointed out that there are five "D's" to marketing research.

1. *Definition.* The first job is to define the problem correctly.
2. *Digging.* This is the hunting out of facts ... digging up

every kind of data, from every possible source, that might be helpful.

3. *Dividing.* Here the facts that are dug up must be divided into various categories and analyzed.

4. *Diagnosis.* The facts in the various categories must then be put together. This means that the facts must be synthesized.

5. *Decision.* Here is where the information that has been defined, dug up, divided, and diagnosed is used to help make an executive decision.

There is nothing magical about marketing research. It is simply the finding out, the factual searching out of information, and the organization of these facts in a sensible, logical way. Remember all the steps that G.E. took to get its electric blankets to us?

"Research is a way of thinking and operating, based on a little less intuition and a little more knowledge," says *McCall's* publisher, A. Edward Miller. In other words, research does not interfere with executive decisions, but may enable executives to make better decisions more effectively; and this may enable us consumers to buy better, more pleasing products.

2. Samples and Surveys

We wanted bigger and gaudier and flashier automobiles in 1956, and smaller, compact cars in 1960. We wanted Ivy League clothing for men and Dior fashions for women in 1955, and the continental look and the "voluptuous aura" in 1960. Increasingly, the makers of consumer products have to try to learn what we consumers want, and where, and when, and how . . . and also why. To learn what makes consumers "tick"—that is what marketing research and motivation research are about.

These are tools by which producers keep in touch with consumers. Years ago we bought what the producers and sellers of goods wanted to produce and sell. But this has changed. Now we insist on having the things *we* want . . . and eventually we get them. It's the job of producers and sellers to find out about us—and what a big job they have!

Marketing research is used to help producers determine what it is that the consumer wants. And while it is true that the answers of marketing research are not and cannot be 100 per cent accurate, nevertheless they represent serious efforts on the part of business to find out what we want. Unfortunately, most consumers don't know of the work being done by business to find out what's on the consumer's mind ... or if they have an inkling that such work is being done, it becomes suspect. Otherwise-intelligent consumers swallow by the bookload a lot of guff about "hidden persuasion," not realizing that 99 per cent of the business firms carrying on consumer research are in earnest in trying to find out what consumers want so that the consumers can get what they want. After all, producers will have greater profits if they can please us.

No matter what methods of consumer surveys are used, the researcher usually tries to obtain a representative sample of consumers for his questioning. This involves the use of highly specialized statistical techniques to find out which consumers should be included in the sample. It is not necessary to investigate or "sample" millions of people in order to find out about them. A few thousand or even a few hundred may be sufficient (and that is one reason that maybe *you* have not been "sampled" recently). By comparison, if you are testing or "sampling" a fruit cake, you don't have to eat the entire cake to determine its taste. By testing (tasting) a small sample (slice), you usually can get a fairly good idea of the quality of the entire population (cake).

There are two limiting factors in every survey ... and they are sufficient to prevent *you* from being sampled. These two factors are time and money. A company just cannot ask every potential or present customer what he thinks about a certain product or idea. Can you imagine how long it would take and how much it would cost if a toothpaste manufacturer were to try to talk to 180 million of us?

A survey must be made with a relatively small "population" or group, made up of people who are representative or typical of the total market or population who buy or might buy the product. Sometimes there will be only 100 people interviewed, and sometimes the number will be in the thousands. The *Life* Study of Consumer Expenditures was a sample of our entire population; and because it was representative (what statisticians call a probability sample), the results could be projected to give the same picture as if the entire population had been questioned. Thus, the conclusions of any survey are based on the interpretation of the results; and the results, in turn, are based on the samples of people; and this sample, in turn, is limited by the factors of cost and time.

Marketing research may involve trying to find out whether a *product* is acceptable to consumers. It may involve a study of *inventories* to find out if products are moving through the "pipelines" of distribution quickly enough. Research may mean studies of *pricing,* to find out how products are doing compared with competition. It may involve such things as pretesting of *advertising.* It may include special studies at the *point of sale* to find out what the relations are between consumer and retailer, or how the consumer shops in a retail outlet.

The manufacturer wants to know as quickly and accurately as possible how well he is doing. Are we buying his products? So he tests a sample of us; and what he finds out is used both in his own behalf and for the ultimate benefit of his consumers. Interviews in person or by phone and mail surveys help him to find out what we are buying and what we want.

One of the things often done in bringing out a new product is to engage in *test marketing*. The manufacturer sets up certain locales as "test markets." These may be Peoria or Harrisburg or Rochester or Dayton or Omaha or a variety of different places suitable for test purposes. The producer then goes into these markets with the new product, tries to sell it, and at the same time "researches" the promotion to find out how he is doing.

The accompanying table lists some of the favorite test markets, and indicates how the cities vary according to the kind of product.

Test Markets *

Product	Category	Company	Test markets used
Bravo	Detergent	S. C. Johnson	Syracuse, Pittsburgh
Kerid	Ear cleaning formula	Blair Labs	Buffalo, Rochester, N.Y.; Columbus, Ohio
Aluminum cook-in container	Packaging	Ekco-Alcoa	Pittsburgh
Scotch-Brite	Scouring pads	3-M	Tulsa, Salt Lake City, Wichita, Kans.
Spree	Soap	Colgate-Palmolive	Western Michigan, Northern Florida, Columbia, S.C.
Air-wick stick	Deodorant	Lever	Kansas City, Providence
MP	Gasoline	Milton Oil Co.	Springfield, Mo.
Baby food warmer	Small appliances	G.E.	Los Angeles, Pittsburgh, Philadelphia
Vapor Brite	Oven cleaner	Copper Brite	Los Angeles
Reisweld	Adhesive	H. B. Fuller	Minneapolis-St. Paul
Charge-it plan	Credit service	F. W. Woolworth	Cleveland
Ready-to-bake coffee ring	Food (baked)	Borden	Pittsburgh; 9-state area of Southwest
Country Chowder	Food (canned soup)	Campbell	Syracuse, N.Y.; Toledo, Ohio; Indianapolis, Minneapolis-St. Paul
K-Concentrate	Food (cereal)	Kellogg	Los Angeles, San Francisco
New Horizon	Food (instant protein)	General Foods	Burlington, Vt.
Western Blend	Food (coffee)	Maxwell House	Denver, Seattle
Instant Mashed and Quick Hash Brown	Food (potatoes)	Pillsbury	Syracuse, N.Y.; Wichita, Kans.; Sacramento, Calif.
Individual beefburgers	Food (meat)	Swift	Los Angeles
Combination Punch	Food (juice)	Sunkist	Fort Wayne, Ind.

* *Printers' Ink,* Vol. 268 (Sept. 25, 1959), p. 66.

Manufacturers of products sold in grocery and drug outlets have access to two different kinds of specialized research services which enable them to learn rather quickly how sales are going. The two different services referred to are offered by the Market Research Corporation of America (MRCA) and the A. C. Nielsen Company.

In the early 1940s MRCA set up its National Consumer Panel. This panel now consists of about 10,000 U.S. families and contains over 33,000 individuals. This panel has been selected in such a way that it is a representative cross section of homes and families in the United States. It reproduces, in miniature, the purchasing habits and characteristics of all families of the United States. This consumer panel can provide regional as well as national information of various kinds.

In each of the families in this consumer panel, a "purchase diary" is kept by the housewife. She writes in this diary all information on a weekly basis relating to the purchases of that family, and includes: date and day of the week; brand names bought; types of container (glass, tin, etc.); number of items purchased; exact weight or quantity; place where purchased (including store name); kind of transaction; and price paid.

This detailed information is collected on a weekly basis by MRCA and processed, so that it is possible rather quickly to give results on food, drug, and household products. MRCA has a weekly, monthly, and quarterly report, and also an annual summary of the reports, so that it is possible to trace various trends in the buying of products. Information is given as to size of family, occupation of the head of the household, general socio-economic level, and other pertinent factors.

The manufacturer can learn the answers to such questions as: Who buys our product? How many people buy it . . . and how many don't? How much do they buy at a time . . . in what sizes . . . when . . . and where? How much of it do they buy in a year? Do they continue to buy it . . . or do they switch to another brand? Do they buy our product alone . . . or divide their purchases among a number of products?

This kind of information is of the utmost importance to an enlightened business executive. It helps to take the guesswork out of his estimates. It changes "guesstimates" to estimates.

The A. C. Nielsen Company also provides many answers to marketing questions, but in quite a different way. This company does not obtain the data from the homes where the purchases are made, but rather from retail outlets where food and drug products are sold.

The Nielsen Retail Index reports are based on data from stores representing the buying activities of over 3 million consumers. The Nielsen Food Index and the Nielsen Drug Index are the most widely known of these services. The store panels (1,600 food stores and 750 drug stores) are accurate cross sections of stores throughout the United States ... with proper representation by geographical areas, county sizes, store types and sizes.

This is not a matter of the stores maintaining diaries, but rather of the A. C. Nielsen Company sending its own auditors into the stores on a regular basis; these auditors take actual inventories, and make audits of invoices covering merchandise coming into the stores. In other words, a Nielsen representative goes into each of the stores and actually counts the stock of whatever products are being studied—stock on the shelves and in storage—and checks over the invoices to find out what products have been bought.

This does not mean that entire stock of each of these grocery outlets is counted; but it does mean that the stock is inventoried for the products of those manufacturers who have bought the Nielsen service, and for the competing brands. Detailed information also is obtained as to the different sizes of the products (for example, 8-, 10-, or 12-ounce cans, etc.), and on price.

The Nielsen Food and Drug Index services reveal the changes occurring in the movement of goods to consumers. They also provide information on movement of goods into retail stores; retail inventories and day's supply; distribution of individual items; retailers' out-of-stock; retail prices; consumer prices;

special sales prices; profit margins; dealer use of displays; redemption of coupons; and the like. Information can also be provided on stock location, shelf position, and shelf facings—all cross-analyzed with consumer sales standings.

Just as it is obvious that information can be obtained this way on a national basis, it is also possible to break up the information on a regional basis, and in other ways. For example, detailed information can be supplied separately concerning the supermarkets, the superettes, and the "Mom-and-Pop" stores. It is possible to break down the information as to whether or not the outlet is self-service. The information can be divided as to chains, supermarkets, and independents.

The Nielsen Company also has developed test-market services via special store panels. These have been used extensively to evaluate new products, new advertising and merchandising programs, and product changes *before* they are launched on a broad-scale basis.

Whereas MRCA gives the manufacturer information as to what the consumer is actually buying at a particular time, the Nielsen service gives the manufacturer detailed information on what is happening in the retail store outlets. In other words, Nielsen also helps to take the guesswork out of the estimates of the business executive, and make "guesstimates" into estimates. Both services are mentioned, to give you some notion of the interest which manufacturers have in us as consumers, and what some of their attempts are to find out what we spend our money for. It may take several months for products to move from factory to consumer; that is why Nielsen and MRCA can give the manufacturer information he cannot find out by watching his own sales.

3. Pass Key to Better Products and Easier Shopping

Obviously the producer is not going to be able to stay in business if he is not making a profit; but in order to make a profitable product, *he must produce what you and I want and need.* And marketing research may help to tell him what our wants and needs are.

That is one of the principal reasons why doors on automobiles are now easier to open and shut . . . why syrup bottles no longer drip . . . why your modern vacuum cleaner does a more efficient job.

Who, then, benefits from marketing and motivation research? If the research is well done, the answer is: everybody, *both company and consumer.* Research helps companies to determine just what kinds and qualities of products are wanted by us consumers. New products are more carefully investigated than ever, and potential "bugs" may be discovered and eliminated before the products ever reach us in the market place.

But you still may ask . . . what value does this have for me? The answer is that research as a tool—although an imperfect one—may aid you a great deal. Many of the ideas which result from research studies are consumers' ideas. Even though many ideas from consumers are discarded because they are not practical, a great many ideas can be used or modified, to help give consumers better products, more adapted to their wants. Through surveys, interviews, and consumer panels, opinions of consumers are evaluated, and their ideas are put into effective practice, modified, or discarded.

This means that we can buy with greater confidence; we are getting products that will be what we expected. Better-engineered products are offered to us; and thus a product will probably last longer than the same product used to, and with fewer maintenance problems.

Companies are continually trying to improve their products. Green Giant has made several improvements in their cans of peas in the last couple of years . . . a product we probably would take for granted was standardized. The Chrysler Corporation makes hundreds of improvements in its various automobiles in the course of a year . . . minute changes individually, but collectively they add to better products year in and year out.

Cheerios has changed significantly over the years . . . not enough to shout about each time, but over the years a perceptibly better product has resulted.

General Motors has been using customer research since the early 1930s. The company wants counsel from consumers as to what they like and don't like about automobiles and automobile products. The object is to find out what people want and, as far as practical, to provide for these wants.

Today big companies such as Procter & Gamble have dozens of young women ringing doorbells all over the United States, trying to find out about consumer purchases and consumer wants and desires. Advertising agencies are continually making surveys to find out what people like and dislike about various products. Retailers ask consumers what they want in clothing, drugs, appliances, furniture, and food in order to understand better what consumers want to buy.

And we, the consumers, also want more information. Why? Because we demand choices among thousands of different products, in all kinds of shapes, colors, and sizes. What's sauce for the marketing executive is sauce for the consumer—both end up with better and more desirable products.

One of the reasons that P & G's liquid cleaner, Mr. Clean, does not slip out of your hands is that information was obtained by asking women which of various differently shaped bottles they preferred.

A few years ago the Philip Morris Co. spent considerable sums of money in trying to find something new for cigarette packages. The bothersome thing about the old package, according to Mr. and Mrs. Consumer, was that it was too difficult to open. Thus, because of you and me and our wants, the "snap-open" pack emerged.

A manufacturer of bleach found that although he had a handle on his bottle to make it easier for a woman to pour, the handle was thought to be uncomfortable, which it actually was. So the design of the handle was changed, and the result was a better-selling product for the producer, and a more convenient product for the consumer.

Will you buy a package of cake mix if it is priced at 39 cents or 69 cents? Does the soap package you see in the store distinguish it from other soaps? These answers are all-important to the manufacturer and to the retailer, but also have important meanings for us consumers. We are able to locate products quickly because of distinctive packages and brand names. We have confidence in certain products because of differences in price.

"The research department studied consumer preferences to determine the optimum size of soap cake to produce, whether one or more sizes was needed, what shape the cake should be, what color was most desirable, what fragrance should be added, the type of package to use, the price at which it should be sold, and the brand name, Dial." This quotation, from the book on marketing research by Profs. Harper W. Boyd, Jr., and Ralph Westfall, suggests the immense area covered by marketing research. Just think of all the decisions producers must go through before their product even gets on the shelf at your local store!

With some of the major electric appliances, sometimes it has been useful to have eventual users "help" to design the product. The use of cross-country clinics, where women can see, feel, and examine "mockups" of ranges has helped Borg-Warner in designing the kinds of ranges best suited to women's wishes. General Electric has used somewhat this same technique—by putting washing machines, dryers, refrigerators, and other appliances in trailers and transporting them around for housewives to examine.

Life considered the idea of lowering the price of the magazine from 25 to 19 cents. To determine whether there would be any increase in newsstand sales and what the general reaction might be, the proposed reduced price of 19 cents was tried out in several communities for a limited time. Perhaps you live in such an area and remember the advertising, and even the cover of the magazine which stated that this offer was for a limited time only. As a result of the sales figures for several months in these test markets, it was decided to reduce the price to 19 cents throughout the United States. The result was that *Life* sales went up several hundred thousand, and millions of *Life* readers are happier to be paying less for the magazine.

For Crisco, eye-movement tests were used along with other techniques. It was found by Louis Cheskin that stars on the package caused excessive blinking (of people, not of the stars). A new package was developed without stars, and people could see the package easier and liked it better.

Good Luck margarine had a small four-leaf clover trademark on one corner of the package. When the clover was made bigger so that it covered almost the whole label, more people bought the margarine.

Here are two additional examples that show how research has helped in solving advertising problems. Special apparatus from the psychological laboratory, designed by Dr. Edmund W. J. Faison, now president of Visual Research, Inc., of Chicago, was used in the projects.

The first example involves the testing of a new copy phrase in advertising the new shaker top on the Morton Salt container. The question was whether the copy phrase would be immediately understood in print advertising.

A test ad which featured the copy phrase or slogan in its headlines was shown in a special flash-exposure box to a number of women shoppers. The advertisement was flashed on for 6 seconds; and then each person was asked to describe what she had seen. For purposes of comparison, the same procedure was repeated with another advertisement which played up the package features themselves rather than the copy phrase.

The results showed that the copy phrase was not quickly understood. In fact, it became meaningful in the first advertisement only after the package feature had been explained by the second advertisement. So it was decided to use television commercials instead of print advertising to introduce the new

Morton package. Thus, after the superiority of the special package feature had been clearly demonstrated, the copy phrase used at the end of the commercial was much more meaningful to consumers.

A second example is that of testing a new package design for the detergent *All*. A new type of cardboard container had been developed that was much stronger than the previous one. It permitted the use of a package with a larger shelf-facing area, but without center bulging. The question was whether the visibility and psychological attributes of the new package were superior to those of the old one. A number of visibility measurements were made—with varying degrees of illumination, periods of exposure, distances, and angles. And housewives were interviewed to obtain their psychological reactions to the designs. The new package was found to be superior to the older package in both visibility and psychological attributes. As a result, the new package design—much better for consumers—went into mass production.

Marketing research is not a sure cure for the many decisions a producer or advertiser has to make. It is far from being as exact as research in physics or chemistry; but it is one step along in building better communication between consumers and producers. It is at least the beginning of a "telephone system" that needs more refinement. Perhaps in the not too distant future, the connection between consumers and producers will be much clearer—maybe we'll be able to dial direct!

Don't take too much stock in the popular but erroneous idea that big business is made up of a lot of scheming "hidden persuaders." Many consumers seem to believe that in the world of big business is an unscrupulous band of hucksters who use mysterious weapons called "marketing research" or "motivation research" to increase their own profits at the consumer's expense.

These kinds of research do not represent a conspiracy against us consumers. They are not attempts to invade our privacy or pry open our minds, so as to use the information against us and make us buy shoddy merchandise. They are sincere attempts by manufacturers to produce better goods ... to please both *us* and *them*.

Most certainly, representatives of business and advertising want to know as much about consumers as possible, in order to increase their own business and their profits. But this knowledge also helps us consumers to have better products and easier shopping.

16

Is Motivation Research the Answer?

1. The Meaning of M.R.

M.R. stands for "Motivation Research." It refers to studies which seek to understand and explain the *why* of people's buying behavior. It refers to the use of psychological methods that encourage a person to disclose information about his fundamental drives and motives which he might not indicate in a straight, direct question-and-answer session.

Most of us don't give exact answers to personal questions, either through embarrassment or a feeling that it is "none of your business," or because we don't consciously know the exact answers. Instead, we often give socially desirable answers. For instance, when asked, "How are you today?" you may feel terrible, but you say, "great" or "fine"—a socially acceptable answer.

Also, sometimes we are so unaware of our true feelings that it is difficult to tell someone else what our feelings are. After all, most of us do not go around engaging in deep introspection as to what our inner or hidden motives are. And many of us are not too good at expressing ourselves and telling exactly what we mean. Why do we claim that we brush our teeth just to prevent decay, when actually most of us brush our teeth mainly *before* breakfast?

Or perhaps we don't want to give true information. Direct questions to a housewife, for example, on how often she vacuums her rugs may lead to slightly exaggerated replies, because she wants to appear as a clean and meticulous housewife. Many people tend to exaggerate their readership of magazines such as *National Geographic* or *McCall's* or even *Good Housekeeping,* and to understate readership of such publications as *True Story, True Confessions,* or *Confidential.*

The problem is—what is really in the consumer's mind? Sometimes this information can be obtained from motivation research. Where does the phrase "motivation research" come from? Actually the term is a misnomer. The phrase "motivation research" refers to what are called "projective techniques," which are used by clinical psychologists to learn something about people's unconscious motives, wishes, desires, aspirations, doubts, fears.

In other words, motivation research is an umbrella phrase, used to cover special techniques such as thematic apperception, picture probe, narrative probe, sentence completion, word association, depth interview, group interview ... methods of exploring our motives. These techniques, used by psychologists for many years in clinical and counseling work, are called "projective techniques"; each will be discussed below. In adapting these methods to consumer research, marketing men coined the phrase "motivation research." Motivation research is not something new or recently invented for purposes of "hidden persuasion," but is a fancy name for projective methods that have been used in psychological clinics for many years.

Clinical psychologists need to know what is on the patient's mind, or what is on the mind of an individual from a counseling standpoint. Years ago clinical psychologists found that just to ask a direct question is not enough ... that talking to a person and asking him to tell what is on his mind is not sufficient. Counselors know that in the first few interviews many people do not even admit what the real problem is. It may take hours of interviewing and counseling before the individual will begin to talk freely about what really is bothering him, or what he *thinks* is bothering him.

Therefore, projective methods have been developed by clinical psychologists. These methods are used to discover as much as possible about a person's characteristic modes of behavior, by presenting him with rather vague or ambiguous stimuli. The theory is that the individual who is being interviewed or tested will in various ways *project* his own personality traits into a situation, and that by examining resulting data the psychologist can discover something about the individual's personality traits which that person might not reveal through direct questioning.

As psychologists Horace B. English and Ava Champney English have said: "Thus, a child's response to an empty sheet of paper and colored crayons may reveal his emotional mood or his more enduring sentiments. The man reminded by a glorious sunset to tell his wife to have bacon for breakfast is presumably revealing certain aspects of his personality."

For use in business, these techniques employ indirect methods of trying to find out what is on the consumer's mind, as contrasted with the more direct methods of simply asking the person outright what he thinks about something. Dr. Lyndon O. Brown, vice-president of Dancer-Fitzgerald-Sample, Inc., advertising agency, gives the following example of a projective technique:

"Housewives were shown two statements, each of which described a laundry product in a different way and were asked, 'Which of these two products would you prefer to use?' Their responses to this direct, subjective questioning were 20 per cent in favor of Statement A and 80 per cent in favor of Statement B. A comparable group of housewives was shown the identical statements but with only a very slight change in the wording of the question to, 'Which of these two products *do you believe most women* would prefer to use?' Their responses to this indirect, projective questioning were 53 per cent in favor of Statement A and 47 per cent in favor of Statement B." In other words, the projective method gave different information than was obtained through direct questioning.

However, do not make the mistake of thinking that just because a projective technique has been used, everything has been learned about a consumer or about a group of consumers. Projective techniques are useful, if their limitations are realized. They are not efficient enough to probe *deeply* into motives and predict our desires exactly. Thus, these techniques often are used *along with* other techniques. It is the total picture, or total pattern, that is most useful.

All of the projective methods use indirect means to try to discover what is on the consumer's mind. Notice that I purposely use the phrase "indirect means," and not "devious means," because marketing men are not trying to use "tricky" methods of persuasion. Motivation-research methods obviously are different from direct questioning of consumers; but motivation researchers are in all sincerity simply trying to find out what you and I and other consumers might want to buy and might be likely to buy, and why we feel the way we do. This is important for both the businessman and the consumer.

2. Projective Techniques

Believe it or not, a motivation-research study made some years ago for a chewing-gum manufacturer concluded that we chew gum because we are a "nation of frustrated breast-feeders." And it was also said that our chewing habits are a "safety valve for impulses related to the infant's pleasure of sucking."

Another absurd example of M.R. was the claim by some psychoanalytically oriented researcher that we like soap because it carries us back to the uterus, arousing "prenatal sensations of being surrounded by the amniotic fluid in our mother's womb." Someone else, apparently in all seriousness, claimed that when a woman bakes a cake she is symbolically recreating the process of giving birth! If this idea were not so ridiculous, we could say that it is no wonder a woman gets so upset when the cake falls.

It is because of interpretations such as these that many a businessman says, "Nuts," when he hears the words "motivation research." All he needs to do is to have heard one or two stories like this and he says: "If that is motivation research, I want nothing to do with it!"

And you can't help but agree with him. Small wonder that one businessman says: "Depth probing, a sneaky, Peeping Tom kind of technique, really digs the dirt. It indicates that most of us are a mass of complexes, compulsions, and contradictions. The only question is whether we are more mixed up when we are conscious or when we are unconscious."

But you should know that *most* motivation research is *not* based on such psychoanalytical interpretations. Actually there are a lot of examples of how projective techniques have been sensibly used, and without the benefit of Freud, Adler, or Jung. In the indirect tests, there are no "right" or "wrong" answers. The aim is simply to provide information about a person's *real* attitudes without self-consciousness, so that the data can be analyzed from a psychological (but not necessarily psychoanalytical) standpoint.

Here are some of the projective techniques, stated in capsule form. The *thematic apperception test* (TAT) uses a drawing of people, and the respondent is asked to tell a story about it. The *picture probe* shows two characters in a cartoon strip, with one making a statement, and with the respondent asked to say what the other character says. In the *narrative probe*, a hypothetical situation in story form is given to the respondent for his comments. The *sentence-completion* method allows the respondent to finish each of a group of incomplete sentences any way he wishes. For *word association*, the respondent is asked to give immediately the first word or group of words that comes to his mind for each word of a series that is read aloud to him rapidly. These and other techniques, including the *depth interview* and the *group interview,* may be used separately or in various combinations.

The *thematic apperception test* is a series of pictures of individuals, somewhat unstructured. I say "unstructured" because there is nothing in the pictures to indicate precisely who the people are or where they are, and the respondent is simply asked to make up a story about them. Who are these people? What are they talking about? What are they saying? How will it all come out?

In other words, each person can *project* into the picture what he himself sees. The theory, then, is that in doing this, a person will reveal something about himself. You see, the *visual sensation* is essentially the same for everybody who looks at this picture; but *perception* is quite different, depending upon your own background, experiences, aspirations, and desires. Within any such story will appear a theme which is a reflection of social pressures, personal desires, pleasant or unpleasant outcomes, social conflicts, feelings of affection, hostility, etc. And on the basis of the stories and of their structure, the motivation researcher makes his interpretations and draws his conclusions.

Another technique of somewhat this same sort is the *picture probe.* The respondent fills in the comments or thoughts of two or more people pictured in a drawing. In a study of attitudes of men toward buying life insurance for their families, each husband was shown a drawing of a husband, wife, and insurance agent. The question was—what is the wife saying and what is the husband thinking? Typical interpretations were: "She might even be saying, 'We could afford a larger amount, dear, don't you think?' And the husband thinks he is being taken advantage of in front of the agent." "You can see that the man isn't too anxious to sign those papers, but he'll get worn down by his wife and the insurance man."

Another drawing showed a wife receiving a $10,000 life insurance check from the agent. Typical comments of husbands: "Boy, will she have a good time! She'll blow the whole thing in less than a year." ... "She's thinking, 'Thank God he died while I'm still young enough to go and hook some other slob—not when I'm 60. Now I'm free!' "

To outward appearances, a husband usually seems quite calm about the purchase of life insurance. But it becomes obvious from interpretations of projective materials that he may have deep-rooted anxieties about his beneficiaries, life insurance agents, and death.

A third example is the *narrative probe*. Here you don't even need a picture or anything of this sort. You just ask the person to respond to a made-up story. In the clinical situation, the psychologist might say to an individual, "By the way, sitting in the next room is a very despicable person. Tell me the traits which this person has." The individual responding is likely to reveal, without realizing it, what he thinks are *his own* most despicable traits. Or contrariwise, the psychologist might say, "Sitting in the next room is an individual who is an unusually fine person. Tell me what this person is like." Again, the theory is that the individual responding will reveal what he regards as the finest traits of *himself*.

This technique enables the respondent to give answers with fewer self-centered implications. For example, in a study made for the State Farm Mutual Automobile Insurance Company, one of the narrative probes used was: "A friend of yours has just bought his first car. He asks you what he should do about getting insurance for it. What would you tell him?" An individual respondent makes an answer ... another makes another answer ... another makes another answer ... and so on; thus, the researcher gathers together a vast array of answers, which he later reads, studies, and analyzes, trying to find out what significant points have been made.

Another projective technique is the *sentence-completion method*, in which an individual is asked to say the very first thing that comes into his mind by completing a sentence. For example, he is given the phrase, "I feel that people ..." and is told to finish the sentence. Try this on yourself right now. Or he is told, "When things get hectic I..." How do you complete the sentence? Or, "When given orders I..." Or "I am happiest when..." "Some day I..." "I become annoyed when they..." You can see that if you would complete sentences such as these with the very first thought that comes to mind, you might reveal some things about your personality that might not come out through more direct questioning.

Since the respondent builds a sentence from a stimulus word or words, clues may be obtained about attitudes toward various ideas or things. One examiner might start out with some very neutral words or phrases and then gradually move to the subject in which he is particularly interested. In a study carried out for Johnson's Wax, respondents were asked to complete the sentences below (the answers made by one respondent are also shown).

Most floor waxes *are too slippery*

The hardest thing about waxing is *cleaning beforehand*

Johnson's Wax *costs too much*

The ideal floor wax *should last a long time*

When I am through waxing *I hope it won't get tracked up right away*

The easiest way to apply wax is to *pour it on and then spread it around with a cloth*

The only thing I don't like about wax is *the smell*

Now, this set of answers by one person alone does not give complete answers as to which of the product's qualities should be stressed in the advertising and promotional work. Naturally the company wants to emphasize those qualities of its product in which consumers are most interested; and so answers from many consumers may provide material that is useful. As a matter of fact, in one of the Johnson's Wax campaigns involving the "no scuff" theme, the phrase "no scuff" actually came from women respondents.

One more instance of a projective technique is the *word-association method*. The respondent is given a series of words and asked to say the very first word that comes into his mind. As a simple example, I say to you "salt." What do you say quickly? "Pepper." I say to you "chair"; you say "table." I say "hot"; you say "cold."

There's nothing mysterious about these examples. But when a psychologist throws in some additional words that are emotionally charged—perhaps the word "love"—perhaps the name of a loved one—perhaps the name of a certain place—this can be quite revealing. This method of evaluation is based on *first* associations made to various words. The nature of the associations and the way they differ from usual responses serve as the basis for interpretation.

As an example, a motivation researcher was asked by a beer company whether this company should use the word "lagered" as one of the key phrases in its advertising. Should the word "lagered" be played up big in headlines? The method used by the motivation researcher was very simple. He read aloud a list of words, with the instruction to give the very first word that comes to mind. And then within the list he had the word "lagered," so that no special attention was directed to it. The results were that 36 per cent of the respondents gave associations like beer, ale, or stout to the word "lagered." Another 38 gave such responses as slow, tired, drunk, lazy, behind, linger, dizzy. The remaining 26 per cent of the respondents gave no answer. Need I say that the word "lagered" was *not* used in the new advertising campaign, for the meaning intended by the manufacturer was not generally understood.

Of course, you might argue that "lagered" could be built up over a period of time and sold to consumers as a meaningful word. An advertising campaign a few years ago played up "dry" beer. In questioning people, it was found that most didn't have the slightest idea what a dry beer is, but after seeing it advertised they thought it was great!

Another example is the *depth interview*. This is a very lengthy, conversational interview with an individual in order to get him to talk freely about all sorts of things that come into his mind. Almost "free wheeling." At some time in your life, you have sat in a bus station, a train station, an airport, or on a public conveyance, and some stranger has poured out to you the intimate story of his life. You just listened—and this is an important requirement in depth interviewing.

Chicago Daily News columnist Sydney J. Harris relates that he was lolling on the front porch of a resort hotel. "A man sat down in the chair next to me, and within five minutes I was told that he lived in Columbus, sold insurance, had four children, belonged to the Elks, was born in Delaware, had attended the Ohio State University, thought his wife was getting too plump, didn't like his son-in-law, and wanted me to be sure to look him up any time I happened to be passing through Columbus."

"He didn't know me from Adam's off-ox, nor did I give his confidence the slightest encouragement beyond a perfunctory politeness. I have met this same man by the hundreds, on trains and planes, in hotel lobbies and lunch counters —and the same autobiographical material starts pouring forth like a gusher that has been repressed for years."

Have you ever had that sort of experience? Or perhaps you yourself have gushed to somebody. Although this is not depth interviewing, it illustrates the *kind* of interviewing that clinical psychologists may engage in, to get an individual to talk freely about himself. This will not be a completely *free* association of ideas; that is, it isn't just *anything* that comes to the individual's mind. But it will be *controlled* association, in that the psychologist may to some extent guide the conversation. He may guide it to the extent at least that he keeps the person on the same general subject, although his role is mainly to be a good listener and occasionally to ask a question. This interview does not use a questionnaire, although it is "structured" or purposeful in that the psychologist will have in mind a series of points to be covered.

This type of interviewing technique in which occasional probing questions are asked is an attempt to uncover the motives which underlie or influence respondent behavior. The interviewer attempts to guide the discussion in certain channels.

Some years ago the editor of a leading woman's magazine wanted to know what it was that women would like most of all to read about, in stories, articles, and special features. The women being interviewed were not told the exact purpose of the interview. The interviewer went into the home and simply said: "I want to talk about women's attitudes. I want to get your views about women in the home." Then gradually she led the discussion around to women's publications, in order to find out what women would like to read in magazines. But in the process the interviewers were told the most intimate details of the lives of the wives and mothers—the extent to which they liked or disliked their husbands or children, or how much the family was in debt—intimate details of this sort. Those interviewed were willing to talk freely to a nice, pleasant, good-listening stranger, much more freely than to a friend or the next-door neighbor. What was learned, of course, about the daydreams, fantasies, wishes, and secret ambitions of women was unusally helpful to the editor in determining what kinds of things his readers would like in a magazine.

Related to this is the *group interview*. This is "depth interviewing" not just with an individual but with a whole group of people sitting together and talking on a subject. In this situation, as with the individual depth interview, the interview may be tape-recorded so that it can be played back later and analyzed precisely as to what was said. Individuals talking freely as a group may develop ideas that might not come out of an interview with one person.

For example, a group of housewives may meet and tell what they want in a certain product. This does not involve great psychological probing, but out of one such tape-recorded interview came the following factors. What the housewives wanted most of all for a certain food product was to have a container with a screw top, rather than something that is hard to pry off . . . to have a very wide-mouthed jar . . . and to have the container marked off so it could be used as a measuring cup.

A lot of different kinds of exploratory techniques have been mentioned, just to give you some slight acquaintance with them. These techniques have considerable meaning in searching for people's motives. The information obtained may affect both the product and the advertising. The techniques may be useful in determining just what factors are most important to consumers, as we shall see in the next section.

3. Motivation Research in Use

Here are some examples of motivation research as used in business.

A manufacturer of food mixes learned from projective techniques that many women felt unhappy about just putting something in the oven and turning on the heat—they didn't want to appear to themselves as lazy, and wanted to feel that they had more of a share in creating the final results. So the product was developed with the different ingredients separated; for pies, for instance, the crust and the filling were packed separately. In this way there could also be greater freedom of choice in cooking, since different kinds of fillings could be combined with different kinds of crusts. This was more acceptable to women.

The M. and M. Candy Company had been promoting candy on the basis of taste and quick energy. But results from projective techniques inferred that most of us consider candy a special reward for having finished a difficult task. M. and M. changed its promotion to the theme: "Make that tough job easier: you *deserve* candy." Apparently consumers then felt better about the candy they nibbled.

The major sales appeal of a book club was the savings that members could realize on the purchase of each book. But projective techniques showed that many joined and ordered a few books, but then felt guilty about not reading them and dropped out of the book club. The appeal was changed to emphasize the club as a means of building a lifetime library, and both the club and its members liked this.

Ry-Krisp crackers used to be presented as a reducing food. But projective techniques showed that this tended to limit the appeal to overweight people, and also failed to convince them because they knew that they would never achieve the sylphlike figures depicted in the Ry-Krisp advertisements. The promotion was changed to emphasis on Ry-Krisp for snacks and as cocktail crackers; this was to the greater satisfaction of both producer and consumer.

For a wax product, TV commercials showed a woman waxing her floors but with an applicator that ended up dirty. Projective techniques revealed that this was disliked by housewives. The new advertising theme stressed clean floors and the maintenance advantages of the wax product, and both manufacturer and consumer liked this better.

On the label on the Star Kist tuna can is a vivid picture of a bearded deep-sea fisherman. Query: What should the image be? Projective techniques indicated that the strong, masculine fisherman had considerable appeal for women shoppers, and the label was not changed to something different. Both men and women shoppers like the label.

A leading airline stressed the *safety* of air travel, and especially its own excellent safety record. But projective techniques revealed that this caused people to worry about the possibility of being killed. Sales appeals were changed to emphasis on amount of time saved, and both the airline company and its travelers were happier.

Studies on cigarette smoking have shown some interesting consumer attitudes. Contrast, for instance, attitudes toward filters in the early 1950s with attitudes today. It was difficult then to get men to smoke filter cigarettes because men thought of filters as "sissy" or effeminate. (Men are interesting human beings. They are the people to whom it was so difficult in the 1930s to sell the idea of having zippers on their trousers! This took years of sales promotion.)

As to cigarettes, motivation research has shown that although smokers cannot distinguish most brands when blindfolded, still they have definite preferences. And research has revealed that most smokers consider their habit morally wrong, filthy, and dangerous . . . yet feel "compelled" to smoke—to prove their strength, sophistication, and sociability, and to experience pleasure.

Following are some examples of M.R. used in connection with three types of beverages—beer, tea, and coffee.

Beer is a product toward which people have fairly clear attitudes. Beer drinkers tend to stay with a brand for an extended period of time—and few people will drink just any kind. Their feelings and beliefs about beer determine the way people buy and drink beer, and the pleasures and dislikes they find in it.

Using projective techniques, one motivation-research study showed that most people thought of beer as a social beverage —not comparable to hard liquor—nor considered a doorway to alcoholism. Beer is a democratic drink and people do not have technical reasons for their beer preferences. The implications were that beer advertising should be aimed at the middle majority. Men are probably the major market in terms of both consumption and brand selection. Some of the most effective appeals are relaxation and refreshment, festivities, informal gatherings, and beer with meals.

One of the most interesting motivation-research studies in recent years was on tea. Depth interviews showed that in the minds of most people, tea was associated with foreigners (Britishers primarily), women, and sissies. The picture many people have of tea is that of two dear old ladies—very prim and proper, and with their pinkies properly poised—drinking their afternoon tea. Tea is thought of as good for sick, nervous, depressed, feminine types of people. For many years the Tea Council, the trade association which promotes the sale of tea, was using slogans to attract people such as: "Tired? Nervous? Try tea."

This was the very thing that reinforced this picture that people had—namely, that tea was for nervous and sick people. You can probably remember some time in your own life when you were so nauseated that you thought you were going to die (or almost hoped you would)—you were, oh, so sick, and then some kind person said, "Maybe you could keep some tea on your stomach!"

Anyhow, the Tea Council took an entirely new approach to promoting tea. A brand new slogan was developed: "Drink it hefty, hot, and hearty! Take tea and see." This was said over and over again on television and radio and in print advertising. The real objective was to get away from the stigma of effeminacy and to give consumers the right idea—that tea is a healthy, strong, manly drink.

Move to a field like coffee, and you have statements made by women under direct questioning as to why they don't serve *instant* coffee: "Oh, instant coffee doesn't taste as good." Actually in a comparison of the best instant coffees and the best regular coffees, it is almost impossible to tell the difference through taste alone.

Psychologist Mason Haire had an interesting idea on this. *Two* separate shopping lists were prepared which were identical in all respects, except that on one there were the words "Maxwell House Coffee," and on the other was "Nescafé." These lists were given to two different groups of housewives, but neither group knew of the existence of the other list. In-

structions were to read the shopping list and then for the
woman to project herself as far as possible into the situation
so that she could describe the type of woman who was buying
the groceries. Each woman was then asked to write a brief
description of the personality and character of the woman with
the shopping list. No special attention was directed to the
coffee. The responses indicated that the woman with Nescafé
on her shopping list was regarded as a poor planner, one who
spends money carelessly and is lazy!

Here is another example. For a certain brand of instant
coffee, the stress was on savings, deals, bargains, and economies.
Projective techniques showed that as a result, most people
thought of the coffee as an inferior substitute for regular coffee.
Appeals were changed, stressing flavor and convenience in
preparation, to the satisfaction of both producer and consumer.

Sanka coffee used to be promoted by playing up the nerve-
jangling, sleep-robbing aspects of coffee. Projective techniques
indicated that most Sanka Drinkers really liked coffee and re-
sented derogatory statements about it. The advertising theme
was changed to indicate that Sanka is a beverage that lets you
drink all the coffee you want without losing sleep; and Sanka
users felt happier.

For Wesson Oil's Snowdrift, it was discovered through M.R.
that housewives felt that the swirl on top of the shortening
inside the can symbolized purity and fluffiness, both desirable
qualities. So the swirl was shown on the label on the outside
of the can, also making it easier for consumers to identify the
can quickly.

Dr. Ernest Dichter, president of the Institute for Motivational
Research, Inc., lists the following methods as a possible approach to the testing of new packaging:

- *Free Association.* The consumer is asked to tell everything that
  comes to his mind.
- *Story.* "Look at this package and make up a story about it,"
  says the psychologist. Such a third-person story permits the
  consumer to express his true feelings without fear of offend-
  ing anyone.

- *Color*. To study colors, the psychologist asks, "How do colors make you feel?"
- *Personality*. To study the package's "personality," the consumer is asked, "When you look at this box, what kind of person are you reminded of?"
- *Slogan*. The entire range of associations with the slogan is probed, and its emotional impact is estimated.
- *Choice Imputations*. The consumer is asked to tell how he thinks other consumers will react to the product.

Here is an example of how a combination of motivation research and "regular" marketing research was used successfully. The work was done for the State Farm Mutual Automobile Insurance Company, which for many years in its advertising had been emphasizing the low cost of its insurance. The problem was to decide whether the same type of advertising campaign should be continued.

Projective techniques were employed and also consumer questionnaires; and the findings resulted in a complete change in the national advertising program. Psychological analysis revealed that most men may unconsciously *resent* an insurance company at the same time that they *accept* it as a protector of individual welfare. Although men were happy not to have had an automobile accident, they were also inclined to resent the fact that they had had to pay for something on which they had had no opportunity to collect!

These and other research findings led to significant changes in the State Farm advertising campaign—the use of longer advertising copy, more space, and an even more factual presentation. State Farm's advertising began to answer important questions about automobile insurance that were in the minds of consumers. Although low cost was still stressed, major emphasis was given to the size and stature of the company. Psychological research indicated the great interest of policyholders in prompt, courteous, and expert service; and so the advertising also began to feature actual case histories as evidence that State Farm offered this kind of service.

Motivation-research methods are designed to obtain infor-

mation from consumers—so as to understand more and more
about our motives—and then to use this information in more
interesting and more persuasive advertising. But this does not
mean that motivation research is as immoral and dangerous as
germ warfare. After all, motivation researchers are not sneaky
Svengalis who burn incense to Dr. Ernest Dichter.

*Motivation research is not the ogre that some sensationalistic
writers have made it appear.* They talk about motivation research as if it is some kind of magic used by businessmen to
seduce consumers into buying things they shouldn't have. This
is just so much hogwash.

Motivation research is simply the application of techniques
that psychologists have known about for a long time ... techniques that business has borrowed in order to have a better
understanding of consumers.

A great advertising copywriter, Walter O'Meara, has said
about motivation research: "I have seen it produce a copy idea
so sound and good that a great many millions of dollars were
spent on it unhesitatingly—and successfully. On the other hand,
I have seen it yield arrant nonsense."

Motivation-research techniques do not always have practical
use. After all, when a man goes on a fishing expedition, he
doesn't always catch fish. When another man uses motivation-
research techniques, he is probing, and hoping he will come
up with some new ideas. He may, or he may not. Or what he
finds may be different from what someone else finds.

Sometimes the interpretations of motivation-research data
may result in conflicting claims. As an example, two different
organizations made motivational studies of prunes. Using projective techniques, one study indicated that most people considered prunes as shriveled, tasteless, and of poor appearance.
They disliked prunes because they were symbolic of old age
(shriveled up); prunes were devitalized, denatured; they were
disliked as a symbol of parental authority; prunes did not have
prestige; prunes were associated with peculiar people, and they
were also associated with hospitals, boarding houses, and the

Army. Another study, using other projective techniques, indicated that the principal hindrance to buying prunes was their laxative quality.

It was concluded from the first study that the laxative attributes of prunes should not be emphasized in advertising prunes, whereas the opposite conclusion was arrived at from the second study, that the health factor and especially the laxative quality of prunes should be played up.

The editors of *Fortune* magazine report that both Dr. Ernest Dichter and Dr. Burleigh Gardner were hired separately to analyze consumer attitudes toward the advertising concepts used by Dial soap. "Dichter concluded that the emphasis on Dial's deodorant powers was all wrong, that it made people subconsciously uneasy about *losing* their own distinctive body odors, and 'scared them away.' He recommended less emphasis on the soap's deodorizing features. Gardner, on the other hand, found consumers well disposed to Dial's messages, and since Dial's deodorizing agent (hexachlorophene) was apparently winning the customers, Gardner advised the company to continue the sales pitch."

Obviously contradictions of this kind, as they get known in the business world, result in considerable skepticism about motivation research. But it is not too surprising to have different interpretations and recommendations from two different M.R. practitioners. Don't you sometimes find different interpretations about what's ailing you from two different M.D.s?

Actually a number of companies have developed some faith in the value of motivation-research findings, although hardly any company would believe that motivation-research findings will provide the entire answer to a problem. After all, *most businesses have been developed without the benefit of motivation research*. But motivation-research findings are used more and more in trying to learn more about us consumers and how we think and act.

17

Women Are Here to Stay

1. Woman's Changing World

The role of woman in American society is constantly changing. During the nineteenth century she was primarily a homemaker, and her main interests were in raising her children and keeping house for her husband. Her duties and contacts outside of the home were limited; and her husband was responsible for how his income was spent. He even did most of the family shopping.

But times have changed. The days of the husband and father as complete "boss" in the home have given way to family discussions, and to attitudes toward woman as an equal partner in marriage. The American woman of today is also better educated than any other woman in the history of mankind. She has great freedom to come and go as she pleases. If she does not marry, there are various careers open to her.

When a woman marries, she and her husband seldom live with parents, as they used to. The young wife takes it for granted that she will move into her *own* home or apartment not long after she is married. Owning and caring for her home demands a lot from her. She may even budget her husband's pay check—unthinkable in grandfather's day—to be sure that it stretches to meet the "easy payments" due, as well as the ordinary expenses of daily living. (In grandmother's day, grandfather took care of all money matters.) The housewife must operate her various machines (home appliances), plan her decorating schemes, shop for the floor covering, wallpaper, and so on ... and probably help her husband do the painting and other do-it-yourself activities.

After all, the median marrying age for women is now twenty years! This means that age eighteen to nineteen is now the age for becoming engaged.

Today's homemaker has to spend a great deal of time away from home—doing the family shopping, providing "taxi" service for husband and children, attending meetings in her community. And more than ever she may be instrumental in her husband's career; she must be able to entertain his business associates and their wives.

Thus, *modern woman faces a dilemma.* Her role is to carry out shrewd, thoughtful planning and activities ... including wise administration of the family budget, assisting in her husband's career, and taking part in community activities. Yet she is also expected to retain her sweet, tender, and alluring femininity. No wonder that after being enthusiastic about premiums and green stamps and "cutting corners" to save, she also needs to buy products that express her femininity to others and to herself. She must reassure herself and others that she is still a female, despite all the more masculine types of activities that society demands of her.

But women are different from men. And *women* are different from *women,* too—that is, the woman of today is quite different in attitudes and hence in buying habits from the woman of yesteryear. Some women are even changeable in their patterns of buying—men talk about women "changing their minds."

Although she basks in being the modern American woman, the partner in marriage, both she and her male often denounce the role of woman as competitor of man. Most women would readily concede that men, if they had the time and inclination, could be good shoppers for the family—they could do anything a woman could (almost) and do it better. But the point is, they don't necessarily want to do all these things—they have well-educated wives and have provided them with the time to do the buying.

This is natural; after all, the wife is the keeper of the home. She is the one who should do the buying of items directly related to general housekeeping . . . which account for some 40 per cent of the family budget. She is co-buyer of all other items in the family budget. This is a modern-day phenomenon, for in bygone days the head of the family (the Man) did his consulting with the older generation. But modern "young marrieds" no longer necessarily live in proximity, either in time or distance, to their parents. So it is quite natural that men consult their wives.

A. W. Zelomek describes another facet of the American male's changing role: "With more and more women working, and with men spending more time at home, it is probable that women's influence over buying will increase while their actual purchasing may decrease. The last stronghold of the American female—the supermarket—has already been heavily invaded by men. Today a woman on a weekend shopping trip not only must compete against other housewives, but also is likely to find her access to the potatoes barred by a strapping six-foot male."

And sweet, matronly ladies are finding competition for their baby-sitting services. A man can watch the children while watching TV, particularly if his wife has put them to bed before going out for a while! He may even dry the dishes and scrub the floors; this is particularly true where both spouses work.

Keeping in mind that "women are women"—they still have the babies and the Cleopatra wiles that attract men—and that "men are men"—they still have a yen for both cars and women —*the roles of American woman and man are becoming in-*

creasingly alike. Even though evidence indicates that women dominate the spending in the United States, they reflect the basic characteristics and aspirations of American males.

Several interesting and reliable studies have been made on who is the decision maker—male or female. It is a matter of fact that economic decisions concerning the home are most commonly made *jointly* by husbands and wives. The results of several studies on decision making, male or female, are quite enlightening, and substantiate that spending is a cooperative endeavor.

About 14 per cent of the family income is dedicated to the family chariot. Who makes the important decisions relative to this necessary convenience? The car is used most often by males, over three-fourths of whom (fifteen years of age and over) have drivers' licenses. However, almost half of the females also possess drivers' licenses. A 1959 survey revealed that 19 per cent of women are personally responsible for the upkeep of one or more of the automobiles in their family. The women used the car mostly for shopping (90 per cent) and pleasure (84 per cent), and also for taking children to school (30 per cent) and going to work (26 per cent).

Even though women are in the drivers' seat so much of the time, men dominate the car-purchase field. The husband is most frequently responsible for the initial suggestion to buy a car; but if there is a decision to postpone, this is a joint endeavor. The man also is more likely to be involved in the decision as to the make of car; and he is responsible for shopping around. Both husband and wife are in agreement that satisfactory past experience, styling, and price are the major reasons stated for car purchase. They are in agreement as to the order of importance of these reasons. They are also both involved in the selection of body style, but the husband (no matter how little he knows about it) likes to be concerned with engine selection. Choice of exterior colors and interior trim is primarily in the wife's domain, and so she can influence the decision on which model.

In spite of being the joint decision maker, however, woman's emotional setup is far different from that of her man, and probably always will be. Bernice Fitz-Gibbon, New York advertising and merchandising consultant and former advertising director of Gimbel's, has vividly described what does *not* appeal to a woman in automobiles . . . "Woman is *not* Sputnik-minded. She's a put-put-nik. She likes to putter, she dawdles. She never worries about whether a car can go fast enough. She does not long for hot, hotter, hottest performance. She does not want a car that can 'flick its tail at everybody else' and 'won't take sass from any other car.' She doesn't want to sit on top of an engine named Fury. She doesn't want a sleek demon of surging horsepower. In other words, a car is not an Instrument of Aggression for her—as it often is for a man. . . .

"And just as she does not respond to blazing take-off, she also does not respond to all the technical nuts-and-bolts stuff: ball joint front suspension, canted blades, twin traction, power-punch pistons, and turbo and torque. She would be horrified at a headline, 'If you hear a thump, it's only your heart.' A woman would be sure it was a broken connecting rod, whatever that is."

The decisions to buy are most commonly joint decisions as to home furnishings, equipment, and appliances, which account for 9 per cent of the family dollars. One study shows 54 per cent of such purchases are joint; 25 per cent are made by the wife only; and 11 per cent by the wife predominantly. Research studies by Prof. George Katona of the University of Michigan Survey Research Center show that conflicts about major decisions to buy or save are much less frequent than mutual adjustment of economic desires.

Another type of study indicates that "when the relative influences of husbands and wives in purchasing appliances are gauged, it is found that husbands and wives are in substantial agreement. Wives apparently understand the roles their husbands play in buying appliances. In reality, however, husbands appear to be as influential in deciding upon the appliances bought as are their wives. Husbands, in fact, are more influential than their wives when it comes to buying television sets and equally influential when it comes to buying refrigerators. The washing machine, however, is more the wife's domain." This study also indicates that husbands are more influential in deciding brands than in initiating purchases.

In the decisions on saving money, a study by Dr. Elizabeth H. Wolgast in the *Journal of Marketing* indicated that in 48 per cent of the cases this was decided by both equally; in 27 per cent of the cases the wife decided alone; in 15 per cent the husband alone.

The trend is toward more and more decision making by women as to how the family money is saved or spent. About 80 out of every 100 new homes are purchased by people under forty years old, and American women are an important influence as to what goes into these homes. Almost three-fourths of all household furniture is sold to homemakers under forty years of age, where women's decisions are so important. And with population and marriages on the rise, women's influence on how money is spent will be greater. From 1950 to 1955, there was an average annual increase in the number of married couples of 291,000; but by the early 1970s the annual increase may be as much as 800,000.

Actually a lot of buying, among both women and men, is for self-reward. Of course, some men think of the buying by their women as self-indulgence. But when you see a woman buy an inlaid coffee table or a jeweled sweater, she is doing the same sort of thing that her male counterpart does when he purchases a portable bar or monogrammed shirts. *Psychological factors, rather than need, are the motivation for most purchases;* and most females like to feel that they are entitled to the best.

2. Woman's Changing Role

It's a woman's world . . . and what's more, MEN have made it so! Man the scientist, man the technologist has created a new world in which woman's ageless role as mother and home-maker has been greatly expanded. The modern American woman's domain is far beyond her home alone.

Over the years, women have become well educated and oftentimes business-oriented—but none the less have managed to cling to important female traits. Both the American male and female have seen the wisdom of the tailor-made American women who complement the American way of life. They are now partners in the present and future of the greatest nation the world has ever known.

In the last century, woman's role was typified as being feminine, delicate, romantic. Marriage was almost a *must* for all girls; and after consummation the marriage was further consummated in endless house work and child rearing. Says Marion Harper, Jr., president and chairman of the board of McCann-Erickson, Inc.: "If a homemaker of 100 years ago could live through a day with a modern woman, following her from one appliance to another, inspecting her wardrobe and dressing table, driving with her to the shopping center, watching in unbelief as she prepares convenience foods, sharing some of her leisure-time pleasures, she might pass a stern moral judgment, or she might come back to life out of sheer delight and astonishment!"

Increasingly we live in a world of automation. Many of us even wonder—who are the masters . . . machines or men? Some of us, both men and women, may lose confidence in our own resources for self-development.

But women are especially affected. Even more than men, modern women may feel the lack of capacity of enjoyment from within themselves, and thus be insecure and anxious. Many have found that the psychological rug of necessity for doing things for their families has been pulled out from under them. It is not surprising that some critics have even denounced women themselves as "examples of mass production."

Descriptions of the modern American woman are often quite controversial. A seemingly embittered Englishman, Eric John

Dingwall, takes the extreme position that the trouble with the American woman is:

- She is obsessed with sex and eternal youth.
- She demands tribute, not love, and her bedroom manners are a "disaster."
- She dominates and browbeats the American male from infancy to marriage.
- She treats her husband as a beck-and-call servant.
- She raises her sons to be mama's boys.
- She has sacrificed her femininity and become frustrated, dissatisfied, resentful, neurotic.

Apparently Mr. Dingwall is upset at the thought of the rising status of women. Perhaps he fears his own ability to cope with basic changes in our culture. Other more sage Englishmen, however, are likely to describe the American woman from a more practical point of view. The American standard of living is greatly enhanced by the fact that Americans use the entire potential of the population—not just the males.

Helena Kuo, a Chinese writer, has remarked that America is a woman's world, a world in which women have succeeded in everything except in the art of being truly feminine. But her description of American women is in an unusual frame of reference. It would be far more accurate to describe American women within the frames of reference of modern America and then relate these traits to her role as the major spender in the family. In fact, American women are responsible for over 70 per cent of the spending in the United States. And this seems to be all right with most men, who like to spend most of their time on the job and in other interests.

More and more, women are permeating all facets of society. Dr. Harold Mendelsohn of the Psychological Corporation of New York says: "This expansion of the female role has gone beyond the wildest fancies of the most ardent of the suffragettes whose battle cry was directed exclusively to political and economic egalitarianism. Was it not G. B. Shaw who said,

'Around the turn of the century, the American woman wanted something very badly—she thought it was the vote.' Expanded education and career opportunities for women plus the increase in leisure made possible by a home labor saving technology have plunged many women into the thick of cultural and community activity, education, philanthropy, and social welfare. . . . More and more we have seen a gradual breakdown of the traditional role of the woman as a homemaker exclusively."

As a matter of fact, about 34 million women keep house, while about 23 million are career women. And women workers will increase 25 per cent, to about 30 million, by 1970, compared with only a 15 per cent increase in the number of working men.

It is interesting to note that the 30 per cent of the married women who are now working hold down over 53 per cent of the female jobs. The 45 per cent of the single gals who work hold down only 24 per cent of the feminine positions. Women hold almost one out of five of the union membership cards. All in all, women in America comprise about one-third of the entire working force. Their median salary is $3,006, compared to $4,720 for men.

In spite of receiving lower salaries than men, American women control 65 per cent of the savings accounts and have 53 per cent of all stocks in their names. Furthermore, women, who outlive their men by about six years on the average, are increasing their wealth . . . and also they are the principal beneficiaries of estates and insurance policies.

Women also outnumber the male descendants of Adam. As of 1960, there were about 89 million possible Stetson customers, but approximately 91 million potential Lilly Daché chapeau customers. By 1980, the chapeau manufacturers will have a heyday, for the females probably will outnumber the males by almost 3 million.

But women are not complacently sitting back to await either

widowhood or Social Security. Not only is the modern female a woman of substantial means, but she has psychological characteristics of great importance:

• The modern American woman has a *mental potential equal to that of man*—and increasingly this is recognized. Her formal education is getting to be almost on a par with that of her male counterpart. As a matter of fact, since the 1920 census, more women than men, percentagewise *and* in out-and-out numbers, attend school through the age of seventeen. Also, while 21 per cent of the male population attends school through the age of twenty, the figure is 15 per cent for the females.

• While working wives are no longer a novelty, many a housewife is still *free to plan a twenty-four-hour day*. She does not always spend some ten hours away from the home, as her husband usually does. Because of this "leisure," she has more time for reading, consulting with neighbors and friends about current problems, watching TV, listening to the radio, and shopping. She has a greater opportunity for self-development of her mental potential. And she likewise has far more opportunity to be in the know about product qualities.

• The working wife has *expanded her horizons* in a different manner. Because of her "automatic" home and good education, many a woman is not only a wife and mother, but a bread winner. She supplies a substantial portion of the family income.

• Because of her education and wider horizons, modern woman is *more secure* in herself. This security is accompanied by decreased desire to seek status and go in for social climbing. She is much more casual in her attitudes, and not so bound by custom as her mother was at the same age.

• She is more *hungry for information* about products than ever before. There are so many new products coming out all the time—and she doesn't always know where to get the answers.

• Modern woman *lives for today as well as tomorrow*. Yes, she is saving, and at the same time she is planning for the future, but there isn't quite so much emphasis on leaving money for the children. Instead, the modern mother is giving her children a better education and more worthwhile experiences that prepare them better to provide for themselves.

• Since *the family is still her chief concern,* she would like to live, or does live, in the suburbs, because this gives the family a good environment and a possibility for extensive friendships. It also reduces the anonymity factor of her own life and that of her family—it gives the family more "togetherness."

• Her education and family interest have developed a *higher level of taste* in woman, American style. Because of a keen desire for quality, price may become secondary, but it is still a key factor in her spending.

• Even though prices are not always the determining factor, she has *more sense about money.* She not only knows where it comes from and where it goes, but she tries to get her value for each dollar spent.

Bernice Fitz-Gibbon says: "Women like neat, clear, straightforward facts which make it easy to compare one store's merchandise with another's. In an ad for a carving board, a woman wants to know, besides the fact that it is $4.95, that it's solid maple, that it is 12" x 18", that it is hand rubbed, with steel wool and then with wax, that it won't warp or split, that the roast holder is chrome and adjustable and removable, that there's a well and tree to capture juices."

• Since she frequently works outside the home, the modern woman is *busy.* She has lots of time problems; her leisure time is becoming more and more crowded. As a result, she is interested in timesavers that better enable her to fill her role as housewife and career woman. Even so, she is able to appear in public looking so affluent that you might think she did not work, and probably would never have to work.

Yes, women today can do lots of things they couldn't do some years ago. They can both sew and swim ... rivet and run races ... cook and converse ... make gall-bladder incisions or driving decisions. Women can do just about anything men can do, and also one thing more—have babies.

Yet the so-called "man in the street" still believes that men and women are two entirely different species of mankind. Not only are they physiologically different, says he (gratefully), but he believes they are different in terms of their thinking: "Women don't think through a problem the same way that men do." And he thinks that women are more emotional than men: "They break down and resort to tears." What are the facts?

As to biological differences, they exist not only in physical structure, sexual equipment, and secondary sex characteristics, but also in activities. Naturally, then, we should expect some differences between the two sexes as a counterpart to differences in physiology. Yet, strangely enough, there are fewer *psychological* sex differences than most people think. Various studies by psychologists have shown this. General intelligence does not favor one sex over the other, and there are only slight differences in ability to perform specific mental tasks. The big differences favoring men come where there are important elements of bodily strength and factors involving other people. Such psychological sex differences as can be found are accounted for, however, not just by differences in physiology, but by differences in childhood training and the influence of our society.

Actually *maleness* or *femaleness* is a biological matter, but more important in understanding the consumer are the personality characteristics of *masculinity* and *femininity*. We are too likely to take it for granted that a male must necessarily think and act aggressively. This leads people to believe that "it's a man's world," and to think that women—simply because of being females—are feminine and passive.

Training of boys and girls, from the cradle on, has a lot to do with how they later behave. A little boy is usually treated as a man-to-be. It is permissible for him to get his fingers soiled, to get dirt on his clothes, to engage in scuffles and fights ("he's a real *boy!"*) and even to say some "nasty" words. But a little girl is trained to be a "little lady," to sit just so, to tuck her dress over her knees, not to engage in rough-and-tumble activities, and even in early years to prepare to become a desirable wife for some man.

Later grown up, a woman may feel extremely dominant, yet not be permitted to achieve dominance status because of living in a "man's world." In fact, over and over again she may have to compensate for her feelings of dominance by using "ladylike" ways. So, when she is spending that 70 per cent slice of her man's income, she may be reflecting feelings of dominance . . . or the exact opposite, passive femininity.

In a speech before the *Advertising Age* Creative Workshop in 1959, Mrs. Charlotte Montgomery, columnist and editor, talked about the modern "Changed Woman." She listed 10 changes that affect today's woman as a spender:

1. *She is more secure in herself.* She has less desire to seek status, to go in for social climbing, to prove she's as good as a man at a job. She's over her resentment of her role as a housewife—though she still cringes at the name "housewife."
2. *She sets less impossible goals.* Her ideals are more attainable. She expects to achieve the modest dreams she dreams.
3. *She is better read, better educated.* Her horizons are broader.
4. *She even comes in different sizes.* This affects her thinking not only about clothes but also about food, hobbies, sports. She feels young longer.
5. *She has better taste.* And this is constantly pushing upward. Much of the time she's shopping for finer things than are offered her.
6. *She has more sense about money.* This means more acumen, and more business experience. She welcomes good advertising, and is highly critical of what she regards as bad advertising.
7. *She has a true understanding of and desire for quality.* This is not to be confused with snobbery or even with earlier standards. She may want plastic dinnerware, but she wants good plastic.

8. *She likes "What's New" as never before.* "Convenient" ... "Easy" ... "Quick" ... "Instant" ... are more and more her *buy*-words.

9. *She expects business to serve her richly, fully, endlessly.* She wants specialized products designed for the pocketbook, size, tastes, and needs of her family. Smaller units and larger units ... with the perfume and without ... chocolate-flavored and plain.

10. *She takes for granted much that is truly amazing.* Remember, she belongs to a generation that grew up with drip-dry, detergents, aerosols, synthetic fibers, frozen foods, and instant mixes. They are "everyday" to her. It takes something more than this to excite her.

It is obvious that, more than at any other time or place in the world, spending is influenced by women and what they think. Even so, the ladies choose to be naive about some of the things that fascinate men—but their sophistication as spenders is slowly but surely increasing. In the meantime, advertisers will be appealing to woman's emotions and intuitions—as well as to the increasingly similar goals of the U.S.A.-styled male and female.

18

There'll Be Some Changes Made

1. Patterns of Today

No wonder it is so difficult for a manufacturer to decide
what to make, and when and how to sell what he makes. He
doesn't know whether or not the consumer will spend his money
for the manufacturer's products.

In many other parts of the world where people do not even
have enough to get full bellies, it is relatively easy to predict
what people will buy or barter because they don't have much
choice. But in our nation, where people have the financial in-
dependence to choose among many things, it is extremely
difficult to guess what is going to be bought at any specified
time. The manufacturer has to make predictions, not just for
tomorrow but for months and years ahead. He does not decide
on a new product, manufacture it, and then try to get it on
the shelves or in the showrooms of the retailer tomorrow. The
development of a new product may take years of planning;
and, therefore, what people are going to be buying several
years from now is already being discussed, argued about, and
planned for in most industries.

A popular subject of discussion in the late 1950s was why
the automobile manufacturers hadn't done things differently,

and why they didn't change their designs completely. The same sorts of questions have been raised about washing machines and other "big-ticket" items. But remember, when a manufacturer is planning production, by the time he has gone to the blueprint stage, and by the time he has his tools and dies and new equipment, he is probably "locked up" in the situation for at least the next year or so. It will probably be a couple of years before he can make drastic changes.

If he is in the business of manufacturing and selling to other manufacturers (not directly to consumers), his guesses are going to have to be years in advance. John L. Gillis, marketing vice-president of the Monsanto Chemical Company, has told me that he is *trying* to estimate what people will buy at least seven years in advance. And in these seven years lots of things can happen, not only to us as consumers but to this shrinking world of ours.

It is no wonder that we sometimes have tremendous over-production of some products. The supply of goods can often be greater than the demand of the "fickle" consumer, who has the right to change his or her mind. But, as Prof. James C. Drury of New York University has suggested, "overproduction of goods might represent underproduction of markets." If a manufacturer finds that his supply of goods is greater than the market demand, he will probably think of this as over-production of goods and therefore cut production, lay off workers, and slash budgets. But if he views his problem as one of underproduction of markets, then he should arrive at an opposite solution: produce more markets, hire more salesmen, and increase advertising budgets.

Because you yourself and your neighbors are highly mechanized, electrified, refrigerated, and automobilized, you probably assume that everybody else is also. But about one out of every ten American families still does not have electrical refrigeration. There are hundreds of thousands of American families who still cook with coal and wood ... who do not have kitchen sinks, bathtubs, or vacuum cleaners. About 25 per cent of our families do not own an automobile; and only one family in eight has two cars.

There may be a naive assumption on your part that almost everybody flies. Do you know how many people in the United States have *never* ridden on a commercial airline? Probably about 70 per cent. The reason the airlines continue in business is that so many of the 30 per cent of us who do fly, fly a great deal.

Ours is a "restless" economy. We have the right to decide *what* we will buy (if anything) and *when* we will buy (if at all). We have constant changes in tastes and desires, and these changes are costly to manufacturers. Along with these changing desires we have the "explosive" situation of a booming birth rate and a tremendous movement to the suburbs and at the very same time a reverse flow of people back to the city. About 20 per cent of all people in the United States change their residence in a year's time. (Of course, this does not mean that 20 per cent of all people move, because some people move about more than others.)

It is no secret that our metropolitan areas have been growing constantly, partly at the expense of the rural areas. But the most important part of this metropolitan growth has been the exodus from the cities to the suburbs. Remarkably, the suburbs have accounted for over 60 per cent of the population growth.

As of 1960, the total population was expanding at an annual rate of about 1.7 per cent. (If that rate of growth continues, we shall have within 59 years *twice* as many people as in 1960 —that is, 360 million instead of 180 million.) But suburban population was gaining at a rate of about 5 per cent a year, as contrasted with a gain in the cities of only about 7/100 of 1 per cent.

In terms of buying power, the difference between cities and suburbs has been even greater than population numbers would suggest. This is logical because, for the most part, the families that go suburban are the more affluent ones.

The effects of this suburbanizing process are striking. The number of people in suburban households tends to be larger than in city households, and these households have greater buying power. The suburbs of the 18 major metropolitan markets which have a city of 500,000 or more represent 15 per cent of all households. But the *Life* study shows that this 15 per cent of households accounts for 21 per cent of all spending for furniture, bedding, and linens; for 22 per cent of expenditures for all home-decoration materials; for 23 per cent of all sporting goods and equipment; and for 30 per cent of all floor coverings.

These shifts to the suburbs have greatly influenced the ways we spend our money . . . have forced us to think not only of three necessities of life—food, clothing, and shelter—but of a fourth, the automobile. The automobile is no longer a luxury for most of us, nor even "visual evidence of success"; it is simply an essential part of our machinery for living.

Note also that there are various kinds of "markets" in which we like to spend our time and money. For example, there is something called the Christmas market, the Easter market, the Mother's Day market, the Father's Day market. There is the do-it-yourself market.

We might even say that there is a "food market." After all, we do like full stomachs, and on a regular basis. The food stores do approximately one-fourth of all retail trade, in dollars. No wonder, when you realize that you can get by with driving an old car or none at all, or wearing older clothes, but you can't get by without eating every day.

With increased prosperity, you might suppose that individual consumption of food has increased. Surprisingly, per capita consumption of food has not gone up in recent years. If you want to know how much you eat per year, it is probably 1,500 to 1,600 pounds of food. This figure seems to be about the same over the years—regardless of increased population, increased buying power, and increased standards of living.

However, three things have happened.

One is that people today are looking for a greater variety of foods than ever before. They are willing to get away from the "old-fashioned" staples and try out new kinds of foods.

Second, a mechanical device called the deep-freeze unit is affecting our food habits. In this freezer we can store everything from a large chunk of a cow to a flock of chickens. And our grocery or supermarket keeps fresh supplies for us in its deep-freeze units.

Third, and partly because of this second factor, we have increased our per capita consumption of meats, poultry, fish, eggs, dairy products, fruits, and vegetables. Even though the total amount of food consumed has not changed, dietary habits have changed—we now have greater variety and better quality of foods.

One of the most important markets is the small-town market, and because so many people have not had the good fortune to have chosen their ancestors in such a way that they could be born in a small town, it might be well to note that over half of the U.S. population is located in towns and rural communities smaller than 10,000. There are about 60 million people who live in towns of less than 2,500. Half of these towns are really small towns, and not just suburbs of large cities.

This does not mean that city markets are unimportant. They certainly are important and will continue to be. Actually, the *trend* is toward bigger and bigger city markets. More and more people are going to live in the huge metropolitan areas.

In considering these big-city markets, take into account not only their metropolitan areas but also what are called "trading areas." A trading area is not a respecter of the way the Rand McNally Company makes maps, or even of the way in which counties and cities and towns are marked out. Trading areas are affected by certain centers of trade which draw people oftentimes out of other counties, out of parts of other counties, or sometimes even out of other states.

In connection with the growth of metropolitan areas and trading areas, the main trend at present is toward the development of about fourteen huge *metropolitan strips of land*. These different strips will within the next few years contain around 60 per cent of our total population, yet will represent only about 4 per cent of our total land area.

I do not need a crystal ball to know that within the next few years the area from Milwaukee, Wisc., to Gary, Ind., is going to be built almost solidly, and this does not mean just along the "industrial Riviera" of Lake Michigan. The "strip" will extend some miles west of the lake.

If you live in or near the New England area, I recommend that you drive south from northern New England, but do not use the new superhighways. Instead, start considerably north and drive as far south as Washington, D.C., on into Virginia— all by old U.S. Highway No. 1. You will find that you will never once be out of a metropolitan area—and this is a strip of several hundred miles. In other words, to talk very much about *the* Boston market or *the* Hartford market or *the* New Haven market or *the* Bridgeport market is not so meaningful as it used to be.

And there are similar strips around Detroit, around St. Louis, around Los Angeles, and so on. What difference does it make that we are getting these great metropolitan strips occupying 4 per cent of the land and containing almost two-thirds of the population? The answer is that this affects tremendously the tastes and preferences of people, and the kinds of things for which they spend their money.

In general, people who live in these areas will tend to be more "sophisticated" than people who live elsewhere. This does *not* imply that people who live elsewhere are dumb or dull. But on the average, there will be a tendency for more aggressive, more alert people to live in areas of this sort.

If you live in an urbanized area, you and your family can satisfy lots and lots of different wants. While it is true that you cannot listen to your tape recorder, stereo hi-fi, and radio . . . watch your television . . . drive your car . . . look at your photographic slides and at your movies . . . and cook outdoors in in-

teresting costumes—*all at the same time*—you will want more
and more opportunity to do lots of different things, and you
will certainly want to do them in a variety of different ways.

For the spenders in our economy, these huge "interurbias"
are the places with *almost infinite possibilities* for variety and
novelty and change.

The marketing of all sorts of products continues to have
enormous possibilities, particularly in the United States where
we are devoted so wholeheartedly to leisure-time pursuits. Because people have more money and more time to spend their
money than ever before, our opportunities are fantastic.

2. Patterns of Tomorrow

Tremendous shopping centers have developed and will be
significant in our future shopping habits. They draw trade from
a wide area ... with their dozens of stores, and probably a
bank, restaurants, and other commercial establishments ...
maybe a movie theater.

Examples: the Plaza Shopping Center in Kansas City, Missouri; the Westchester Shopping Center in Los Angeles; Hills-
dale south of San Francisco; Northgate in Seattle; Northland
near Detroit; the Cross County Center in Westchester County,
New York; Old Orchard and also Edens Plaza, in the northern
suburbs of Chicago. Shopping centers no longer concentrate
within the city limits, but are on the ouskirts, or out in the
suburbs, or even beyond the suburbs—and with convenient
parking space and one-stop shopping so that you can buy
in a number of different places, almost at the same time.

In addition to this type of one-stop shopping at shopping
centers, a similar situation has grown up with the supermarket. Incidentally, where did the idea come from—of the
supermarket? It is a business which is characteristically American. You can now find an occasional supermarket in the Latin
American countries but usually with U.S. capital backing. And
European nations are just beginning to have supermarkets of
any consequence.

Why have they mushroomed so in the United States? One answer is that we have had the enormous growth of good highways, and the development of automobiles on a scale unsurpassed by any other nation. With this we have had the movement of our population toward the more urban areas, plus general dissatisfaction among retailers with inefficient retailing methods.

Another factor is that the supermarkets and chain stores have been able to offer price appeals. But even more important, they have offered improved retailing practices: prompt and courteous service, plus clean, modern, attractive, and well-located stores, plus good-quality merchandise in relation to price. Central ownership, central management, central buying, central warehousing, central storing, and centralized advertising—these can make a considerable difference in the efficiency and quality of a retailing operation.

In addition to women buyers, men are now buying in the chains and supermarkets on a scale never dreamed of twenty years ago. And when papa goes shopping with mama in the food stores, the sales ticket zooms upward. Papa sees all sorts of delicacies and oddments which appeal to him, and he thinks he really ought to stock up on these and have them in the refrigerator or deep freeze for special snacks.

The psychological appeal of the supermarket is enormous because you, the individual shopper, not only have your choice in nonfood items as well as food items, but you can also take your time in buying and are under no pressure from any salesclerk. Interestingly enough, as I mentioned in an earlier chapter, a large number of the items bought in the supermarkets are bought on impulse.

In order to save time and effort, you and I have learned to organize our buying habits into multi-purpose shopping trips, and to "cluster" our purchasing within small geographical areas.

Dealing with consumers, either directly or through intermediaries, are about 10 million different producers and distributors, over 4.6 million business concerns, almost 5 million farms, some 150,000 Government agencies, and an unknown number of individuals who provide professional services, run one-man businesses, or do part-time retailing.

Professor Reavis Cox of the Wharton School of Finance and Commerce, and former president of the American Marketing Association, says: "Nothing is more astonishing about modern man's way of life than the extremes to which he has carried the process of jamming himself down into a few densely crowded cities." The reasons for most of us living in a surprisingly small fraction of the total U.S. land are complex. But one important influence, as Professor Cox says, is that cities "make it possible for consumers to come into physical contact easily and in rapid succession with the large number of places at which they collect the goods and services delivered to them by the economy's assembly lines."

Along with these developments "scrambled merchandising" has also come about. That is, retail stores that used to sell only certain kinds of merchandise now sell lots of different kinds. A hardware outlet stocks items that can be found in food stores and drugstores. A drugstore sells grocery products and hardware items. A food store sells drug products and even some hardware products.

For example, more toothbrushes are sold in food outlets than in drugstores. And the sale of cigarettes in food outlets is greater than through any other source!

Food retailers are steadily increasing their share of the drug and toiletries business. According to Arthur C. Nielsen, Jr.: "In 1957, food stores accounted for 34% of the sales of a representative group of twenty proprietary and toiletry commodities. By 1959, this figure had increased to 51%." Why this trend in the so-called food outlet? It's very simple: higher markup and greater profits than on food products.

As for the approximately fifty thousand drugstores in the United States, practically all of them sell merchandise that does not require any compounding of prescriptions. Actually only about a fifth of a drugstore's income comes from prescriptions. It comes instead from the soda fountain and from the sale of cosmetics, candy, magazines, tobacco, hardware, and so on. Here we find more and more scrambled merchandising. And the same is true of the variety stores, the so-called "five-and-tens."

The Katz drug chain of Kansas City, Missouri, was one of the pioneers in scrambled merchandising. Today the Katz stores are like small department stores, all on one floor. In the greater Los Angeles area is a chain called Thrifty Cut Rate Drug Stores. In their stores you are able to buy clothing, drugs, foods, hardware—you can almost name it, and there it is, in a huge store all on one floor, looking like an overgrown supermarket. As another example, Webb's City in St. Petersburg, Florida, has attained national fame for scrambled merchandising on a tremendous scale.

So, you begin to wonder . . . what is retail shopping going to be like in the 1970s and 1980s? Probably several things will happen.

Great shopping centers will continue to be built on the outskirts of cities. No wonder, when you consider the millions of people who will be moving to suburbia. Dr. Philip M. Hauser of the University of Chicago says that of a possible increase of 80 million persons in population between 1950 and 1980 in standard metropolitan areas (large cities and their suburbs), only 16 million will be added to the population of central cities, and the remaining *64 million* will be added to the suburbs! Furthermore, of the 64 million added to suburbia, about 29 million will be added to incorporated areas of suburbia—but the remaining 35 million will be added to what now is exurbia and interurbia, that is, what today is the open country, and unincorporated parts of metropolitan rings.

There will also be a *return to the city* among many older people, especially fathers and mothers whose children are now grown. These are the people who originally moved to the suburbs because they wanted the kiddies to have more fresh air and sunshine and live in a "good neighborhood." The number of people in the age group fifty-five and over will increase several million during the 1960s; and this may help the rebirth of some of the central shopping areas of the cities.

Also, *consumers are going to be much better educated* in the years ahead. For 1980, it is estimated that for the adult population 11 per cent of the twenty-five-years-and-over population will have finished college, and 60 per cent high school, just about double the percentages at the present time.

As to other changes, Wroe Alderson, an outstanding marketing authority, predicts: "Summer air conditioning will become as commonplace as winter heating. Forms of entertainment will be improved and multiplied. The drudgery of child care will be partially alleviated. The hazards of fire and of household accidents will be greatly reduced. Medical care will be regular and directed more at prevention than cure. The family psychiatrist may become almost as common as the family doctor. Many households will make use of such outside services as accounting. Families will still have problems but they will be the problems of the rich rather than the poor, since nearly everyone will be rich by the standards of 1880."

And we'll also find *changes in our patterns of shopping*. Not only in the growth of shopping centers both in suburbia and in the city . . . but in the ways shopping is done. Nothing seems more antiquated than the present method of making a purchase in a retail store. The next time you buy something as simple as a handkerchief, take note of the fantastic number of minutes spent by the clerk filling out forms and sales slips and getting change while you, the customer, *wait*. Electronic controls and the development of electronic systems of communication, not even invented yet, ought to be possible within the retail stores.

Finally, as our cities sprawl even further and their exact outlines disappear into a blurred image, there will be a blurring of the image of retail outlets. Supermarkets will expand more and more beyond foods into other packaged goods . . .

maybe even into clothing and appliances. And the so-called discount houses—formerly the retail terror of the postwar world—will become more and more like department stores.

In other words, *"scrambled merchandising" will increase.* The head of one of the largest grocery chains in the St. Louis area tells me that it is going to be increasingly difficult to tell what his stores are, as contrasted with some of the drug chains and hardware chains. "You will be able to come into any store of my grocery chain, and you will find food, drug, and hardware items; and I'm sure that you can then go into the stores of the leading drug chains and you'll find more and more food items, more and more hardware items, and so on."

What else for the future? Will the sporting-goods store and the hardware store, or even the gas station, become logical outlets for frozen foods? Will the department store borrow a page from grandfather's book, and, forsaking the white heat of competition in appliances, return to the old idea of really extensive and varied food departments? Will supermarkets install automatic vending machines in their parking lots, for use of nighttime and week-end shoppers?

Whatever the future, we can be sure of one thing—there'll be some changes made.

19

Your Future Is Here

1. The Soaring Sixties

Millions more people, especially youngsters and oldsters ... better-educated people ... with more money to spend ... for more products and services—that is the picture for the "soaring sixties."

If people keep on marrying at the rate of the past few years, half of the 210 million population of 1970 will be wedded, and will have established over 55 million homes. Yes, our future is going to be a crowded one. So what about our population which continues to grow ... up, out, and around?

Most of the population *increase* probably will be concentrated in 24 states, principally Western and Middle Western states: California, Oregon, Washington, Montana, Idaho, Nevada, Arizona, Utah, Colorado, New Mexico, Texas, Wisconsin, Illinois, Michigan, Indiana, Ohio, Florida, Virginia, Maryland, Delaware, New Jersey, Connecticut, Alaska, and Hawaii. Within most of these states will be great metropolitan "galaxies," which by 1970 will be amassing population at a rate that will eventually net over two-thirds of our 1980 population ... and at least 60 per cent of this two-thirds will be suburbanite. It is understandable that cities, slated for only a 30 per cent increase, will not grow so fast as suburbia—unless they grow *up* instead of out, for the borders of most cities are well defined.

This increasing density of population in relatively small areas has great significance to us consumers. Not only is the geographic location of population of great importance, but the age structure of our population is beginning to resemble an hourglass—with heavy concentrations among the senior-citizen and teen-age divisions. By 1970 the fifteen-to-nineteen-year-old group will increase by 46 per cent, and the twenty-to-twenty-four-year-olds will increase some 55 per cent, while the over-sixty-five bracket will be up 26 per cent. However, the thirty-five-to-forty-four group will actually *decrease* 4 per cent.

In the working-age group—twenty through sixty-four years of age—will be 106.5 million people compared with 95 million now, an increase of 13 per cent. To borrow some words from the bees, the "workers" will have increased by 12½ million, and the "drones" by 21 million. In other words, *there will be fewer persons providing for more persons.* This demand on fewer persons may actually preclude a reduction of work hours, and we may have to forego more leisure. As living standards rise, workers may have to work harder.

All this explosive human multiplication is not limited to the United States. Foreign consumption of our products and state-side consumption of foreign commodities will be affected by a vast increase in world population. The *increase per day* in world population is equivalent to the population of Savannah, Georgia (120,000); so we can say that the world is adding 365 Savannahs a year. This means lots more consumers, producers, and keen competition. And the competition is of an unusual type, for our standard of living will continue its rapid upgrade, while most of the rest of the world is just getting a start.

Today we have 6 per cent of the world's population and produce about 50 per cent of the free world's output of raw materials. Along with a growth of population go many changes in social patterns. One of the more important is the development of two-generation living units, that is, homes without grandparents, aunts, or uncles under the same roof with parents and their children. By 1970, largely because of the war babies and the postwar babies of the 1940s, new homes will be formed at the rate of 1.2 million a year.

By 1970 our annual college enrollments will have increased by at least 80 per cent. As Peter F. Drucker, management consultant, says: "If the birth rate was the most important economic event of the last few years, the second most important was the steady increase in the number of full-time and part-time college students."

And the entire school population will increase by 23 per cent by 1970, compared with a 17 per cent increase in the entire population. Not only will there be more young people in school, but also a catapulting emphasis on adult education, and "taking an evening class."

Over the years, the members of the family—both children and adults—may be getting so many diplomas that there will hardly be space to hang them all . . . even in the two-car garage.

Keeping in mind that there will be more people in school, there is the possibility of equality of opportunity for education . . . rather than just equality of education. In other words, we might learn to educate people to their capacity, with more capable people receiving education to satisfy their capacities. If this trend becomes an actuality, not only will we have well-educated average people, but we'll have some superbly educated bright people.

So while many people are predicting an increasing mass market, we must also keep in mind that, even though both average and bright people will have considerable amounts to spend on goods, there will still be many differences in tastes according to different levels of capacity. The people in the "upper" market will have been satisfied with the quality of the products they have been able to buy and are buying—and so they'll be looking for the new and different: helicopters, bathing suits that inflate with the "lap" of a large wave, golf balls that "buzz" when they land in the rough, and many other out-of-this-world innovations. The "uppers" won't be perfecting the quality of their town houses—they'll already be "perfect"—but the "middlers" will still be absorbed in making their apartments and houses more attractive.

As our world shrinks, we'll become more interested in the lands across the waters. Young Americans and many adults already are learning more about the other cultures of the world and are beginning to learn foreign languages. And we are becoming more interested in world politics, geography, and other ways of life. This in turn increases our wants for many foreign commodities—note the already booming market in foreign automobiles, sewing machines, radios, cameras, office equipment, wools from England, handmade shoes from Italy.

Evening classes for adults will interest us not only in the surrounding world but in learning "How to Do It." We'll be learning to paint, make jewelry, upholster furniture, write short stories, decorate cakes. Yes, *education will be the spark that ignites the fuse of explosive leisure time.*

There is also a possibility that increased education may temper our interest in material things in life. There is an outside chance that good literature, opera, symphony, and art may come into their own within the next decade. Since money is no longer going to be the main symbol of social class, emphasis on other facets of life may come into vogue. In the past, an education too often has been just having a degree or diploma; but since most people will now have at least a high school diploma, we may put a far greater emphasis on broader education in the arts.

Not only is our population erupting and getting more information, but our national economy is expanding. The national economy can be measured by the Gross National Product (GNP), which is the total national output of all goods and services at market prices. By 1970, our GNP will be at a high of at least $700 billion, perhaps $750 billion, compared with about $500 billion for 1960. With a 210 million population in 1970, there will be a tremendous spurt in family income. Only a cataclysmic war or other major catastrophe can prevent this. Family income, adjusted for change in the value of the dollar, already has gone up 50 per cent in the last ten years ... and the end is not in sight.

In 1959 the number of family units with $4,000 to $7,500 of income annually was about 22 million. Within this group there were well over 7 million family units with more than $6,000. The number of family units under the $4,000 mark has declined, both relatively and absolutely.

By 1970 there will be a *doubling of family units with incomes of more than $7,500,* to about 25 million families. They will comprise nearly two-fifths of all consumer spending power. The middle-income units, whose spending power dominated the markets of the early 1950s, will have only 28 per cent of the disposable income by 1970 ... down from 43 per cent in 1947.

Yes, at least $7,500 yearly will be in the pockets of 45 per cent of all families by 1970! The middle-income families will be another 39 per cent, and those with less than $4,000 will be only 16 per cent of the population. Note that three-fifths of the over-$7,500 families of 1970 will also be over $10,000.

No longer does all the money go for food and clothes and rent and automobiles. People can afford to take a vacation *or* save for college tuition. They can afford to go out to the movies *or* give a party at home. Andrew Heiskell, chairman of the board of Time, Inc., says: "By 1970, beyond question, the 45% of all families whose after-tax incomes is $7,500 or more, will control more than 60% of all expendable dollars, and will be able to choose not just clothes and cars and entertainment. They'll be able to select an entire way of life."

We have covered a lot of figures in a very few pages. So let's summarize what lies ahead for the next dynamic decade:

Population: By 1970, there will be nearly 210 million in-

dividuals—an increase of some 17 per cent during the sixties.

Education: Annual college enrollments will double by 1970, at which time there will be some twenty-two million college-educated Americans.

Income: Personal income will grow until, by 1970, the average family income will approach $7,500 (after taxes and in 1959 dollars).

Goods and Services: The per-person gain in national output will be 33 per cent for the decade, with the total gross national product rising to some $700 to $750 billion by 1970.

The People: We shall continue to have the most affluent society in the world, or in all history.

The Market: Higher standards and tastes will dominate the new market. With higher intellectual level, people will be more interested in quality. And they will have the income to use discretion in their buying. We are coming into what might be called the great *Age of Discretion*—in which vastly dissimilar industries will be competing for the consumer's discretionary dollar. More than half the personal income will be discretionary by 1970.

2. Blueprint for Tomorrow

How will all these facts and figures affect you and your spending in the coming years? Many of the events that determine your future already have happened.

• In the next decade, as at present, about two-fifths of the population (43 per cent, including the employable unemployed) will be supporting the remaining three-fifths. Thus, our standard of living will continue to be greatly dependent on a combination of manufacturing and marketing abilities.

• The pet prediction of many economic soothsayers is that there will be a tremendous increase in the leisure-time market. It should be remembered, however, that most of the leisure time will be available to the youngsters and oldsters.

- We may go through a decade of fads in material possessions ... with our much-moneyed populace alternately bestowing honors upon higher education, yachts, original paintings, solar heating, swimming pools, or whatnot.

- It is possible that the next decade may see an even greater trend toward savings.... with the ownership of securities being a sign of "having arrived."

- It also will be possible for almost anyone to live in any style to which he or she *wants* to be accustomed. The laborer can spend his money in the usual way; or he may decide to maintain a higher cultural standard of living.

- The American people may decide that they want a much higher standard of "public" living to go along with the swelling standard of "private" living. *Architectural Forum* has predicted a $285 billion budget for public building by 1968. This will be expended for hospitals (many more are needed for the greater numbers of babies and of oldsters); for colleges; for civic centers.

- There will be even more super-duper superhighways. At the beginning of the century there was almost no paved highway in the United States; but there is now enough paved highway in the United States to cover all the New England states solidly and completely ... and that still isn't enough.

- Purchasing of your basic commodities will be much more simple. Not only will there be even more self-service, but there will be a much wider array of automatic dispensers. You may be able to buy your socks or stockings from a machine that may resemble today's soft-drink or coffee machines—by pushing buttons for size, length, color, and fabric. And when you pay for a standard item, you'll simply put in your money, and out will come your purchase—wrapped, of course—along with your change and sales receipt.

- Most basic commodities will be inventoried and reordered directly by an IBM-type system. In this manner, you'll rarely be disappointed because your store is temporarily out of stock.

- Since 60 per cent of the population will be over sixty-five or under twenty-one, there will be many more products with special appeal for these two age groups.

• Because of higher levels of education, consumers will be better qualified to make decisions without the aid of a salesperson, and they will be greatly helped by advertising, which is a tremendous force in the dissemination of product information. In fact, we'll become more dependent on advertising, much of which will have to meet the standards of our better-educated society.

• Factors other than income will become more important than ever in determining what we'll spend our money for. Such sociological factors as occupation, location of household, education, and family size always have influenced both how much we spend and for what. But with income becoming more evenly distributed throughout the population, sheer ability to buy will become less and less important, and the sociological forces will become more and more important in determining what we buy.

A further look into the late 1960s augurs great scientific developments, many of which are already in the blueprint stage. Recent predictions by *Fortune* magazine included a comprehensive theory of elementary particles; test-tube creation of a living cell; detailed understanding of the aging process; computers with brainlike attributes; substantial control over tornadoes and hurricanes; a cure for cancer; a 2,000-miles-per-hour airliner; a small flying car; accurate 90-day weather forecasts; fresh water from sea water at acceptable cost; nuclear power in most of the United States; rocket mail and rocket freight service; and a man on the moon.

For each new basic service or technical or scientific achievement, there are hundreds of seen and unforeseen ways in which they may be incorporated into our everyday living. We'll have all-electronic cooking ranges, with radar waves to cook the inside of a roast in a matter of seconds, without browning the surface . . . disposable tableware, to eliminate dishwashing . . . fully portable TV sets, operating from batteries which will be recharged from an electric outlet . . . tiny high-fidelity speakers of exceptional range and brilliance . . . a combination auto-aircraft-boat . . . electronic safety devices for automobiles which will avoid dangerously approaching cars . . . gas turbine trucks . . . tires with detachable, replaceable treads . . . foods sterilized by gamma rays . . . self-lighting cigarettes . . . paper clothes that can be thrown away after a few wearings . . . air purifiers . . . gas-less automobiles . . . smokeless heat . . . automatic public conveyances . . . houses that may not need to be painted.

Here is a possible picture of the 1970s, painted by *Newsweek:*

"Waking to cool, 1970-style music from a tiny phonograph built into her pillow, the housewife yawned, flicked a bed-side switch to turn on the electronic recipe-maker, then rose and stepped into her ultrasonic shower. While sound waves cleaned and vigorously massaged her, breakfast got itself ready in the kitchen. The recipe-maker, taking its cue from a menu coded on a punch card, perked the coffee, dropped six eggs from the egg compartment into a bowl, mixed them with a dish of milk, and scrambled them.

"Breakfast done, the housewife turned on the central vacuum cleaner, which sucked dust from all the rooms through special ducts. She switched on the video phone, scanned the list of groceries and prices that appeared on the screen, and enunciated into the mike: 'Two pounds of chopped chuck, one pound of butter, three artichokes, a bunch of bananas.' An electronic brain at a warehouse downtown punch-registered the tape-recorded order and printed up a copy, with the housewife's name and address, for the deliveryman.

"Outside, the electronic lawn mower gave a barely audible clank, and began to mow the lawn in a pre-programmed pattern. Its electric-eye scanner, sweeping the grass tops hourly to determine when the grass needed cutting, had picked up solid returns.

"While this is hardly likely to be the 'typical American home' ten years from now, all of these push-button devices, and hundreds of other equally futuristic gadgets, are far past the dream stage. Prototypes for some (ultrasonic dishwashers, hands-free telephones) already exist; others are now being developed. And there are businessmen who are firmly convinced that all are close to being commercially feasible."

More than any other time or place in the history of the world, we can now live in the future. In all other environments of time and space, people have lived for the future, but with a grim present ... or they have merely subsisted for each day, with no future to look forward to even on the distant horizon.

We can live relatively carefree today and still be certain of a better tomorrow. And our grandchildren have an even brighter future—which may be out of this world, both figuratively and literally.

When we re-examine the wonders of the past decade, we can better appreciate the rapidity with which developments of the future will be arriving. In 1949 consumers could already buy television sets, air conditioners, dishwashers, clothes dryers, power lawn mowers, high-fidelity phonographs, LP records, tape recorders, Polaroid Land Cameras, and automobiles with automatic transmissions. Then the 1950s brought power steering and power brakes to automobiles, and stereophonic sound to phonograph records.

In 1949 we knew only about nylon; now we can choose among Orlon, Acrilan, Dynel, Verel, Creslan, Darvan, Zefran, Dacron, Kodel, and Teron. And polyethylene (plastic bags) is a product of the fifties. Latex-based paints for the do-it-yourself market were most popular; and Fiberglas set the style in pleasure boats. And vinyl plastics are now an everyday phenomenon in place of linoleum and asphalt.

In December, 1957, *U.S. News & World Report* PREDICTED the following items during the next ten years: big jet airliners; atomic power plants, operating on a commercial basis; diesel-power for many autos, small and cheap to run; space vehicles of many kinds, including rockets to the moon; solar batteries, using energy from the sun to run appliances; limitless water supplies, by low-cost conversion of sea water; pocket radios about the size of a watch; picture-frame TV, so thin it can be hung on the wall; home air conditioning as a low-cost device added to the furnace; vast highway networks to crisscross the United States; new clothing materials that will not wear out or catch on fire; new medical cures and techniques to control heart disease and high blood pressure.

These were predictions for ten years ahead, but *in only two years* the jet airliners were a reality; the first atomic power plant was in operation; diesel-powered autos were running in Germany; solar batteries to operate radios were a reality; solar energy was used to recharge the rockets to the moon; the first salt-water converter had been developed; pocket radios about the size of a watch were possible with the new transistor batteries; air conditioning had become available at relatively low cost; and the tollways, freeways, and superhighways were ribboning the cities and the countryside.

It doesn't take long today for an idea to become a reality. It is no wonder that we have faith in the imagination—we can dream of almost anything, and it may become a reality. *The greatest discovery of America is still before us!*

Some Suggested Readings

Chapter 1. What's on the Consumer's Mind?

Britt, Steuart Henderson, "The Strategy of Consumer Motivation," *Journal of Marketing*, Vol. 14 (April, 1950), pp. 666–674.

Dichter, Ernest, "What Are the Real Reasons People Buy Today?" *Sales Management*, Vol. 74 (Feb. 1, 1955), pp. 36–38, 86–89; and Vol. 74 (Feb. 15, 1955), pp. 46, 48–50, 52–55.

Chapter 2. Consider Your Motives

Britt, Steuart Henderson, "The Application of Social Science Findings to Advertising," *American Management Report No. 15.* New York: American Management Association, 1958.

Guthrie, Edwin R., *The Psychology of Human Conflict.* New York: Harper & Brothers, 1938.

McGregor, Douglas, " 'Motives' as a Tool of Market Research," *Harvard Business Review*, Vol. 19 (Autumn, 1940), pp. 42–51.

Maslow, A. H., *Motivation and Personality.* New York: Harper & Brothers, 1954.

Chapter 3. What Do You Want?

Editors of *Fortune, U.S.A., The Permanent Revolution.* Englewood Cliffs, N.J.: PrenticeHall, Inc., 1951.

Katona, George, *The Powerful Consumer.* New York: McGraw-Hill Book Company, Inc., 1960.

Chapter 4. The Consumer Is King

Luce, Henry L., "The Character of the Businessman," *Fortune*, Vol. 56 (August, 1957), pp. 108–109, 182, 185.

Martineau, Pierre, "Social Classes and Spending Behavior," *Journal of Marketing,* Vol. 23 (October, 1958), pp. 121–130.

Potter, David M., *The People of Plenty.* Chicago: University of Chicago Press, 1954.

Rainwater, Lee, Richard C. Coleman, and Gerald Handel, *Workingman's Wife: Her Personality, World and Life Style.* New York: Oceana Publications, Inc., 1959.

Chapter 5. Business Is Your Business

Drucker, Peter F., *The Practice of Management.* New York: Harper & Brothers, 1954.

Drury, James C., "Is Your Problem Overproduction or Underproduction of Markets?" *Printers' Ink,* Vol. 260 (July, 1957), pp. 19–22, 58.

Mazur, Paul M., *The Standards We Raise,* New York: Harper & Brothers, 1953.

Zelomek, A. W., *A Changing America: At Work and Play.* New York: John Wiley & Sons, Inc., 1959.

Chapter 6. Spend Your Money and Take Your Choice

Ferber, Robert, "Our Changing Consumer Market," *Business Horizons,* Vol. 1 (Spring, 1958), pp. 49–66.

Martineau, Pierre, "It's Time to Research the Consumer," *Harvard Business Review,* Vol. 33 (July–August, 1955), pp. 45–54.

Mortimer, Charles G., *Two Keys to Modern Marketing.* Scarsdale, N.Y.: The Updegraff Press, Ltd., 1955.

Sapir, Edward, *Fashion, The Encyclopedia of the Social Sciences,* Vol. 6, pp. 139–144. New York: The Macmillan Company, c. 1930.

Veblen, Thorstein, *The Theory of the Leisure Class.* New York: Modern Library, Inc., 1934.

Chapter 7. You Have the Money and the Time

"$41-Billion for Fun: Who Sells Most to Leisure Market—and Why," *Printers' Ink,* Vol. 268 (July 10, 1959), pp. 25–31.

Green, Arnold W., *Sociology: An Analysis of Life in Modern Society,* 2d ed. New York: McGraw-Hill Book Company, Inc., 1956.

Havemann, Ernest, "Why Nobody Can Save Any Money," *Life,* Vol. 46 (June 15, 1959), pp. 120–132.

Silberman, Charles E., "The Money Left Over for the Good Life," *Fortune,* Vol. 60 (November, 1959), pp. 134–137, 240–242, 247–248.

"What People Are Spending Their Money for Now," *U.S. News & World Report,* Vol. 46 (May 18, 1959), pp. 58–59.

Chapter 8. Who Spends For What?

LIFE Study of Consumer Expenditures: A Background for Marketing Decisions, Vol. 1. New York: Time, Inc., 1957.

Ostheimer, Richard H., "Who Buys What? *Life's* Study of Consumer Expenditures," *Journal of Marketing,* Vol. 22 (January, 1958), pp. 260–272.

Whyte, William H., Jr., and Editors of *Fortune, Is Anybody Listening?* New York: Simon and Schuster, Inc., 1952.

Chapter 9. Vive la Product Différence!

Johnson, Samuel C., III, "S. C. Johnson's New Products Profit from Screening, Sponsors, Product-Plus," *Printers' Ink,* Vol. 262 (Feb. 7, 1958), pp. 33–34, 38.

Phillips, Charles F., and Delbert J. Duncan, *Marketing Principles and Methods.* Homewood, Ill.: Richard D. Irwin, Inc., 4th ed., 1960, Chap. 23.

Chapter 10. Are They Tops or Flops?

Hepner, Harry W., *Modern Marketing: Dynamics and Management.* New York: McGraw-Hill Book Company, Inc., 1955, Chap. 10.

Chapter 11. What Do You Imagine?

Martineau, Pierre, *Motivation in Advertising.* New York: McGraw-Hill Book Company, Inc., 1957.

Chapter 12. You Learn through Advertising

Borden, Neil H., *The Economic Effects of Advertising.* Homewood, Ill.: Richard D. Irwin, Inc., 1942.

Britt, Steuart Henderson, "Subliminal Advertising—Fact or Fantasy?" *Advertising Age,* Vol. 28 (Nov. 18, 1957), pp. 103–104.

———, "Subliminal Advertising," *Advertising Agency Magazine,* Vol. 51 (May 23, 1958), pp. 14–16.

Cone, Fairfax M., "Advertising Is Not a Plot," *The Atlantic,* Vol. 201 (January, 1958), pp. 71–73.

Eldridge, Clarence E., "Advertising Effectiveness—How Can It Be Measured?" *Journal of Marketing,* Vol. 22 (January, 1958), pp. 241–251.

Mayer, Martin, "What Is Advertising Good For?" *Harper's Magazine,* Vol. 216 (February, 1958), pp. 25–31.

McGarry, Edmund D., "The Propaganda Function in Marketing," *Journal of Marketing,* Vol. 23 (October, 1958), pp. 131–139.

Myers, Kenneth H., "Have We a Decline in Advertising Appropriations?" *Journal of Marketing*, Vol. 23 (April, 1959), pp. 370–375.

Simon, Morton J., *The Advertising Truth Book*. New York: Advertising Federation of America, Inc., 1960.

Wiseman, Mark Huntington, *The New Anatomy of Advertising*. New York: Harper & Brothers, 1959.

Chapter 13. Your Stores Have Personalities

Lunding, Franklin J., " 'Heart Appeal' in Grocery Advertising," *Journal of Marketing*, Vol. 24 (October, 1959), pp. 74–76.

Martineau, Pierre, "The Personality of the Retail Store," *Harvard Business Review*, Vol. 36 (January–February, 1958), pp. 47–55.

Chapter 14. How About Price?

Dean, Joel, "Pricing Policies for New Products," *Harvard Business Review*, Vol. 28 (November, 1950), pp. 45–53.

Wharton, Don, "Beware the Phony Price-tag 'Bargain'!" *Reader's Digest*, Vol. 73 (December, 1958), pp. 40–42.

Chapter 15. Marketing Research Can Help

Boyd, Harper W., Jr., and Ralph Westfall, *Marketing Research: Text and Cases*. Homewood, Ill.: Richard D. Irwin, Inc., 1956.

Crisp, Richard D., *Marketing Research*. New York: McGraw-Hill Book Company, Inc., 1957.

"How New-product Test Cities Are Selected," *Printers' Ink*, Vol. 268 (Sept. 25, 1959), pp. 66–68.

Lucas, Darrell Blaine, and Steuart Henderson Britt, *Advertising Psychology and Research*. New York: McGraw-Hill Book Company, Inc., 1950.

Reed, Vergil D., "How to Get the Most out of Marketing Research," *Advertising Agency*, Vol. 48 (January, 1955), pp. 64–66.

Chapter 16. Is Motivation Research the Answer?

Britt, Steuart Henderson, "Why It's Best to Use 'Combination Research,' " *Printers' Ink*, Vol. 249 (Oct. 22, 1954), pp. 60–66.

———, "Four Hazards of Motivation Research: How to Avoid Them," *Printers' Ink*, Vol. 251 (June 17, 1955), pp. 40, 45, 48.

Ferber, Robert, and Hugh G. Wales (editors), *Motivation and Market Behavior*. Homewood, Ill.: Richard D. Irwin, Inc., 1958.

Martineau, Pierre, *Motivation in Advertising*. New York: McGraw-Hill Book Company, Inc., 1957.

Newman, Joseph W., *Motivation Research and Marketing Management*. Boston: Harvard University Graduate School of Business Administration, Division of Research, 1957.

Smith, George Horsley, *Motivation Research in Advertising and Marketing.* New York: McGraw-Hill Book Company, Inc., 1954.

Chapter 17. Women Are Here to Stay

Dingwall, Eric John, *The American Woman.* New York: The New American Library of World Literature, Inc., 1957.

Kluckhohn, Clyde, *Mirror for Man.* New York: McGraw-Hill Book Company, Inc., 1949.

"What the U.S. Woman Has Accomplished," *Life,* Vol. 41 (Dec. 25, 1956), pp. 22–170.

Wolff, Janet L., *What Makes Women Buy.* New York: McGraw-Hill Book Company, Inc., 1958.

Wolgast, Elizabeth H., "Do Husbands or Wives Make the Purchasing Decisions?" *Journal of Marketing,* Vol. 23 (October, 1958), pp. 151–158.

Chapter 18. There'll Be Some Changes Made

Alderson, Wroe, "Here's How Stores Will Face It," *Nation's Business,* Vol. 43 (November, 1955), pp. 85–90.

Cox, Reavis, "Consumer Convenience and the Retail Structure of Cities," *Journal of Marketing,* Vol. 23 (April, 1959), pp. 355–362.

Chapter 19. Your Future Is Here

"America at Work—Prospects," *Newsweek,* Vol. 54 (Dec. 14, 1959), pp. 86–100.

Editors of *Fortune, Markets of the Sixties.* New York: Harper & Brothers, 1960.

Hauser, Philip M., "The Challenge of Tomorrow's Markets," *Journal of Marketing,* Vol. 24 (July, 1959), pp. 1–7.

Parker, Sanford S., and Lawrence A. Mayer, "The Decade of the 'Discretionary' Dollar," *Fortune,* Vol. 59 (June, 1959), pp. 136–138, 260–264.

Acknowledgments

A great many individuals, organizations, book publishers, periodicals, and newspapers have provided useful ideas, or have given me permission to quote from them or refer to their work. In addition to those mentioned in the preface, entitled WHAT THIS BOOK IS ABOUT, I wish to acknowledge the aid of the following:

INDIVIDUALS AND ORGANIZATIONS

Wroe Alderson
PRESIDENT
ALDERSON ASSOCIATES, INC.

Dr. Harold P. Alspaugh
DIRECTOR, RATE AND DATA DIVISION, STANDARD RATE & DATA SERVICE, INC.

Paul D. Allman
PRESIDENT
THE CRACKER JACK CO.

Dr. Gordon W. Allport
PROFESSOR OF PSYCHOLOGY
HARVARD UNIVERSITY

Dr. Ira D. Anderson
ASSOCIATE DEAN
SCHOOL OF BUSINESS
NORTHWESTERN UNIVERSITY

Peter Aptakin
MARKET RESEARCH DEPARTMENT
LIFE

Frank Armour, Jr.
PRESIDENT
H. J. HEINZ COMPANY

Andrew L. F. Armstrong
VICE PRESIDENT
COMPTON ADVERTISING, INC.

Stanley L. Arnold
PRESIDENT
ARNOLD AND ASSOCIATES

H. W. Baldock
DIRECTOR, MEDICAL RELATIONS
E. R. SQUIBB & SONS

Lee S. Bickmore
PRESIDENT
NATIONAL BISCUIT COMPANY

Fred J. Borch
VICE PRESIDENT AND GROUP EX-
ECUTIVE, CONSUMER PRODUCTS
GROUP, GENERAL ELECTRIC
COMPANY

Neil H. Borden
PROFESSOR OF MARKETING
GRADUATE SCHOOL OF BUSINESS
ADMINISTRATION, HARVARD
UNIVERSITY

Charles F. Borgard
DISTRICT REPRESENTATIVE, CHI-
CAGO, GENERAL ELECTRIC
COMPANY

Dr. Lyndon O. Brown
SENIOR VICE PRESIDENT
DANCER-FITZGERALD-SAMPLE, INC.

Rex M. Budd
DIRECTOR OF ADVERTISING
CAMPBELL SOUP COMPANY

Leo Burnett
CHAIRMAN OF THE BOARD
LEO BURNETT COMPANY, INC.

Edward C. Bursk
EDITOR
THE HARVARD BUSINESS REVIEW

Walter W. Candy, Jr.
PRESIDENT
BULLOCK'S, INC. (LOS ANGELES)

Dr. Hadley Cantril
SENIOR COUNSELOR
THE INSTITUTE FOR INTERNA-
TIONAL SOCIAL RESEARCH

Reginald T. Clough
PROMOTION DIRECTOR
THE READER'S DIGEST

Fairfax M. Cone
CHAIRMAN OF THE EXECUTIVE
COMMITTEE, FOOTE, CONE &
BELDING

William N. Connolly
VICE PRESIDENT
S. C. JOHNSON & SON, INC.

Dr. Reavis Cox
PROFESSOR OF MARKETING
WHARTON SCHOOL
UNIVERSITY OF PENNSYLVANIA

Dr. Ross M. Cunningham
ASSOCIATE PROFESSOR OF MAR-
KETING, SCHOOL OF INDUSTRIAL
MANAGEMENT, MASSACHUSETTS
INSTITUTE OF TECHNOLOGY

Draper Daniels
EXECUTIVE VICE PRESIDENT IN
CHARGE OF CREATIVE SERVICES,
LEO BURNETT COMPANY, INC.

Donald David
COPYWRITER
CAMPBELL-EWALD COMPANY

Dr. Joel Dean
PRESIDENT
JOEL DEAN ASSOCIATES, INC.

Gerald F. DeLashmutt
CUSTOMER RESEARCH STAFF
GENERAL MOTORS CORPORATION

Pierre A. de Tarnowsky
EXECUTIVE VICE PRESIDENT
WARNER-LAMBERT PHARMACEUTI-
    CAL COMPANY

Dr. Ernest Dichter
PRESIDENT
INSTITUTE FOR MOTIVATIONAL
    RESEARCH, INC.

Eric John Dingwall
AUTHOR

Alex Dreier
ABC COMMENTATOR

Dr. Peter F. Drucker
PROFESSOR OF MANAGEMENT
GRADUATE SCHOOL OF BUSINESS
NEW YORK UNIVERSITY

Dr. James C. Drury
PROFESSOR OF MARKETING
NEW YORK UNIVERSITY

Peter Ehlers
ACCOUNT EXECUTIVE
KETCHUM, MACLEOD & GROVE,
    INC.

Clarence E. Eldridge
MANAGEMENT CONSULTANT

Victor Elting, Jr.
VICE PRESIDENT, ADVERTISING AND
    MERCHANDISING, THE QUAKER
    OATS COMPANY

Dr. Horace B. English
PROFESSOR OF PSYCHOLOGY
OHIO STATE UNIVERSITY

Grover W. Ensley
EXECUTIVE VICE PRESIDENT
NATIONAL ASSOCIATION OF MU-
    TUAL SAVINGS BANKS

Dr. Edmund W. J. Faison
PRESIDENT
VISUAL RESEARCH, INC.

Dr. Robert Ferber
RESEARCH PROFESSOR OF ECONOM-
    ICS, UNIVERSITY OF ILLINOIS

Louise Field
RESEARCH ASSOCIATE
THE TWENTIETH CENTURY FUND

Bernice Fitz-Gibbon
PRESIDENT
BERNICE FITZ-GIBBON, INC.

Dr. Edwin B. George
ECONOMIST
DUN & BRADSTREET, INC.

Dr. Richard Glenn Gettell
PRESIDENT
MOUNT HOLYOKE COLLEGE

John L. Gillis
MARKETING VICE PRESIDENT
MONSANTO CHEMICAL COMPANY

Dr. Arnold W. Green
PROFESSOR OF SOCIOLOGY
THE PENNSYLVANIA STATE UNI-
    VERSITY

Dr. Mason Haire
PROFESSOR OF PSYCHOLOGY
UNIVERSITY OF CALIFORNIA,
    BERKELEY

Marion Harper, Jr.
CHAIRMAN OF THE BOARD AND
    PRESIDENT, McCANN-ERICKSON,
    INC.

Neison (Wishbone) Harris
FORMER PRESIDENT
THE TONI COMPANY

Sydney J. Harris
COLUMNIST
CHICAGO DAILY NEWS

Dr. Eugene L. Hartley
PROFESSOR OF PSYCHOLOGY
THE CITY COLLEGE OF NEW YORK

Dr. Ruth E. Hartley
DIRECTOR, SPECIAL RESEARCH
    PROJECTS, THE CITY COLLEGE
    OF NEW YORK

Dr. Philip M. Hauser
CHAIRMAN, DEPARTMENT OF SO-
    CIOLOGY, UNIVERSITY OF CHI-
    CAGO

August Heckscher
DIRECTOR
THE TWENTIETH CENTURY FUND

Dr. Harry Walker Hepner
PROFESSOR OF PSYCHOLOGY
SYRACUSE UNIVERSITY

Dr. Cyril Herrmann
VICE PRESIDENT
ARTHUR D. LITTLE, INC.

Dr. John J. Honigmann
ASSOCIATE PROFESSOR OF ANTHRO-
    POLOGY, UNIVERSITY OF NORTH
    CAROLINA

Dr. Rossall J. Johnson
ASSOCIATE PROFESSOR OF INDUS-
    TRIAL MANAGEMENT, NORTH-
    WESTERN UNIVERSITY

Earl W. Kintner
CHAIRMAN
FEDERAL TRADE COMMISSION

Dr. Arthur W. Kornhauser
PROFESSOR OF PSYCHOLOGY
WAYNE STATE UNIVERSITY

Arthur B. Langlie
PRESIDENT
McCALL CORPORATION

Thomas W. Lapham
VICE PRESIDENT
YOUNG & RUBICAM, INC.

Herbert A. Leggett
EDITOR
ARIZONA PROGRESS

Charles C. Lehman
SENIOR ANALYST
DANIEL STARCH AND STAFF

Martin Levin
EDITOR, "THE PHOENIX NEST"
SATURDAY REVIEW

Dr. Theodore Levitt
LECTURER ON BUSINESS ADMINIS-
    TRATION, GRADUATE SCHOOL OF
    BUSINESS ADMINISTRATION,
    HARVARD UNIVERSITY

Dr. Robert D. Loken
ASSISTANT TO THE PUBLISHER
LIFE

Joseph Lorin
VICE PRESIDENT
GREY ADVERTISING AGENCY, INC.

Henry R. Luce
EDITOR-IN-CHIEF
TIME, INC.

Earle Ludgin
CHAIRMAN OF THE BOARD
EARLE LUDGIN & COMPANY

Franklin J. Lunding
CHAIRMAN OF THE BOARD
JEWEL TEA CO., INC.

Dr. Paul I. Lyness
ADVERTISING AND MARKETING
    CONSULTANT

Jack Mabley
COLUMNIST
CHICAGO DAILY NEWS

Dr. Ruth P. Mack
ECONOMIST
NATIONAL BUREAU OF ECONOMIC
    RESEARCH

Alan R. Martin, Jr.
MARKETING DEPARTMENT
LIFE

C. Virgil Martin
PRESIDENT
CARSON PIRIE SCOTT & CO. (CHI-
    CAGO)

Pierre D. Martineau
DIRECTOR OF RESEARCH & MAR-
    KETING, THE CHICAGO TRIBUNE

Dr. A. H. Maslow
CHAIRMAN, DEPARTMENT OF PSY-
    CHOLOGY, BRANDEIS UNIVERSITY

Lowell B. Mason
LAWYER
FORMER MEMBER OF FEDERAL
    TRADE COMMISSION

M. M. Masterpool
MANAGER, HOUSEWARES DIVISION
    ADVERTISING AND PUBLICITY,
    GENERAL ELECTRIC COMPANY

Paul M. Mazur
INVESTMENT BANKER
LEHMAN BROTHERS

Thomas B. McCabe, Jr.
DIRECTOR OF MARKETING SERV-
    ICES, SCOTT PAPER COMPANY

Dr. Edmund D. McGarry
PROFESSOR OF MARKETING AND
    ECONOMICS, THE UNIVERSITY
    OF BUFFALO

Dr. Robert N. McMurry
PRESIDENT
THE MCMURRY COMPANY

Dr. Harold Mendelsohn
ASSISTANT DIRECTOR
MARKETING & SOCIAL RESEARCH
DIVISION, PSYCHOLOGICAL COR-
PORATION

Fredrick R. Messner
VICE PRESIDENT
G. M. BASFORD CO.

Mrs. Charlotte Montgomery
CONSULTANT AND COLUMNIST FOR
GOOD HOUSEKEEPING

Henry Morgan
RADIO AND TV PERSONALITY

Thomas C. Morrill
VICE PRESIDENT
STATE FARM MUTUAL AUTOMO-
BILE INSURANCE COMPANY

Charles G. Mortimer
CHAIRMAN
GENERAL FOODS CORPORATION

Dr. Kenneth H. Myers
PROFESSOR OF INDUSTRIAL MAN-
AGEMENT, SCHOOL OF BUSINESS,
NORTHWESTERN UNIVERSITY

Dr. Jean Namias
ASSOCIATE PROFESSOR IN ECO-
NOMICS AND STATISTICS, ST.
JOHN'S UNIVERSITY

Dr. Joseph W. Newman
ASSOCIATE PROFESSOR OF BUSI-
NESS ADMINISTRATION, GRADU-
ATE SCHOOL OF BUSINESS, STAN-
FORD UNIVERSITY

Arthur C. Nielsen, Jr.
PRESIDENT
A. C. NIELSEN COMPANY

David Ogilvy
PRESIDENT
OGILVY, BENSON & MATHER, INC.

Ralph P. Olmstead
VICE PRESIDENT IN CHARGE OF AD-
VERTISING, KELLOGG COMPANY

William A. Patterson
PRESIDENT
UNITED AIR LINES

James O. Peckham
EXECUTIVE VICE PRESIDENT
A. C. NIELSEN COMPANY

Peter G. Peterson
EXECUTIVE VICE PRESIDENT
BELL & HOWELL COMPANY

Knowles L. Pittman
ASSISTANT PUBLIC RELATIONS
MANAGER, KRAFT FOODS

Alfred Politz
PRESIDENT
ALFRED POLITZ RESEARCH

A. L. Powell
DIRECTOR OF PUBLIC RELATIONS
THE PILLSBURY COMPANY

C. James Proud
PRESIDENT AND GENERAL MAN-
AGER, ADVERTISING FEDERATION
OF AMERICA

Dr. Lee Rainwater
PSYCHOLOGIST
SOCIAL RESEARCH, INC.

Dr. William J. Regan
ASSISTANT PROFESSOR OF MARKET-
ING, SAN FRANCISCO STATE COL-
LEGE

Frank D. Register
EXECUTIVE ASSISTANT
NATIONAL CONFECTIONERS ASSO-
CIATION

William A. Reynolds
TREASURER
AMERICAN CARPET INSTITUTE

Dr. David Riesman
PROFESSOR OF SOCIOLOGY
HARVARD UNIVERSITY

Harvey H. Robbins
SECRETARY
INSTITUTE FOR BETTER PACKAGING

Curtis Rogers
PRESIDENT, CONSUMER PANEL DI-
VISION, MARKET RESEARCH
CORPORATION OF AMERICA

Dr. Beardsley Ruml (deceased)
*Was director of several com-
panies*

Erwin A. Salk
PRESIDENT
SALK, WARD & SALK, INC.

David Sarnoff
CHAIRMAN OF THE BOARD
RADIO CORPORATION OF AMERICA

Harry F. Schroeter
DIRECTOR, GENERAL ADVERTISING
DEPARTMENT, NATIONAL BIS-
CUIT COMPANY

F. J. Schwaemmle
DIRECTOR, INFORMATION SERVICES
DELTA AIR LINES, INC.

Walter D. Scott
EXECUTIVE VICE PRESIDENT
NATIONAL BROADCASTING COM-
PANY, INC.

James J. Sheeran
MERCHANDISING REPRESENTATIVE
TATHAM-LAIRD, INC.

Dr. Muzafer Sherif
DIRECTOR, INSTITUTE OF GROUP
RELATIONS, UNIVERSITY OF
OKLAHOMA

Warren Smith
SECRETARY-TREASURER
THE HAT INSTITUTE

Cecil D. Southard
FORMERLY VICE PRESIDENT IN
CHARGE OF WHOLESALING,
BUTLER BROTHERS

Hal Stebbins
PRESIDENT
HAL STEBBINS, INC.

Dr. John B. Stewart
ASSISTANT PROFESSOR
GRADUATE SCHOOL OF BUSINESS
ADMINISTRATION, HARVARD
UNIVERSITY

Samuel J. Sugerman
PRESIDENT AND GENERAL MAN-
AGER, KAUFMANN'S DEPART-
MENT STORES (PITTSBURGH)

Dudley J. Taw
VICE PRESIDENT, DRUG RELATIONS
MCKESSON & ROBBINS

H. H. Timken, Jr.
CHAIRMAN OF THE BOARD
TIMKEN ROLLER BEARING CO.

William D. Tyler
EXECUTIVE VICE PRESIDENT IN
CHARGE OF CREATIVE SERVICES,
BENTON & BOWLES, INC.

Allen Wagner
DIRECTOR, PUBLIC RELATIONS
GENERAL FOODS CORPORATION

James M. Wallace
EXECUTIVE VICE PRESIDENT
N. W. AYER & SON, INC.

Dr. Henry C. Wallich
PROFESSOR OF ECONOMICS
YALE UNIVERSITY

Dr. Ralph L. Westfall
PROFESSOR OF MARKETING
SCHOOL OF BUSINESS
NORTHWESTERN UNIVERSITY

Don Wharton
STAFF WRITER
THE READER'S DIGEST

William H. Whyte, Jr.
ASSISTANT MANAGING EDITOR
FORTUNE

Henry O. Whiteside
VICE PRESIDENT
J. WALTER THOMPSON COMPANY

Mark Huntington Wiseman
AUTHOR AND ADVERTISING CON-
SULTANT

Albert J. Wood
PRESIDENT
A. J. WOOD RESEARCH CORPORA-
TION

A. W. Zelomek
PRESIDENT
INTERNATIONAL STATISTICAL BU-
REAU, INC.

BOOK PUBLISHERS

(For permission to quote from the books indicated)

Gerald Duckworth & Co., Ltd.:
   Eric John Dingwall, *The American Woman: A Historical Study,* copyright
   1956.

Harper & Brothers:
Paul M. Mazur, *The Standards We Raise,* copyright 1953.
Mark Huntington Wiseman, *The New Anatomy of Advertising,* copyright 1959.

Holt, Rinehart and Winston, Inc.:
Eric John Dingwall, *The American Woman: A Historical Study,* copyright 1956.
Gordon W. Allport, *Personality: A Psychological Interpretation,* copyright 1937.

Richard D. Irwin, Inc.:
Neil H. Borden, *The Economic Effects of Advertising,* copyright 1942.
Harper W. Boyd, Jr., and Ralph Westfall, *Marketing Research: Text and Cases,* copyright 1956.

Alfred A. Knopf, Inc.:
Eugene L. Hartley and Ruth E. Hartley, *Fundamentals of Social Psychology,* copyright 1952.

Longmans Green & Co.:
Horace B. English and Ava Champney English, *A Comprehensive Dictionary of Psychological and Psychoanalytical Terms,* copyright 1958.

McGraw-Hill Book Company, Inc.:
Arnold W. Green, *Sociology: An Analysis of Life in Modern Society,* copyright 1956.
Harry Walker Hepner, *Modern Marketing: Dynamics and Management,* copyright 1955.
John J. Honigmann, *Culture and Personality,* copyright 1954.
Pierre Martineau, *Motivation in Advertising,* copyright 1957.

Oceana Publications, Inc.
Lee Rainwater, Richard C. Colemen, and Gerald Handel, *Working Man's Wife,* copyright 1959.

The Ronald Press Company:
Lyndon O. Brown, *Marketing and Distribution Research,* copyright 1955.

Simon and Schuster, Inc.:
Editors of *Fortune, The Amazing Advertising Business,* copyright 1957.
William H. Whyte, Jr., *The Organization Man,* copyright 1956.

The Viking Press, Inc.:
Thorstein Veblen, *The Theory of the Leisure Class* (Modern Library, 1934).

John Wiley & Sons, Inc.:
A. W. Zelomek, *A Changing America,* copyright 1959.

The World Publishing Company:
Lowell B. Mason, *The Language of Dissent,* copyright 1959.

PERIODICALS AND NEWSPAPERS

Advertising Age

Architectural Forum

Arizona Progress

Business Horizons

Chicago Daily News

Fortune

General Features Corporation

Harvard Business Review

Journal of Consulting Psychology

Journal of Marketing

Life

Nation's Business

Newsweek

The Nielsen Researcher

Printers' Ink

Psychological Review

The Reader's Digest

Sales Management

Saturday Review

The Wall Street Journal

Index

Abercrombie & Fitch, 168
Abundance of goods, 50–51
Acuity, visual, 113, 208
Advertising, 51, 103, 147–167
  answers to criticisms, 151–159
  and brand names, 132, 135
  and consumer decisions, 166, 263
  consumer defenses against, 150
  effectiveness of, 41, 42
  ethical, 154–157, 161–164
  exaggerations in, 149, 154–156
  examined by FTC, 161–162
  expenditures, 148, 153–154
  five goals of, 161–164
  growth of, 166
  lack of, in product failure, 121
  long-range, 164–166
  and national income, 153
  necessary for business growth, 159–160
  need for repetition, 159–160
  of new products, 106
  objectives of, 161–164
  opposition to, 151–159
  orientation of, 164
  problems solved by research, 207–209
  as source of information, 59, 156, 158–159, 166
  and store image, 172, 174
  "subliminal," 157–158
  types of, 164–165
  "word-of-mouth," 59
Advertising Age Creative Workshop, 242
Age structure, of population, 43, 257
Alderson, Wroe, 254, 271

All detergent, 209
Allport, Gordon W., 138
American Dental Association, 60
American Marketing Association, 75
American Medical Association, 60
American Motors, 119, 145
American Psychological Association, 4
American Way of Life, key principles of, 51–52
Appliances, 95, 234–235
Architectural Forum, 262
Architecture, and store image, 172–173
Arden House, 30
Armour, Frank, Jr., 116
Arnold, Stanley, 173
Arts, greater emphasis on, 259
Atlantic & Pacific (A&P), 133
Attitudes, of consumers, 21, 86
  and frame of reference, 10–14
  and regionalism, 17–18
  of salespeople, 175–178
  of women, changing, 230–232
Aunt Jemima mixes, 109
Automation, 236
Automobiles, 90, 247, 251
  compact, 119
  design, uniformity in, 25–26
  imagery in selling, 142–146
  major reasons for purchase, 233
  and social status, 66, 143
  and women, 234

Ban, 123
Bardot, Brigitte, 61, 64

Batten, Barton, Durstine & Osborn, Inc. (BBDO), 120
Beer, studies on, 68, 224
Behavior, purchasing, 15, 86–101, 168–178
Believability, as problem in advertising, 161, 163
Ben Franklin variety stores, 72
Benton and Bowles, 151
Better Business Bureau, 58, 185
Bickmore, Lee S., 103
Birdseye, Clarence, 119
Blanket, electric, 182–183, 193–196
Bonwit Teller, 171
Book club, and motivation research, 223
Borch, Fred J., 38
Borden, Neil H., 154, 269
Boyd, Harper W., Jr., 196, 207, 270
Brand loyalty, 133–136
Brand name, advantages to consumer, 131–132
    confidence in, 58
    defined, 131
    generic vs. specific, 128, 139
    and product success, 133
Brand principles, 132
Brands, advertised, favored by consumer, 158–159
    and choice, 40
    as defense against phony pricing, 185
    private, 132–133, 159
    as psychological guide to buying, 136
    and store image, 174
Brisk, 104
Britt, Steuart Henderson, 267, 270
Bristol Myers, 123
Brown, J. A. C., 10
Brown, Lyndon O., 213–214
Bullock's, 176
Bureau of Home Economics, 60
Bureau of Standards, 60
Burnett, Leo, 155, 163
Burnett, Leo, Company, 113–114, 141–142, 151
Bursk, Edward C., 150
Business, dependence upon consumer, 54–56
    and motivation research, 229
    need for advertising, 160
Business conditions, American, 50
Buying, five decisions faced by consumer, 161

Buying, impulse, see impulse buying
    installment, as way of life, 189
    intentions compared with actual purchases, 128
    nonprice basis, 186
    as self-reward, 235
    see also spending
Buying decisions, joint, 232–235
Buying habits, changing, 75
    determined by product images, 139
    effect of social status, 68–69
    of women, 231
Buying power, difference between cities and suburbs, 246

Cadillac, 26, 140
    as ego-building possession, 143
Camay soap, 13, 141
Campbell Soup Company, 180
Campfire Marshmallow, 114
Candy, Walter W., 176
Cantril, Hadley, 12, 13
Caveat emptor, 58, 60
Caveat vendor, 60
Charge accounts, 188
Cheer detergent, 108
Cheerios, 206
Cheskin, Louis, 141, 208
Childhood conditioning, and adult attitudes toward spending, 18–19
Children, and food expenditures, 93
    and habits, 18–19
    as significant factor in spending, 100
Choice, and advertising, 160
    basis of, 161, 166
    confusion of, 40–41
    freedom of, 23–24, 34, 124, 244
    as power of consumer, 60
    and higher prices, 191
    range of, 36, 38–42
Chrysler Corporation, 142, 145, 205
Cigarette smoking, studies on, 224
Cities, consumers in, 252
    return to, 253
Clarksdale Press Register, 128
Clinics, cross-country, in marketing research, 207
Coffee, studies on, 225–226
Cokesbury College, 84
Coleman, Richard C., 268
College enrollments, increasing, 97, 258

Color, in packaging, 108
and sales, 194–195
and store image, 173
Communication, between consumer
and manufacturer, 196
between consumers, 59
research and, 209
Community, influence on spending, 45–46
Competition, of brands, 132
for consumer dollar, 67, 257
as deterrent to false advertising, 162
and new products, 123
"nonprice," 186
and pricing, 180
as protection for consumer, 60
Cone, Fairfax M., 163, 269
Confidential, 212
Conformity, 18, 37
Consumer, all-importance of, 35–48, 55
benefits to, 160
and buying decisions, 161
defenses against advertising, 149–150
"educability" of, 181
favoring advertised brands, 158
as free agent, 152
ideas of, 205
illogical behavior of, 117–118
and imagery, 140
influence on pricing, 186
influence on producers, 160
mind of, 1–9, 211–213
opinions of, 37
problems of, 32–33
U.S., profile of, 97–101
unpredictability of, 9
Consumer Products Group, 38
Consumers Research, Inc., 60
Consumers Union, 60
Consumption, conspicuous, 65, 125, 187
in reverse, 66
total expenditure, 77
Container Corporation of America, 115
Convenience, kinds expected by consumer, 70–71
Continental (car), 66
Copy phrase, testing of, 208
Cosmetics, use of, varying with locality, 71
Cost, affected by demand for convenience, 71

Cox, Reavis, 252, 271
Craftsmanship, 47–48
Credit, importance to consumer, 189–190
installment, cost of, 189–190
Credit and borrowing, 52
Crisco, 131, 208
Crisp, Richard D., 270
Cultural group, and behavior, 18
Cunningham, Ross M., 135
Customers, kinds of, and retailers, 171

David, Donald, 138
Dayco Corporation, 2
de Tarnowsky, Pierre A., 159
Dean, Joel, 181–184, 270
Decision making, by women, 235
Deep-freeze units, 248
Demand, created by advertising, 152
estimated, and amount of education, 96
steps in, 181
Desires, fundamental, 6
Dial shampoo, 109
Dial soap, 13, 191, 229
Dichter, Ernest, 112, 226, 228, 229, 269
Dingwall, Eric John, 236–237, 271
Discernible difference, see under Product
Discount houses, 255
Discretion, Age of, 261
Distribution, see Marketing
Do-it-yourself projects, 28
Dog food, and locality, 72
"Dollar ballots," 36
Dollars, discretionary, 76
Dominance status, and buying habits, 242
Dreier, Alex, 53
Drucker, Peter F., 258, 268
Drug stores, and scrambled merchandising, 252–253
Drury, James C., 245, 286
Duncan, Delbert J., 269
Duncan Hines, 111
"duPont's law," 109
"Durables," spending for, 78

Economic growth, lag in, 84
Economy, affected by decisions to buy, 103
full-employment, 67

Economy, highly competitive, 60
   "restless," 246
Edsel (car), 122, 145
Education, 261
   adult, 260
   and buying habits, 93, 94–97, 101
Education, of consumers, 254
   equality of opportunity for, 258
   increasing trend to, 43
   lack of financing of, 33
Eldridge, Clarence E., 161, 269
Electric mixers, 13
Electronic controls, in stores, 254
"Emotional pull," 8
Emotions, of women, 233
Empathy, in successful salesman, 177
English, Ava Champney, 213
English, Horace B., 213
Ensley, Grover W., 75
Entrepreneur, 35
Ethics, of advertising, 155–157, 163
Expenditures, average family, pie
      chart, 99
   distribution by annual household
      income (table), 91
   eight major types of, 87–88
   see also Buying; Spending
Experience, new, desire for, 6
Experiment, in frame of reference, 12
   willingness to, 20
Exurbia, 253

FTC see Federal Trade Commission
Fads and fashions, 60–67, 191, 262
   psychology of, 67
   reversal of, 64
Faison, Edmund W. J., 115, 208
Fashions, see Fads and fashions
Federal Trade Commission, 58, 60,
      161–162, 185
Ferber, Robert, 67, 268, 270
Fiberglas, 265
Fibers, synthetic, 265
Filling stations, and service, 188
Fitz-Gibbon, Bernice, 234, 240
Flash-exposure box, 208
Florsheim Shoe Company, 2
Food, consumption of, 247
   expenditures, 93
   gourmet, 48
   regional preferences in, 72
   research on, 133–134

Food and Drug Administration, 60
Foods, variety of, 247
Ford, 26, 144, 145
Ford, Henry, 39
Ford Motor Company, 66
Foreign commodities, 259
Fortune magazine, 51, 81, 229, 263, 267,
      271
FR-8, 180
Franklin, Benjamin, 76

GNP see Gross National Product
Gadgets, 33, 82
Gaines Dog Research Center, 72
Gallup & Robinson, Inc., 128
Gardner, Burleigh, 229
Gasolines, and brand loyalty, 135
   imagery of, 137
General Electric Company, 140, 194–
      196
General Foods, 103
General Motors, 145, 206
George, Edwin B., 189
Gettell, Richard G., 34
Gillette Company, 122
Gillis, John L., 245
Goldblatt's, 171
Good Housekeeping, 212
Good Housekeeping Institute, 60
Good Luck margarine, 208
Government agencies, and product in-
      formation, 60
Greeley, Horace, 43
Green, Arnold W., 83, 268
Green Giant, 205
Grey Advertising Agency, 117, 197
Grocery chains, and store image, 169
Gross National Product, 259, 260
Guthrie, Edwin R., 267

Habits, 15–16
   dietary, changing, 248
   set patterns of, 19
Haire, Mason, 12, 225
Handel, Gerald, 268
Harper, Marion, Jr., 236
Harris, Nieson ("Wishbone"), 122
Harris, Sydney J., 220
Harvard Business Review, 16, 150, 181
Hathaway shirt, 141
Hats, men's, 71

Hauser, Philip M., 253, 271
Havemann, Ernest, 268
Heckscher, August, 33
Heinz, H. J., Co., 121
Heiskell, Andrew, 55, 260
Hepner, Harry W., 119, 269
Herrmann, Cyril, 17
Hertzler, Joyce O., 17
Hexachlorophene, 229
Home, and leisure time, 81–83
Home Testing Institute, 141
Homogeneity, of consumer market, 90–91, 98
Honigmann, John J., 174
Housewives, and spare time, 27
Human nature, variation of, 17–18

IBM systems, and inventory, 262
Ideas, free association of, 15
Image, of corporation, 146
    mental, 21
    product, 112, 134, 137–146
        and advertising, 164, 165
        correlated with brand name, 139
    of public utilities, 127
    of self, and buying attitudes, 14
    store, 190–191
Image-building campaign, 140
Impulse buying, 21, 74, 109, 128–129, 251
Income, of average family, 44, 49, 78
    increasing, 260
    changes in distribution of, 44
    discretionary, 36
Income, disposable, 75
    low, 33
    percentages spent, 68
    personal, 261
    power of, 55
    and spending habits, 26
Indexes, of consumer markets, 3
Inflation, 32
Ingenuity, needed for successful marketing, 54
Ingredient, priceless, 130–136
Insecurity, and buying habits, 25
Institute for Motivational Research, Inc., 112, 226
Institute for Research in Mass Motivation, 2
Instruments, psychological, for testing packages, 113–114

Insurance, automobile, advertising, 227
Intelligence, of men and women, 241
International Association of Machinists, 79
Interurbias, 250
Interviews, with consumers, 127
    depth, in motivation research, 216
    group, in motivation research, 216
    in marketing research, 200
    techniques of, 86–87
Inventories, study of, in marketing research, 200

Jantzen, 131
Jell-O, 131
Jewel Tea Company, 132–133, 170
Johnson, Samuel C., III, 269
Johnson's Wax, 107, 218
Journal of Marketing, 119, 140, 153, 235
Judgment, rapidity of, 138

Katona, George, 234, 267
Katz drug chain, 253
Kellogg Company, 114
Kintner, Earl W., 155
Kluckhohn, Clyde, 271
"Koolfoam," 2
Kornhauser, Arthur W., 8
Kraft foods, 104
Kuo, Helena, 237

L.S.C.E. see Life Study of Consumer Expenditures
Labor force, percentage of women, 43–44
Laboratory, consumer-reaction, 113–114
    marketing, 126–127
    psychological, 208
Langlie, Arthur B., 132
Language, of advertising, 155
    symbolic function of, 14
Leadership status, and education, 96
Legibility, of package, 113
Lehman, Charles C., 148
Leisure, American love of, 84
Leisure time, 26, 27, 79–85, 259
    of women, 239
Lerner, Max, 84
"Leveling process," 25
Lever Brothers, 13
Levitt, Theodore, 83

Life magazine, 103, 271
  Marketing Laboratory, 126–127
  price of, 207–208
Life Study of Consumer Expenditures,
    28, 39, 86–89, 93, 95, 200, 247, 268
  over-all purpose of, 86
Lifebuoy soap, 141
Lighting, and store image, 173
Likes and dislikes, of consumer, 8
Liking (term), meaning of, 21
Locality, and consumer demands, 71
London, Jack, 141
Lord & Taylor, 171
Loyalty, brand, *see* Brand loyalty
    customer, 190
Lucas, Darrell Blaine, 269
Luce, Henry R., 55, 267
Lucky Strike, 140
Ludgin, Earle, 123
Lunding, Franklin J., 170, 270
Lux soap, 13, 141

M. and M. Candy Company, 222–223
M.R. *see* Research, motivation
MRCA *see* Market Research Corpora-
    tion of America
Mabley, Jack, 190
McCabe, Thomas B., Jr., 116
McCall Corporation, 132
McCall's, 60, 97, 198, 212
Macy's, 171
McGarry, Edmund D., 148, 151, 269
McGregor, Douglas, 267
Mack, Ruth P., 9, 31–32
McMurry, Robert N., 177
Maier, Norman R. F., 41
Man, as social being, 7
Man the Consumer, 7–8
Manufacturers, and advertising, 154
  and marketing research, 69
  problems of, 69
Market, buyer's, 53
  city, 248
  "class," no longer existing, 89
  food, 247
  of future, 261
  leisure-time, 261
  middle-class, 26
  small-town, 248
Market Research Corporation of Amer-
    ica, 202–204

Marketing, advertising as tool of, 154
  contrasted with production, 56
  defined, 53
  factors involved in, 53
  as principal job of modern executives,
    54
  problems of manufacturer, 72
  revolution in, 49–54
  and the social sciences, 56
  test, 200, 201
  see also Selling
Marketing research, *see under* Research
Markets, kinds of, 247–248
  location of, as major economic prob-
    lem, 55
  and people, 56
  test, list of (table), 201
Marlboro, 141–142
Marshall, Alfred, 25
Marshall Field, 171–172
Martin, C. Virgil, 171
Martineau, Pierre, 16, 66, 139, 171, 172,
    268, 269, 270
Maslow, A. H., 18, 267
Mason, Lowell B., 162
Mass production, dependence upon con-
    sumption, 51
  made possible by advertising, 152
Mayer, Lawrence A., 271
Mayer, Martin, 269
Mazur, Paul M., 55, 268
Mead, Margaret, 83
Medicines, and frame of reference, 12
Men, and supermarkets, 251
Mendelsohn, Harold, 237
Mental pictures, and reality, 14
Merchandising, "scrambled," 252–253
Messner, Fred R., 108
Meters, 113
Middle-income groups, 74, 76, 92
  and education, 95
  expenditures, 39
Middle majority, 25, 42–48
  increase in, 67
Middle West, 43
Miller, A. Edward, 97, 198
Mr. Clean, 206
Mobility, of consumer, 55
Money, no longer symbol of social class,
    259
Money sense, of women, 240
Montenier, Jules, 123

Montgomery, Charlotte, 242
Moralists, and credit economy, 189
Morgan, Henry, 149
Mortimer, Charles G., 70, 160, 268
Morton Salt Company, 106
Motivation research, see under Research
Motives, in buying, 1–22
Myers, Kenneth H., 153, 269

Names (product and company), in decisions to buy, 146
Namias, Jean, 119
Narrative probe, 215, 217
National Consumer Panel, 202
National Geographic, 212
National Industrial Conference Board, 84
National Tea Company, 133
Necchi sewing machine, 187
Needing (term), meaning of, 21
Needs and wants, 39
    and buying, 23–34
    limitlessness of, 31
Nervous system, autonomic, 16
Newman, Joseph W., 5, 270
Newsweek, 264–265, 271
Nielsen, A. C., Company, 117, 133, 134, 203–204
Nielsen, Arthur C., Jr., 252
Nielsen Retail Index, 203
Nieman, Marcus, 171
Nouveau riche, 65

Obsolescence, "built-in," 125
    psychological, 124–126, 190
    as threat to products, 123
Occupation, and spending habits, 46
Ogilvy, David, 2, 58
O'Meara, Walter, 228
Ostheimer, Richard H., 269
Overproduction, 245

Packard, 144
Package, as sale-clinching factor, 109
Packaging, 29, 103
    consumer preferences in, 110–115
    interviews with housewives, 111
    and marketing research, 208
    and percentage of selling price, 115
    research, 141
    as silent salesman, 107–115

Packaging, standards for, 112
    testing of, 113–115, 208–209, 226–227
Panels, consumer, 127, 202
Parents' Magazine, 60
Parkay margarine, 104
Parker, Sanford S., 271
Patterson, William A., 175
Peckham, James O., 158
Penetration-price method, 184–185
Pepsi-Cola, 140
Personality, human, 139–140
Personality, of product, 112
    of salespeople, and store image, 174, 176
    of stores, 168–178
Personality characteristics, and buying, 17, 68
Persuasion, "hidden," 199, 209
Philip Morris Co., 206
Phillips, Charles F., 269
Picture probe, 215, 217
Pillsbury Company, 114
Play, versus work, 83
Pledge, 107
Plenty, era of, 36
Point-of-purchase displays, 174
Point-of-sale studies, 200
Polaroid cameras, 117
Politz, Alfred, 31, 118
Population, changes in, 42–43
    increasing, 261
        annual rate of expansion, 246
        by region, 256
Postpurchase anxiety, 177–178
Potter, David M., 268
Predictions, by manufacturer, 244
Prejudices, and buying patterns, 19
Prestige, and choice of automobile, 143–146
    and decisions to buy, 161
    and store image, 170, 190
Price, 179
    cut, 186
    and decision to buy, 240
    effect of packaging, 115
    fictitious, 185
Price, and new product, 121
    not only determining factor, 186, 190
    range of, 181
    stabilized by brands, 131
    steps in estimating, 181–184
    and supermarkets, 251

Prices, in terms of work involved, 1914
    and 1955, 180
Pricing, policies, 182–184
    reduced, 184–185
    studies of, 200
Printers' Ink, 82, 268, 270
Procter & Gamble, 13, 102, 206
Production, of goods, contrasted with
    marketing, 56
Productivity, increased, and deflated
    dollar, 180
Products, attitudes about, 105
    choice of, increasing, 40
    competing, 41
    discernible differences, 102–107, 115,
        124
        consumer's need for, 41
    home testing of, 126
    information about, 58–60
    life cycle of, 117, 184
    marketing, and consumer test, 126–
        129
    new, 28–29, 103, 136
        and advertising, 159
        demand for, 259
        development of, 107, 120, 182–183,
            244
        and established brand names, 131
        failure of, 116, 120–126
        and family of other products, 182
Products, new, search for, 129
    personality of, 112
    and symbolic associations, 140
Profits, and marketing research, 204
Progress, symbolized by brand name,
    132
Projections, psychological, and car
    ownership, 144
Projective techniques, 213, 222, 226–227
Promotion, lack of, in product failure,
    121
Prosperity, and consumer's decision to
    spend, 79
Prudential Insurance Company, 140
Psychological factors, as motive for
    buying, 235
Psychological studies, need for, 17
Psychologists, hostility to, 4
    industrial, number of, 4
    and motivation, 4–5
Psychology, 4
    and research methods, 211

Public buildings, budget for, 262
Public Health Service, 60
Purchase diary, 202
Purchasing power, long-term trends in,
    25
Puritan traditions, and leisure time, 84
Push-button devices, 264

Quality, and brand name, 132
Quaker Oats, 111–112
Questionnaires, consumer, 227

Radio, and complaints about adver-
    tising, 149
Rainwater, Lee, 47, 268
Rambler (car), 15
Reader's Digest, 185
    and advertising, 148
Readings, suggested, 267–271
ReaLemon, 109
Reasoning, logical, and decisions to
    buy, 15
Recession, 32, 50
Recognition, desire for, 6
Recreation, 80–81, 83
    and spending, 28, 82, 84, 89
Reed, Virgil D., 267
Reference, frames of, 10–15
Regan, William J., 29
Regionalism, and basic attitudes, 18
    and sales emphasis, 109
Regions, and food expenditures, 94
    and market-location characteristics,
        100
    and marketing research, 204
    see also Locality
Research, marketing, 193–210
    defined, 198
    differing from market research, 197
    factors in, 196
    five "D's" of, 197–198
    services, 204
    motivation, 211–229
        compared to marketing research,
            197
        defined, 211
        examples of use in business, 222–
            229
        not psychoanalytical, 215
    product, 4
    as a tool, 205

Response, desire for, 6
Retail-outlet studies, 126
Retailers, type of appeal of, 171
Revlon, 109, 111
Riesman, David, 66, 83, 177
Risks, in business, 69
"Robber barons," 36
Romney, George, 119
Roper, Elmo, 141
Ruml, Beardsley, 38, 55
Ry-Krisp, 223

Safeway stores, 102
Saks Fifth Avenue, 171
St. Regis Paper Company, 103
Sales, dependent upon proper pricing, 180
    and estimating price, 181
Sales Management magazine, 159
Sales points, in advertising, 164
Sales volumes, influenced by competitive pressures, 38
Salesclerks, effect on shoppers, 175
Sample, probability, 200
Sampling, in marketing research, 198–204
Sanka coffee, 128, 226
Sapir, Edward, 268
Sarnoff, David, 103
Saturday Review, 149
Savings, controlled by women, 238
    decisions on, 235
    effect on spending, 76
    trend toward, 262
School population, increasing, 258
Schweppes Tonic, 3
Scientific developments, future, 263
Sears, Roebuck, 172
Security, desire for, 6
    and women, 239
Self, evaluation of, and purchasing, 17
Self-service, 51, 59, 133, 170
    importance of advertising in, 166
    increasing, 262
    and packaging, 108–109
Selling, as crux of industry's problem, 51, 52
    in mind of consumer, 1
    personal, 159, 162
    retail, 176
    starting with advertising, 159, 165
Sentence-completion method, 215–216

Service, cost of, 188
    importance to consumer, 187
    problem of, 32
Shaw, George Bernard, 237
Sheaffer Pen Company, 2
Sherif, Muzafer, 13
Shirts, men's, 29–30
Shoes, men's, 2
Shoppers, wants of, 176–177
Shopping, comparative, 58
    and self-service, 59
    future patterns of, 250–253
    one-stop, 250
Shopping centers, 250
Shopping habits, American, 52
Shopping lists, use of, 127–128
Signs and symbols, influence on buying, 15
Silberman, Charles E., 268
Simmons Beauty Rest, 136
Simon, Morton J., 269
Skim-the-cream price policy, 182–183
Slichter, Sumner, 84
Sloan, Alfred P., 196
Slogan, advertising, 195
    as builder of product images, 138
Smith, George Horsley, 270
Snorkel pen, development of, 2
Snowdrift (Wesson), 226
Social distinctions, by likes and dislikes, 48
Social patterns, changing, 257–258
Social Research, Inc., 47
Social status, and buying patterns, 17, 19, 63, 68–69
    of stores, 172, 175
    and use of leisure time, 81, 83
Sociological factors, and spending, 263
Soft drinks, 3, 118
Sophistication, of consumer, and advertising, 155
    in trading areas, 249
Southard, Cecil D., 72
Spending, annual household average, 87
    changes from 1936 to 1956, 90
    discretionary, 74, 76
    as expression of consumer attitudes, 87
    factors influencing, 45–46
    influence of women, 234, 237, 243
    investment by manufacturer, 120

Spending, and leisure time, 81
  patterns of, 89–94
  ratio by income groups, 92
Spending, rise of, 75
  trend toward, 76–77
  see also Buying; Expenditures
Spending habits, changing with in-
  come, 26
  uniformity in, 68
Spending power, increasing, 26
"Spiff," 191
Sports, increased participation in, 83
Squibb, E. R. and Sons, 130
Standard of living, American, 32, 51,
  237
  higher, 262
Star Kist tuna, 223
Starch Reader Impression Studies, 148
State Farm Mutual Automobile Insur-
  ance Company, 227
Status, see Social status
Stebbins, Hal, 155
Steelworkers, earnings of, 76
Stewart, John B., 17
Stopette, 123
Stores, department, and service, 188–
  189
  image (personality) of, 168–178
  personnel, 169
  psychological identification with,
  172
Stripe toothpaste, 128
Studebaker-Packard, 145
Studies, of economic decision making,
  233
  psychological, 2
Substitution, brands as protection
  against, 131
Suburban living, relation to spending,
  100
Suburbs, 82, 240, 246
Sugerman, Samuel J., 168
Superhighways, 262
Super Market Institute, 103, 173
Supermarkets, 232, 250
  atmosphere, 190
  and impulse buying, 109
  problem of layout, 173
  psychological appeal, 251
  and store image, 169
Surveys, in marketing research, 198–
  204

Symbols, in advertising, and store
  image, 174

Tastes, changing, 240, 246
Taw, Dudley J., 191
Tea, studies on, 225
Tea Council, 225
Technological changes, and buying, 28
Television, and complaints about ad-
  vertising, 149
Test markets, see under Markets
Testing, of products, by consumer, 126–
  129
Tests, eye-movement, 208
  used in projective techniques, 215–
  216
Thematic apperception test, 215
Thomas, W. I., 5
Thorndike, E. L., 20
Thrift, attitude to, 76, 151
Thrifty Cut Rate Drug Stores, 253
Timesavers, interest in, 240
Timken Roller Bearing Company, 160
"Togetherness," 240
Toni Company, 122
Toothpaste, salt, 106–107
Trade-mark, defined, 131
Trading areas, 248–249
True Confessions, 212
True Story, 212
Twentieth Century Fund, 166
Tyler, William D., 140

Unconscious factors, and motives, 15
Underconsumption, 66
Uniformity, trend toward, 25–26
United Auto Workers, 79
U.S. Department of Labor, 75, 76
U.S. News & World Report, 265, 268
Unnecessities, defined, 38–39
  psychological, 30

Value, symbolized by brand name, 132
  test of, and price tags, 186
Vanderbilt, Commodore, 69
Variety, and price, 29–30, 191
Veblen, Thorstein, 7, 268
"Veblen's disease," 66
Vending machines, 118, 262
Visibility measurements, 209
Visual Research, Inc., 115, 208

Wage rate, high, 51
Wales, Hugh G., 270
Wall Street Journal, 77, 78, 115
Wallich, Henry C., 31
Wants, *see* Needs and wants
Watson, John B., 19
Webb's City, 253
Westfall, Ralph, 196, 207, 270
Westinghouse, 131
Wharton, Don, 270
"What's My Line?" (television show), 123
Whirlpool, 124
Whitehead, Commander Edward, 3
Whyte, William H., Jr., 78, 269
Wiseman, Mark Huntington, 165, 269
Wolff, Janet L., 271
Wolgast, Elizabeth H., 235, 271
Woman, modern, dilemma of, 231
Women, changing role of, 235–242
  as consumers, 230–242
  increasing employment of, 43

Women, median marrying age, 231
  mental potential equal to men, 239
Wood, Albert J., 189
Word association method, 215–216
Words, influence on purchasing behavior, 14–15
Work day, pattern of, 26
Work force, percentage of women, 238
Work week, average, 79
  of professional groups, 81
Workers, blue-collar, 68–69, 175
  homes of, 75
  as new leisure class, 81
  white-collar, 68–69, 175
Working-age group, 257
Working class, 47
Working conditions, mental, 11

Young and Rubicam, 151

Zelomek, A. W., 52, 74–75, 82, 232, 268